Offshore

Offshore outsourcing—the movement of jobs to lower-wage countries—is one of the defining features of globalization. Routine blue-collar work has been going offshore for decades, but the digital revolution beginning in the 1990s extended this process to many parts of the service economy too. Politically controversial from the beginning, "offshoring" is conventionally seen as a threat to jobs, wages, and economic security in higher-income countries, having become synonymous with the dirty work of globalization. Even though the majority of corporations make some use of offshore outsourcing, fearful of negative publicity most now choose to manage these activities in a discreet manner. Partly as a result, the global sourcing business, reckoned to be worth more than $120 billion, largely operates under the radar, its ocean-spanning activities in low-cost labour arbitrage being poorly documented and poorly understood.

Offshore is the first sustained investigation of the workings of the global sourcing industry, its business practices, its market dynamics, its technologies, and its politics. The book traces the complex transformation of the worlds of global sourcing, from its origins in the new international division of labour in the 1970s, through the rapid growth of back-office economies in India and the Philippines since the 1990s, to the development of "nearshore" markets in Latin America and Eastern Europe. Recently, this evolving process of geographical and organizational restructuring has included experiments in "backshoring" within low-cost, ex-urban locations in the United States and a wave of software-enabled automation, which threatens to remove labour from many back offices altogether. In these and other ways, the offshore revolution continues.

Jamie Peck is Canada Research Chair in Urban & Regional Political Economy and Professor of Geography at the University of British Columbia, Canada. His research interests include labour studies, economic restructuring, neoliberalization, and urban transformations. Elected to the fellowships of the Royal Society of Canada and the Academy of the Social Sciences, Jamie Peck has been the recipient of Guggenheim and Harkness fellowships, and received the Royal Geographical Society's Back Award for contributions to economic geography. He is the managing editor of the journal *EPA: Economy and Space* and the coordinator of the Summer Institute in Economic Geography.

Offshore

Exploring the Worlds of Global Outsourcing

Jamie Peck

OXFORD

UNIVERSITY PRESS

OXFORD
UNIVERSITY PRESS

Great Clarendon Street, Oxford, OX2 6DP,
United Kingdom

Oxford University Press is a department of the University of Oxford.
It furthers the University's objective of excellence in research, scholarship,
and education by publishing worldwide. Oxford is a registered trade mark of
Oxford University Press in the UK and in certain other countries

© Jamie Peck 2017

The moral rights of the author have been asserted

First published 2017
First published in paperback 2019

Published in the United States of America by Oxford University Press
198 Madison Avenue, New York, NY 10016, United States of America

British Library Cataloguing in Publication Data
Data available

Library of Congress Cataloging in Publication Data
Data available

ISBN 978–0–19–872740–8 (Hbk.)
ISBN 978–0–19–884172–2 (Pbk.)

For Joyce

Acknowledgments

I am grateful to the Social Sciences and Humanities Research Council of Canada for supporting the research reported here, in part through the grant "Outsourcing expertise" (410-2009-1172) and in part through the Canada Research Chairs program. Thanks to Kean Fan Lim and Elliot Siemiatycki for research assistance, to Eric Leinberger for his cartographic work, and Jeanne Yang for decrypting. My hosts in the Department of Geography at the National University of Singapore provided a stimulating and supportive environment during my time there as Lim Chong Yah visiting professor. For discussions around the issues explored here I am grateful to Neil Coe, Martin Hess, Nik Theodore, Henry Yeung, and to all those working in and for the outsourcing complex who found the time to talk to me. The early interest, unswerving professionalism, and impressive patience of Clare Kennedy and David Musson at Oxford University Press are much appreciated. And not least, my thanks to Peter Dicken, for inspiration.

Contents

Contents

List of Figures

List of Tables

List of Abbreviations

BPO   Business process outsourcing
CGI   Clinton Global Initiative
CEE   Central and Eastern Europe
COP   Certified Outsourcing Professional
FTE   Full-time equivalent
HfS   Horses for Sources
IAOP   International Association of Outsourcing Professionals
ICT   Information and communications technologies
IT   Information technology
ITO   Information technology outsourcing
KPO   Knowledge process outsourcing
NIDL   New international division of labor
RNC   Republican National Committee
RPA   Robotic process automation
SLA   Service level agreement

1

Introduction

Going Offshore

"These days, outsourcing seems to be everywhere," begins *Outsourcing for Dummies*, an addition to the popular franchise of how-to manuals. "It is no longer a force somewhere out there, on the horizon, that may or may not come this way. It has arrived."[1] And it is everywhere, apparently, not because each and every job function is about to be bundled up and traded on an international market, flying friction-free to some cheaper location, but because the incipient logic of outsourcing exhibits a range and reach far beyond the circumstances of any one "offshoring" event. "Work will be done where it makes the most sense" is the mantra of Nandan Nilekani, the founder and former CEO of the Indian outsourcing firm Infosys,[2] and the man credited with introducing bestselling author Thomas Friedman to the millennial revelation that the world had become "flat," for corporations, for competition, and for technology. Routine blue-collar work had been moving offshore for decades, of course, but the information and communication technology (ICT) revolution beginning in the 1990s radically extended the process to many parts of the service economy. For economists like Frances Cairncross, this technological breakthrough meant that "[c]ompanies will locate any screen-based activity anywhere on earth, wherever they can find the best bargain of skills and productivity," threatening millions of once-secure jobs in higher-wage labor markets but opening up new opportunities for developing countries in a wide range of online economies.[3]

---

[1] Ashley (2008: xv).

[2] Worthen, B. (2007) What the world is flat means to IT outsourcing. *CIO Magazine* May 1, accessed at <http://www.cio.com/article/2439122/outsourcing/what-the-world-is-flat-means-to-it-outsourcing.html>, August 1, 2015.

[3] Cairncross (2001: xi).

The rise of transnational outsourcing—in its commonplace and largely pejorative form, as the "offshoring" of jobs from high-cost countries to lower-cost locations like India, China, and the Philippines in search of the advantages of "labor arbitrage"—has hardly been the subject of universal celebration. Hailed as a transformative business practice by corporate titans like Jack Welch of GE, celebrated as one of the most significant management ideas of the twentieth century by the *Harvard Business Review*, and presented as the harbinger of a new age of emancipatory globalization by opinion formers like Thomas Friedman,[4] outsourcing has also been widely denigrated for its role in "destroying" middle-class jobs in North America and Western Europe, as a root cause of inequality and insecurity, and as the malevolent work of a treacherous class of "Benedict Arnold CEOs" bent on profit maximization by any means necessary, unflinching in their exploitation of cheap-labor strategies in the race to the global bottom. Candidates for elected office have learned to mention the poisonous o-words of offshoring and outsourcing only when distancing themselves from the practices—or better still, attaching them to their opponents.[5] Public opinion polls, particularly in North America but also in higher-income countries more generally, reveal persistently negative attitudes, across all demographics and affiliations, to offshore outsourcing, which is popularly seen as a significant threat to jobs, wages, and economic security.[6] The phenomenon has duly acquired a social currency, albeit as a signifier for a singularly antisocial practice.

Yet none of these seems to have put much of a dent in the growth in offshore outsourcing, which may have been born as a new-age corporate innovation but which has since become an everyday business strategy. A widely quoted (but difficult to verify) claim from the consulting firm Accenture is that outsourcing, mostly to overseas partners, is now practiced by between 80 and 90 percent of Fortune 500 corporations.[7] The global sourcing market is reckoned to be worth in the region of $120–145 billion annually, the trade in information-technology and business-process outsourcing (ITO and BPO) having grown robustly since the late 1990s. The capitals of the multipolar world that is being (re)made by the transnational sourcing of tasks, work, commodities, and functions are illustrated in Figure 1.1. They

[4] See Sibbet, D. (1997) 75 years of management ideas and practice 1922–1997. *Harvard Business Review* supplement 75(5): 1–10; Welch, J. and Welch, S. (2006) Outsourcing is forever. *Business Week* July 31: 88; Friedman (2005); and Farrell (2006).
[5] See Dobbs (2004); Phillips (2012); Moore, M. (1996) *Downsize This!* New York: Crown; Smith, H. (2012) *Who Stole the American Dream?* New York: Random House.
[6] See Public Citizen (2015) *U.S. Polling Shows Strong Opposition to More of the Same U.S. Trade Deals from Independents, Republicans and Democrats Alike.* Washington, DC: Public Citizen; German Marshall Fund (2007) *Perspectives on Trade and Poverty Reduction.* Washington, DC: GMF.
[7] Around half of these Fortune 500 companies outsource to India alone, where the "offshore" workforce exceeds 3 million. See Corbett (2004) and Poster and Yolmo (2016).

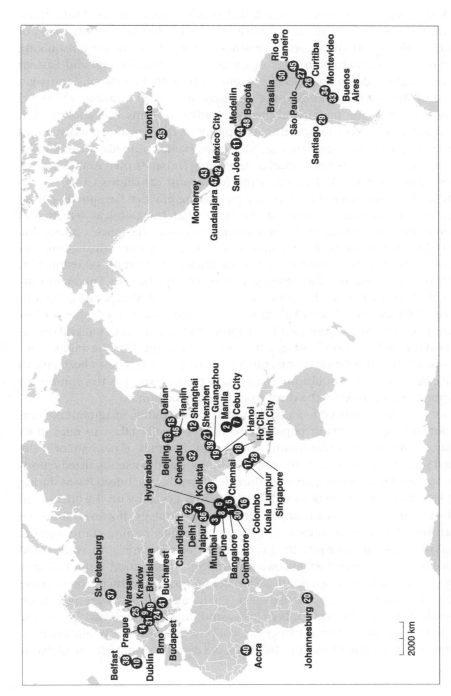

Figure 1.1 Top 50 global outsourcing sites, 2016
Source: author's rendering from Tholons 2016 global rankings

include a range of now well-established sites in India and the Philippines, where the outsourcing of IT and business services has become the basis of strategically important national industries. But rapidly maturing outsourcing economies can also be found across Latin America and Central and Eastern Europe (CEE), focused on cities like Dublin, São Paulo, Kraków, and Santiago. Some of the newer entrants to the rankings of top-100 locations for global sourcing, which are updated annually by advisory firms like Tholons, call attention to just how radical this remapping of the global economy might prove to be: they include Managua, Nicaragua; Halifax, Canada; Jakarta, Indonesia; San Antonio, Texas; Córdoba, Argentina; Dubai, United Arab Emirates; Recife, Brazil; Leeds, UK; Durban, South Africa; and Valparaiso, Chile.

What has long since ceased to be a pioneering practice has quietly passed into the mainstream—quietly in the sense that the political sensitivities around the issue mean that few corporations will announce outsourcing deals in press releases. In a paradoxical sense, offshore outsourcing has become an "internal" matter for the significant proportion of companies that, in some form or other, engage in the activity. Thomas Friedman now remarks that the practice has become so systemic, such a corporate commonplace, that executives "rarely talk about 'outsourcing' these days"; they are just getting on with the ongoing work of supply-chain transformation and organizational reconstruction.[8] Meanwhile, on the "outside," in the public consciousness and in political debate, offshore outsourcing has never been able to shake its negative connotations. Many have come to see it as the epitome of corporate ruthlessness—the dirty work of globalization.

Outsourcing now occupies a curious place in the public imagination. "Fear of outsourcing," which in popular discourse is usually taken to refer to its offshore variant, is extraordinarily widespread. In times of permanently elevated socioeconomic insecurity, populist rhetoric and sensationalized reporting can quickly turn this into something like a panic—as indeed it was during the U.S. presidential elections of 2004 and 2012. Dwelling on the "threat" of outsourcing for partisan advantage can be a risky strategy, however, since the usual bromides of mainstream economic policy (like training grants and tax breaks) are plainly unequal to the challenge of responding to what could prove to be seismic and widespread dislocations. In the short term, this may work as an attack term, or a political slur, but serious policy discussions around the issue remain few and far between. Public anxiety levels are not much helped, either, by the remarkably elusive and unstable "facts" of the matter, for which no systematic statistics are collected. (Indeed, it is questionable whether the net outcomes of outsourcing decisions are properly calculable at

---

[8] Friedman, T. (2012) Made in the world. *New York Times* January 29: SR11.

all, given that they are rarely about simply moving the "same" job from location A to location B, but typically involve job redesign, decomposition, and recomposition, new divisions of labor, and complex changes in the relationships within and between "sending" corporations, intermediaries, and service providers.) On top of these statistical complications, the negative political optics of outsourcing have contributed to a tacit policy of corporate quietude, or at least pragmatic discretion.

As a result, outsourcing is a high-profile political issue that remains in something of a fog. And although it will likely prove to be very important for labor markets and for corporate structures, its characteristic modes of operation are decidedly low profile. In comparison to earlier waves of internationalization and globalization, according to a recent scholarly assessment:

> What is happening now through outsourcing is much more obtuse, tenuous, and varied, straddling the lines of ethics and legality. It involves a full range of activities—in terms of industry, occupation, and tasks—from high skilled and high paying, to low skilled and subsistence wages. [Furthermore] what makes outsourcing especially distinctive is the extent to which it pushes the boundaries of what can (and should) be considered labour.[9]

Offshore outsourcing has become a normalized business practice, with effects that are incremental and ongoing. It short-term effects and medium-term reach may have both been subject to inflation, in the hands of pundits and politicians, which has not been helped by the corporate vow of silence that (partly as a result) envelopes the practice. This may not mean, however, that the transformative effects are necessarily being underestimated, even if they are routinely misrepresented. Indeed, the social, organizational, and economic implications of this quiet revolution are becoming increasingly evident, now that it is reckoned that around one third of all jobs in the United States might, in principle, be "offshorable," affecting occupations as diverse as accountancy, legal research, university teaching, and medical transcription.[10] Offshore outsourcing is compounding the "hollowing-out" phenomena in the high-wage economies of North America and Western Europe, where it has been operating in conjunction with automation, technological change, and "lean" models of corporate restructuring, to erode the demand for middle-income, middle-skill jobs.[11] It seems to be on the way to becoming

---

[9] Poster and Yolmo (2016: 583).

[10] See Blinder and Krueger (2008, 2013) and the discussion in Blinder (2009). These issues are further examined in Chapters 2 and 5.

[11] On forces and forms of labor-market restructuring, see Cappelli et al. (1997), Oldenski (2014), Theodore (2016), and also Stiglitz, J. (2009) The global crisis, social protection and jobs. *International Labour Review* 148(1–2): 1–13; Autor and Dorn (2013) The growth of low skill service jobs and the polarization of the US labor market. *American Economic Review* 103(5): 1553–97.

a macroeconomic phenomenon of real significance, having already become, in a curious sense, a cultural phenomenon.

The ocean-spanning "industry" that has grown up with and around outsourcing quickly learned to operate, whenever and wherever it could, under the radar, and to recoil from public (and research) scrutiny. Small armies of operations managers, consultants, technical facilitators, advisors, and enablers have been mobilized to make offshore outsourcing work. The world that they have made and that they inhabit, styled here as the "outsourcing complex," is the principal concern of this book. Those working in this new field of paraprofessional practice, the shapers of a significant new market for corporate services, have little reason to call attention to what they are doing. Theirs is a largely private world. After a brief period in the vanguard of the globalization project, in the 1990s and early 2000s, this fast-growing and increasingly sophisticated arm of the globalization business has tended to remain in the shadows. The shock of the new having passed, outsourcing no longer quite excites the passions, as it once did, of gurus and futurologists, or management-school "thought leaders." The issues confronting this maturing field of corporate practice are increasingly operational and organizational in nature. Some of them could be considered mundane, were they not so consequential.

What corporate clients like about offshore outsourcing, in addition to its role as a mechanism for lopping off between one and two thirds of hourly labor costs, while optimizing processes and trimming headcounts at the same time, is that they get to determine the terms of trade, terms that are typically enshrined in performance-based contracts with vendor companies and then imposed, often quite unilaterally, on these suppliers and, in turn, on their arm's-length workforces. However, what is less often properly calibrated, in advance at least, are the many "hidden costs" of outsourcing engagements, which are almost guaranteed to become a source of (new) frictions and frustrations, including issues of quality control, system integrity, communications, and coordination. For all parties involved this is difficult and demanding work, marked by a great deal of decidedly suboptimal practice, even if much of the underperformance is masked by substantial savings on the bottom line. As outsourcing has become a basic operational necessity, it has also become a zone of prosaic middle management, with its own communities of rather stressed practice, its own vernacular languages, and its own corporate folklore.

As those in the business will freely confess, "implementing an outsourcing [project] successfully is complicated . . . If it wasn't, the tales wouldn't thrive the way that they do."[12] For a while, it had seemed like rudimentary "out of the box" outsourcing strategies could work miracles in terms of financial

---

[12] Ashley (2008: xv).

savings and efficiency improvements, but over time this terrain has become more, rather than less, difficult to work. As an industry commentator recalls:

> When offshore came along, the cost of operation was so much lower [than in-house or onshore delivery] that even badly planned offshoring [projects] could absorb the mistakes and still show a significantly lower cost of operation. At least for a while… [Soon] managing a mature outsourced operation became more of a challenge than the exciting early days, and little by little the program lost value. Today, many programs that started off with problems or that developed problems over time, or simply ceased to be a priority, became examples of failed outsourcing. Many outsourcers simply want to change the name, but keep working the same way.[13]

Working with offshore service providers, after the deals have been signed, the cost savings booked, and the attentions of senior executives have shifted elsewhere, has in practice often descended to a mundane, daily struggle over performance indicators, quality control, and error rates. As outsourcing practices have become normalized, they have become part of the everyday operational grind in many companies. Meanwhile, the work of that small army of managerial facilitators, in the outsourcing industry proper, has to be focused on the unrelenting task of delivery in a context of an operating environment defined by narrow margins, creeping commoditization, and persistent organizational stress. Insights into the prosaic realities of offshore outsourcing can be (over)heard at industry events and gatherings (although usually away from the plenary stage), and they find expression in some corners of the specialist business media (especially the more unruly and unregulated of the practitioner blogs). Discretion being the watchword, however, most of those involved usually opt for a low profile; if there is dirty laundry, much better that this remains an internal matter.

Correspondingly, direct research access to outsourced operations, if it is granted at all, is generally restricted to industry-friendly investigators; even basic data, most of which is privately collected, tends to be confined to the prohibitively priced (yet only occasionally reliable) reports of consultancies and advisory firms; much is deemed market sensitive or proprietary and is not shared at all. As a result, this is a "new" global industry that the world knows relatively little about, beyond (often misleading) impressions, negative press coverage, management-consultancy spin, and the dry and self-edited outputs of industry-aligned researchers. While there is no shortage of workplace conversation and media speculation about offshoring, the fact remains that the vast majority of outsourcing engagements are managed from behind confidential

---

[13] Niccolls, C. (n.d.) Outsourcing: Is this the end? *About.com*, accessed at <http://outsourcing.about.com/od/feasibility/a/Outsourcing-Is-This-The-End.htm>, January 12, 2016.

contracts and corporate firewalls. In higher-income countries, where offshoring entered the public consciousness as a threat, almost everyone thinks they know about outsourcing, or claims to know someone who has been "outsourced,"[14] yet the phenomenon itself remains shrouded in misinformation if not menace. On those rare occasions when corporate outsourcing practices are described in close detail, these typically take the form of rather stylized business-school case studies, skewed towards success stories and models of innovation—which presumably was the basis upon which access was granted. True, some economists are beginning to develop ground-truthed estimates of the overall scale of the phenomenon,[15] and there is some excellent ethnographic work from the laboring end of outsourcing supply chains, for example in Indian "body shops,"[16] but there has been remarkably little discussion of how the newly formed outsourcing "industry" functions in and across its transnational theater of operations, of the form and consequences of anti-outsourcing politics and discourse, or of the structure and dynamics of the globalizing "market" for outsourced services.

Approaching the Outsourcing Complex

Offshore is an exploratory expedition into this somewhat veiled and privatized world, an examination of a fast-growing industry-cum-profession that has grown up with a particular aversion to the limelight. It draws upon four years of research, funded by the Social Sciences and Humanities Research Council of Canada and conducted first hand by the author, in the online and offline worlds of the outsourcing complex. This has involved a program of interviews, mainly in North America and Asia; observations at a series of conferences, meetings, and webinars involving outsourcing professionals and paraprofessionals in the United States, Latin America, and Asia; extensive documentary and historical analysis; and the tracking of industry blogs, market reports, and media. Candor and openness, it has to be said, are in somewhat short supply here, so triangulating across sources and sites in a search for persistent patterns, telling moments, and apt illustrations has been a somewhat improvised methodological necessity, which has drawn on an array of "middle-range" sources, mostly in the absence of reliable aggregate data at the big-picture scale or sustained access to managerial spaces at the ethnographic scale. Especially useful in this respect, where face-to-face interviews can only

---

[14] See Uchitelle (2007).
[15] See, for example, Blinder and Krueger (2013), Oldenski (2014), and the further discussion in Chapters 3 and 7.
[16] Good examples are Upadhya and Vasavi (2008) and Nadeem (2011).

go so far (due to selection bias in favor of relatively unproblematic engagements and the presence of various layers of commercial confidentiality or sensitivity), have been the various sources of what might be called industry "chatter." While this will sometimes include public relations and straightforwardly promotional content, the talk at industry conferences, in the trade magazines, and on the specialist blogs and websites will often be frank and direct, in its recurring and familiar forms conveying a strong sense of the aspirations, concerns, and frustrations of those working in and around the outsourcing complex. Piecing together information and insights from a range of sources, the goal has been to shine a light on the political economy of the outsourcing business, the structure, dynamics, and day-to-day operations of the outsourcing complex, and the psyche as well as the practices of those involved in designing and managing outsourced operations in this cross-border economy.

Rather than some righteous indictment of the dirty work of globalization, *Offshore* is a preliminary exploration of one of the interior, veiled worlds of corporate globalization, the outsourcing complex. It seeks to bring into the realm of the visible some of the work that is necessary to *make globalization work*, not so much as an heroic domain of corporate strategy but as a space of ordinary—stretched and stretched out—management. The visions, hopes, and aspirations of those working in the outsourcing complex are very much at issue here, in the sense that these speak to how this world is structured, in whose interests, and within what constraints. They also reflect the ambient anxieties of management, the context of persistent operational stress, and relentless competitive restructuring, where margins are characteristically thin and futures are uncertain. Correspondingly, a basic goal of the book is to reveal something of the *character* of the outsourcing business, in a sociological and even psychological sense, as well as in more strictly "economic" terms, to render somewhat more real a complex of actors, organizations, and activities that is characteristically positioned, metaphorically speaking, just over the horizon. To this end, some preliminary work of definition and clarification is in order.

If outsourcing entails "the allocation of risk and responsibility for performing a function or service to another entity," and *global* sourcing involves the extension of the attendant bundle of business, employment, and contracting practices across national borders, those in the trade will also acknowledge that, to put it mildly, "outsourcing means something different to different people." Developing the point, the author of *Outsourcing for Dummies*, Ed Ashley, breaks it down this way:

> Some see [outsourcing] as a synonym for lost jobs, while others see it as a great way to save money and offer improved services. No matter what, it is often controversial and sometimes brings stress to all involved.

9

> The word *outsourcing* stimulates emotion in a lot of people. Some will tell you that the word is French for "firing people." It is understandable because the early years of outsourcing often involved companies blindly transferring work to outsourcers ... [But] I have yet to hear of a [business] leader who pursued outsourcing because he or she wanted to fire people. [They are doing it] for sound business reasons ... Conversely, I've heard countless tales of outsourcing engagements gone awry. Many such situations have been highly publicized, making the stigma associated with outsourcing even worse.[17]

Not surprisingly, those in the outsourcing industry bristle at their portrayal as hard-nosed, mean-spirited "lift and shift" merchants, with a purpose no more noble than the cutting of costs and the exploitation of cheap labor supplies. They understand, of course, that theirs was an industry founded on a promise, made to executives, that a new cadre of offshore vendors could take over the routine operations of client companies, delivering them at much lower cost and with little fuss (the "your mess for less" model). But they also know that this is complicated and challenging work, very often bringing "stress to all involved." Nevertheless, labor arbitrage (or what translated in the *Dummies* guide as "a fancy term for taking advantage of wages that are cheaper elsewhere") has always been, and seems set to remain, an elemental rationale of the global sourcing business. This basic function of cutting and suppressing costs remains fundamental, a defining feature of offshore outsourcing, even as its conventions and practices become increasingly sophisticated, even as service offerings, project-management techniques, and governance arrangements have been enriched, and even as there has been a gradual climb up value chain and occupational hierarchies, into more complex and skilled fields of work.[18] Despite all of this, the stigma remains.

It is true that outsourcing practices and processes have become increasingly refined and robust, and the business of the outsourcing complex these days is about much more than capturing one-time savings on the bottom line for corporate clients. At the same time, however, the quasi-markets that have been constructed around globally outsourced services and functions remain highly price-sensitive—especially where thousands of providers (or "vendors") are fighting for the same contracts and where the products that they are selling remain fairly standardized and substitutable. Yet the streamlining and standardization of organizational systems and business processes—in order that tasks can be deskilled, decomposed, and decoupled from more expensive "onshore" locations—is integral to how this business works. The

---

[17] Ashley (2008: 25–6). Ed Ashley, like many in the newly styled occupation of "outsourcing professionals," has a varied background in international management, ICTs, and management consultancy, and now earns a living as a consulting advisor, helping companies design, operate, and think about these complex operations.

[18] Ashley (2008: 31).

outsourcing industry therefore appears to be doomed to grapple with a basic contradiction, that its own effectiveness in rationalizing, routinizing, and redesigning work tasks, in order to deliver and manage lean operations at a distance, tends to facilitate the very commoditization that the vendors of outsourced services aspire to transcend, in their efforts to move into higher value-added, more trust- or relationship-based, and less price-sensitive markets. For their part, the corporate buyers of outsourced services, who invariably dominate these profoundly competitive supply chains,[19] have grown accustomed to demanding "more for less"—more quality and consistency, shorter turnaround times, and added extras in the shape of augmented services—all with rolling, year-on-year efficiency gains. If this is not delivered, corporate buyers will often switch to another provider, the "winner" of a yet more tightly prescriptive and demanding bidding process. And still, these corporate buyers are, by all accounts, rarely satisfied, even as they know they are making life difficult for vendors and their staff. No wonder that outsourcing engagements are reported to "bring stress to all involved."

One of the reasons that the corporate clients tend to be unhappy, apparently much of the time, is that they have learned that the promised savings on unit labor costs are often diminished—sometimes significantly—by that bundle of "hidden costs, such as those associated with managerial coordination, operational quality, and contractual disputes.[20] Field reports from the early years of the outsourcing boom have revealed that the primal urge to extract cost reductions and efficiency gains by offloading non-core tasks to low-cost providers, and then effectively abdicating managerial responsibility, led to all manner of system failures and service-delivery problems that really should have been anticipated—a phenomenon that has been called the "black hole of outsourcing."[21] According to industry insider Ben Worthen, writing in *CIO*, the magazine for chief information officers:

> When a company first engages an outsourcer with offshoring capabilities, it is usually thinking one thing: reduce costs. True, the labor arbitrage can be

[19] Increased competition amongst vendors means that outsourcing has become a "buyers' market" (Hätönen and Eriksson, 2009: 143). On the structure and dynamics of outsourcing markets, see Chapter 4. On the question of outsourcing and global supply chains, see Gereffi (2006) and Coe and Yeung (2015), and the further discussion in Chapter 2.

[20] On the so-called hidden costs of outsourcing, see Barthelemy (2001) and Larsen et al. (2013). See also Stringfellow, A., Teagarden, M. B., and Nie, W. (2008) Invisible costs in offshoring services work. *Journal of Operations Management* 26(2): 164–79; Reitzig, M. and Wagner, S. (2010) The hidden costs of outsourcing: Evidence from patent data. *Strategic Management Journal* 31(11): 1183–201.

[21] Mullin (1996: 29). Mullin explains the black-hole problem as follows: the "early rush to cut costs [resulted] in the complete disintegration of the outsourced processes' original management structure," corporate clients' virtual abdication of managerial responsibility for outsourced processes having created an "environment where suppliers manage the relationship," often not very well, and sometimes disastrously.

staggering... But the initial cost savings often mask long-term problems. Most companies tend to outsource processes without examining their quality and efficiency. They generally hope—or contractually demand—that the outsourcer fix things for them. Indeed, after the first year of an engagement... companies [tend to] to focus less on cost savings and more on flexibility and agility. That takes time, money and management attention—and may blow away the initial cost savings.[22]

The typical response on the part of corporate clients, as a substantial number of first-generation outsourcing engagements began to turn sour, was to hold vendors' feet to the fire, but even if this approach yielded some short-term gains (minus the cost of lawyers' fees), it would seldom lead to productive and constructive relationships in the longer run. And so the next move on the part of a corporate client might be to rotate the contract, suitably revised and "tightened," to another vendor, after which something like the same dispiriting experience would often be repeated. Ironically, as the global vendor market itself became more crowded and competitive, the front-end costs of rotating providers were generally falling, even as the concealed costs of poorly designed or executed outsourcing engagements remained stubbornly high. For their part, even if offshore vendors were understandably prone to minimizing or obfuscating the true costs of organizational coordination and downstream delivery in their sales pitches to corporate clients—no doubt genuinely hoping that any additional downstream costs could be minimized—they were at the same time subject to intense competitive pressures (both from peer providers and from corporate clients) to keep promising more for less.

The global sourcing market, even as it has matured, continues to be riven by problems of operational stress, creeping commoditization, and periodic failures of managerial coordination, such that the business of the outsourcing complex—even as there is more of it, even as the parties learn to execute better—remains inherently challenging, if not endemically fraught. This is not a business for amateurs, or for executives in search of an easy life. Those in the outsourcing complex with years of accumulated experience (and the air-miles credits to show it) have been working to gain recognition for their practical knowledge and vernacular expertise, along the way constituting a start-up profession of sorts. This has been something of an uphill task, however, since so much of the outsourcing business has become a delegated and relegated problem of *and for* middle management. It follows that the circulation and codification of what passes for expertise, or field knowledge, in the outsourcing complex tends to occur laterally and somewhat haphazardly, in and around

---

[22] Worthen, B. (2007) What the world is flat means to IT outsourcing. *CIO Magazine* May 1, accessed at <http://www.cio.com/article/2439122/outsourcing/what-the-world-is-flat-means-to-it-outsourcing.html>, August 1, 2015.

these middle layers of operational management, as opposed to being passed down from well-recognized sources of authority. Expertise tends to be practical, tacit, and idiomatic; its domain of application will often be organizationally particular or task specific; anything resembling a successful formula or "secret sauce" will be swiftly appropriated and then stylized by the consulting and advisory companies that have colonized the field, but in truth few believe that universal fixes or magic bullets really exist.

The practical knowledge and ordinary expertise concerning how to make outsourcing engagements work (or at least work incrementally better) tends to exist in a rather disorganized and privatized form within the community of outsourcing paraprofessionals, and in the heterogeneous universe that is the outsourcing complex, with its interconnected networks of advisory and consulting firms, specialist intermediaries and service providers, and third-party vendors. The most valuable knowledge is accumulated through years of learning by doing, and amongst those managers, consultants, and advisors with track records spanning multiple assignments, many clients, and many geographies. Recognizing this, corporate buyers commonly turn to third-party vendors and specialist service providers, as repositories of operational expertise, in what has become the prevailing governance model in the offshore outsourcing business:

> The range of reasons [for using third-party vendors to deliver outsourcing projects] include the increasing availability of service providers offering not only standardized [packages], but also more specific and knowledge-intensive product development and analytical services ... However, as business services are becoming more commodified, more providers are able to offer services at low costs which decreases incentives for client firms to internalize the delivery of these services, and which also decreases the costs of switching providers ... [C]ompanies recognize that managing outsourcing activities is not their core competence and that [specialist vendors] can provide the advantages of economies of scale and scope ... [Yet despite] the increase in the commoditization of services and the growing trend towards selecting third party providers, clients continue to report major managerial challenges in implementing offshore outsourcing projects.[23]

There are echoes here of the way in which the earlier rise of temporary employment services—a now pervasive form of *domestic* outsourcing—reduced labor costs and externalized certain risks, but also complicated lines of responsibility and control in "triangulated" employment relationships, in which the temp agencies are typically the intermediating third party.[24] Global

---

[23] Manning, S., Lewin, A. Y., and Schuerch, M. (2011) The stability of offshore outsourcing relationships. *Management International Review* 51(3): 381–406, pp. 383, 385.

[24] On triangulation, see Gottfried, H. (1992) In the margins: Flexibility as a mode of regulation in the temporary help service industry. *Work, Employment and* Society 6(3): 443–60. On the

outsourcing engagements take this intermediary role, quite literally, to another scale altogether. They necessitate coordination not only between organizations but across borders, and often across languages, cultures, and time zones; and they invariably involve larger, more complex, and longer-term deals. If temp agencies have found their work, since the 1970s, amid the flux of contingency, as their client firms sought to achieve flexibility and manage volatility while rightsizing their operations and tightening budgets, outsourcing vendors have subsequently been engaged in the business of externalizing—on a long-term if not semi-permanent basis—significant elements of the operations of client companies. The stakes, and the management challenges, tend to rise accordingly.

Rather than some discrete phenomenon, global sourcing is consequently tied up with a host of transformative changes in corporate organization, management strategy, and purchasing behavior, impinging not on the boundaries of individual firms but of entire industries and indeed economies. There are many gray areas (and blurred boundaries) here, and so some clarification of basic terminology is called for. Across the matrix of corporate make-or-buy decisions in domestic and offshore markets that are summarized in Table 1.1, the transnational variety of this activity involves the sourcing of labor inputs and services from overseas vendors or suppliers. It entails transactions that exceed the boundaries both of the (purchasing) firm and those of the national economy in which that firm is located. In this respect, global sourcing represents an organizational and employment form that is not one but two steps removed from the model of the integrated domestic firm (cell A in Table 1.1), reflecting a *combination* of the decision to outsource (as in cells C and D) with the decision to internationalize (as in cells B and D).

Table 1.1. Spaces of outsourcing: global sourcing versus its others

	Domestic	Offshore
In-house	A The integrated firm	B Corporate transnationalization
	Both core and secondary activities are managed within the organizational boundaries of the firm, sited within a domestic economy	Establishment of overseas divisions or "captive" centers. Transnational firms with functions that span national borders
Outsourcing	C Domestic sourcing	D Global sourcing
	Buying in inputs and services from local (in-country) suppliers and providers	Sourcing inputs and services from overseas vendors and suppliers. Interfirm contracting and collaboration across national borders

political economy of the temp "industry," domestically and internationally, see Peck and Theodore (1998, 2002), Theodore and Peck (2002), and Peck et al. (2005).

14

Mainstream accounts of economic globalization and corporate transformation will often describe a unidirectional trajectory, away from the integrated firm operating within a domestic economy (cell A) to various forms of internationalization, subcontracting, and partnering (cells B through D), but even if this accounts, broadly speaking, for the direction of travel, it will routinely underestimate the organizational and sociological implications of venturing into cell D, the offshore world of global sourcing. The latter are the concerns of this book. As will become clear, rather than some single-event, unidirectional "move," the embrace of offshore outsourcing represents a threshold-crossing moment in what is a complex, evolutionary process both for individual firms and the wider economy—one that brings in its wake a series of cascading consequences (and contradictions) for organizational structures, for technology utilization, for job design and employment, and for business location.

If the corporate drivers of outsourcing have been evolving, so too have the dominant practices and discourses of the outsourcing complex itself. It is more than two decades now since the prevailing model of offshore outsourcing began its long journey from what early commentators described as "a desperate means of cutting costs to a more subtle strategy of partnering with service suppliers that perform critical, but non-core functions," a move from a merely transactional to a more relationship-based or transformational approach, which would cut ever more deeply into near core and even core business functions and labor forces through processes of corporate unbundling and horizontal partnering.[25] This transition—from transactional to transformational outsourcing—may represent a generalized direction of change across the outsourcing complex, but it is a journey that continues to be an extremely challenging one, while only a small minority of best-in-breed engagements come close to approaching the hallowed goal of "transformation." The transition summarized in Table 1.2 is more appropriately understood, therefore, as partly realized tendency (and indeed an aspirational vision) rather than a stabilized achievement. Transformational outsourcing represents a high-road model to which most involved in the industry aspire, in some form or other, but which has been difficult to realize in a sustained or comprehensive manner. "Transactional" imperatives—associated with the original, cost-cutting, arbitrage-based rationale for outsourcing—have been stubbornly persistent, even as services have been enriched, as vendors have become more sophisticated, and as engagements have become more complex. An industry that was formed and forged by the logic of commoditization has been striving continuously to transcend the

---

[25] Mullin (1996: 29). See also Sako, M. (2006) Outsourcing and offshoring: Implications for productivity of business services. *Oxford Review of Economic Policy* 22(4): 499–512.

Table 1.2. Modalities of outsourcing: between the transactional and the transformational

	Transactional	Transformational
Rationale	*Cost reduction*, efficiency gains, and profit maximization; focused on transfer of routine "lift and shift" operations; intended to take out costs for the benefit of "onshore" client firms	*Organizational transformation*; dynamic efficiencies, shared product, and service development; redesigning business processes; enhancing organizational capabilities
Relationships	Arm's length, *price-oriented* transactions with vendors; purchaser-provider relationships; rudimentary contracts	Strategic collaborations and *partnerships* with vendors; evolutionary and performance-based contracting; asset and technology transfers
Logic	Vertical *disintegration*, adoption of lean structures, and the shift from "make to buy"	Corporate "*unbundling*," and the shift from secondary to increasingly core functions
Competences	Focus on core competences within client firms; outsourcing of secondary activities and *routinized* tasks	Mutual development of dynamic competences across organizations; vendors and suppliers build *shared* competences
Labor	*Arbitrage*: tapping into low-wage labor pools/locations as a substitute for existing functions and operations at lower cost	*Access* to specialized knowledge and talent pools, in order to leverage competitive advantages
Processes	*Standardized* solutions, combining lower-cost labor with basic automation and rule-bound systems	Increasingly *customized* and complex solutions; focus on higher value-added operations and functions
Skill	*Downgrading* dynamic prevails: fragmentation and routinization of outsourced tasks and functions; centrifugal deskilling	*Upgrading* dynamic prevails: vendors and suppliers move up the value chain, taking on more complex tasks; decentralized upskilling
Vendors	As *providers*; "your mess for less" business proposition; early market entrants focus on price-based strategies	As *partners*; strategic coevolution with clients; deep and mature infrastructure of increasingly sophisticated vendors
Geographies	*Offshore*; spatial stretching of supply chains, principally from higher- to lower-cost locations	"*Multishore*" (re)combination and reintegration of offshore, nearshore, and onshore operations

constraints imposed by price-based competition and the associated pattern of asymmetrical relations with the dominant class of corporate buyers, but so far with only limited success.

While the outsourcing industry likes to convey the impression, at least in terms of its own public-relations image, that it has matured away from the cheap-labor model, the hard-to-escape reality is that cost suppression remains an existential condition. In part, this can be put down to managerial (and shareholder) pressures emanating from the corporate clients that effectively determine the rules of engagement, who largely set prices, and who dominate the trade, but it also reflects the structure of these extended supply chains, which reach far and wide into developing-country markets, creating conditions of competitive crowding and cost undercutting amongst third-party vendors.[26] While there is certainly some evidence of movement towards more transformative models of outsourcing, based on the principles of high performance, shared competences, and service enrichment, competitive conditions mean that these are still delivered on low-cost terms. There is very little "fat" in outsourcing contracts, even as the expectations (and demands) of corporate clients in terms of quality continue to escalate. It is neither accurate nor fair, in each and every context, to portray outsourcing operations as bottom-feeding activities, consistent with the industry's acquired reputation for handling the dirty work of globalization, but what seems to be indisputable is that this is some of the more *difficult* work of globalization, for the managers of these operations as well as for the workers employed within them.

This is a story of actually existing globalization somewhat at odds with the well-known tales about the so-called death of geography courtesy of the leveling effects of technology and competition. It is true that outsourcing occupies a somewhat deregulated space, sharing with other offshore worlds, for instance those in finance and taxation, a certain culture of discretion, sometimes bordering on secrecy.[27] But this is hardly a featureless, free-market landscape, a product of undiluted corporate will. On the contrary, the turbulent landscapes of the outsourcing complex testify to the ongoing challenges of working offshore, and of managing at a distance. Rather than the death of geography, this has involved the creation of new economic geographies and the continual remaking of *spatial* divisions of labor.[28] In turn, reading this changing landscape can offer insights into the unfolding of corporate strategies and the evolution of competitive dynamics, not as some one-way process but as an often contradictory trajectory of restructuring. Using the outsourcing complex as its sprawling case, this is the approach of the book.

Some of the principal geographical vectors were easy enough to discern at the start: in the early 1970s, what was dubbed the new international division of labor (NIDL) involved the relocation of routine manufacturing activities to Latin America and Eastern Europe, and later on to China and beyond; subsequent waves of outsourcing activity, beginning in earnest in the mid-1990s, were focused on services, as an array of back-office, finance and accounting, and information-technology jobs went to India and then to the Philippines. But subsequently, a combination of rising costs in some of the "first-tier" outsourcing locations, coupled with the coordination challenges associated with the governance of long supply chains and management of

---

[26] Gereffi, G. and Fernandez-Stark, K. (2010) The offshore services value chain: Developing countries and the crisis. In Cattaneo, O., Gereffi, G., and Staritz, C., eds, *Global Value Chains in a Postcrisis World: A development perspective*. Washington, DC: International Bank for Reconstruction and Development/World Bank, 335–72.

[27] See, especially, Palan (2003), Brittain-Catlin (2005), and Urry (2014).

[28] The classic account is that of Doreen Massey (1984).

far-off operations, led to a reevaluation of what would become known as "nearshore" locations—immediately adjacent to the largest of the corporate-buyer markets of North America and Western Europe, and even some selective "onshoring" of mission-critical, highly iterative, or boutique activities into lower-wage regions of the United States. Most recently, a wave of software-based automation, known as robotic process automation (RPA), has begun to sweep across this moving landscape, raising a new set of concerns about labor displacement and leading some to predict that the "final destination" for the outsourcing business might not be some (even) lower-cost location, but instead the "noshore" space of cloud-based operations.

Tracing some of these movements and countermovements in the evolving business of global sourcing, *Offshore* begins from the vantage point of those sites—the corporate capitals of North America and Western Europe—from which "offshore" locations were first envisioned and targeted, and from which the supply chains of the industry are still for the most part controlled. These are the sites, moreover, from which the impetus to undercut established labor contracts, wages, and conditions originated, and where the politics of offshore outsourcing remain at their most fraught. From this point of departure, the book heads out into the outsourcing complex itself, as a newly constituted space (or "platform") of paraprofessional activity, norm setting, networking, and negotiation, to investigate how the industry works, and how it regards and regulates itself. And then, the later chapters of the book focus on the geographical, technological, and organizational restructuring of the global sourcing business, tracing and accounting for its evolutionary complexity and recurring contradictions—all the way out to the imagined location of "Robotistan," the posthuman land beyond labor arbitrage that in some feverish visions is portrayed as the industry's terminal destination. Whether or not this vision of wholesale labor displacement/replacement by way of automation comes to pass, the urgent discussions and strategic positioning that it has (already) provoked speak to the threats that confront the outsourcing complex, as its principals grapple with a fast-arriving future.

The Book Ahead

Complementing the work that is beginning to assemble a picture of outsourcing at the macroeconomic scale, and at the level of individual workplace, *Offshore* sets out to understand the organizational and sociological character of the outsourcing complex, as a rapidly evolving transnational industry-cum-market, as a capacity-making "infrastructure," and as a maturing domain of managerial practice. The processes and practices of the outsourcing complex operate (by definition) across national and organizational boundaries, and as a result tend to be marked by a certain liminality—which is only compounded by the reputational deficits that attach to this often misunderstood and maligned work. From time to time, there have been efforts to renovate and upgrade the image of the industry, but cleaning up someone else's mess for less remains a less than glamorous if not Cinderella activity, an association that is hard to miss on those occasions when the industry gathers, for one of its regular "world summits," in the incongruous location of the Disney World resort in Orlando. The outsourcing industry at work (and play) will be encountered here in Chapter 4.

Prior to that, however, there is some work to do properly to position global outsourcing in its historical and political context. This begins with Chapter 2, which presents an abbreviated (modern) history of outsourcing, from the identification of the NIDL in the 1970s, through the ascendancy of outsourcing as an innovatory business practice from the late 1980s and into the 1990s, to the rancorous "offshoring" debates of the last decade. The chapter provides a genealogical and political-economic commentary on the rise of global outsourcing, from an epiphenomenon of the crisis of competitiveness facing some of the major manufacturing firms of North America and Western Europe in the 1970s, through the digital revolutions of the 1990s and the opening up of white-collar outsourcing markets, to the construction of the contemporary outsourcing "industry," with its peculiar (but constitutive) mix of strong growth, corporate regularization, political stigmatization, and second-class status.

Political representations of outsourcing are the concern of Chapter 3. By way of a deconstruction of presidential campaign discourse in the United States, the chapter explores the politics of offshore outsourcing, as seen from onshore. The accusation of "shipping jobs overseas" has established a singular cultural frame through which the practice of outsourcing has been (negatively and also preemptively) judged. In 2004, the uproar created by the George W. Bush Administration's inadvertent blunder into the outsourcing question turned this into something approaching a third-rail issue in U.S. politics. This set the tone and the terms for an even less substantive rerun in the campaign of 2012, when Barack Obama's challenger, Mitt Romney, was branded "outsourcer in chief," thanks to his presence at the alleged scene of the crime, Bain Capital, and some of the early forays into offshore outsourcing through the private-equity restructuring business. Presidential candidate Donald Trump proposed to outlaw the practice, no less. In its relatively short but checkered history, *offshoring* has provided a stage for an unedifying form of political theater in U.S. presidential campaigns. But in this context it has been more of a substitute—rather than an occasion—for the substantive debate of economic policy options. The profoundly cyclical, often cynical, and ultimately inconclusive nature of U.S. outsourcing debates calls attention to their symbolic form, to their apparently visceral connection to underlying sources of economic uncertainty across the working and voting public at large, and to what has become an extended condition of bipartisan detachment from the fundamental policy issues of trade and employment.

Following these explorations of the constitutive outsides of the outsourcing phenomenon, Chapter 4 enters the outsourcing complex itself. This multidimensional socioeconomic formation spans industrial sectors, occupations, management fields, organizations, and countries, being part industry, part profession, and part market, although it also exceeds (and confounds) each of these analytical templates. Concerned with the nexus of discourse, practice, and organizational dynamics, the chapter departs from the issue of the negative political framing of outsourcing "at large," in order to examine the shared mindsets, modes of (self-)organization, and business practices that have grown up around the outsourcing complex itself. This means taking account of the "infrastructural" role of the outsourcing complex, its functions as an enabler of disaggregated corporate structures and "extruded" modes of management, and the evolving competitive dynamics of outsourcing markets. Outsourcers dream of self-transformation, under the signs of continuous innovation, respectful partnership, and talent mobilization, but this high-road vision is persistently frustrated by the industry's own conditions of existence, based as these continue to be on cost suppression and undercutting, low-wage labor arbitrage, and the top-heavy control of supply chains (and therefore market conditions) by corporate buyers. This means that the industry's search for respect (and professional status) has a forlorn and futile air.

Outsourcing, fundamentally, has always been about the search for cheaper labor, and therefore cheaper locations. This drove the initial rounds of outbound investment in India and China, and then into other countries, as well as down to second- and third-tier cities—to what those in the industry call "new geographies." More recently, there has been a significant movement, especially of voice-based services and financial processing, to a number of nearshore locations in Latin America and CEE, coupled with a more limited, but nonetheless loudly trumpeted, move to "backshore" some activities to certain lower-cost locations in the United States, especially in the rural South. Chapter 5 explores these shifting geographical priorities, rationalities, and horizons, and what they reveal about the locational (and cultural) preferences of corporate clients, as mediated through the phalanx of service providers and advisors that comprise the outsourcing complex. There is more than a little irony in the fact that the upstart business of "rural sourcing" in the United States is being promoted, including by former presidents Bill Clinton and Barak Obama as a "new" industry well suited to the less developed corners of the sunbelt South and the economically lagging parts of the Midwest, where economic development officials will now boast of wage and production costs that have become competitive with those found offshore. The fact that this is partly due to (sometimes exaggerated, but nonetheless real) wage inflation in some of the established capitals of offshore outsourcing, especially in India, coupled with long-run wage suppression in the United States, speaks to the inherently bumpy and circuitous nature of what is sometimes portrayed as a one-way race to the bottom. The bottom, it follows, may not be where we think it is ... In fact, a significant backwash effect may be underway, across the globalizing labor markets that have been made and remade by outsourcing networks, as expressed in the sustained growth of nearshore markets. Centered on Latin America and the CEE region, adjacent to the global centers of demand for outsourced services, nearshore zones have been registering high rates of growth, driven not only by a new generation of domestic suppliers from the "new Bangalores" of Mexico, the Czech Republic, El Salvador, Poland, and many of their neighbors, but also from the constantly moving global networks of some of the Indian pioneers of outsourcing 1.0.

If nearshore servicing of corporate clients in North America and Western Europe represents an outsourcing future that has already arrived, Chapter 6 looks into a future that even some in the outsourcing sector seem to fear— robotic process automation or RPA. *Robota* is a Czech word for a Central European regime of serfdom or forced labor. The word first acquired its con-temporary meaning—*robot*, as some kind of automated, posthuman agent—in a 1920s play by Karel Čapek and subsequently in the genre-shaping fiction of Isaac Asimov. It took some time for life to truly imitate art, but the recent development and rapid commercialization of labor-displacing software 'bots, under the banner of RPA, has been prompting the sort of socioeconomic futurology that would not be out of place on the science-fiction shelves. Walking this line between prophetic fiction and prospective fact, Chapter 6 focuses on a recent outbreak of *robophobia* amongst established BPO and ITO providers in India, the Philippines, and beyond, where RPA is being read by some as a possibly terminal threat to the incumbent business model (predicated on arbitraged, routinized, and low-cost labor), and by others as an invitation to new markets for the design and delivery of cyborg business-services systems.

The question of whether the offshore outsourcing business is on the road to "Robitistan," the farthest shore for distanciated work, brings the discussion full circle to recurring debates around the "end of work." These have recently found expression in the apocalyptic forecast that almost half of the current jobs in the U.S. economy could, in principle, be automated virtually out of existence— maybe onshore, maybe offshore, or somewhere in between. Whether or not the robots arrive in anything like these numbers, software-enabled automation seems certain to have a significant impact on the globalized sphere of digitally reorganized work. To some degree, it can be seen as a genuine substitute for offshore outsourcing, since the routinized tasks on which outsourcers originally built their markets have already been "primed" for automation. Not only does this represent, for some observers, a potential "killer" of extant models of long-distance outsourcing; rather ironically it is also being promoted as a politically palatable "alternative" to offshoring for client companies in high-income countries. In these locations, the combined and cumulative effects of software automation and offshore outsourcing represent a structural change that is arguably comparable with the onset of deindustrialization in the 1970s, with massive implications not only for corporate structures, occupational profiles, and work practices but also for social structures.

These explorations anticipate a conclusion that in the circumstances can really be no conclusion at all. For the restless logics of relocation that have been expressed through offshore outsourcing represent but one episode in ongoing processes of global restructuring. The protracted birth of the outsourcing complex has been about more than the production of a new industry or would-be profession; it has been about the build-out and consolidation of a new organizational infrastructure, or platform, for the transnational redistribution and routinization of work. It has changed, and will continue to change, the terms of trade in globalizing labor markets, impacting not only the location of employment but also the design and definition of jobs themselves, along with their remuneration, security, and social status, with wide and deep implications for regional economic development, corporate geographies, and local living standards. The outsourcing complex has established a kind of globalized matrix for the functional decomposition and geographical redistribution of work tasks, fragmenting and automating jobs, driving down costs and wages, and enabling new forms of long-distance labor-market competition. The stage has therefore been set for an accelerated period of restructuring in corporate, organizational, and employment systems. "Going offshore" has not been a one-time locational shift. Rather, it marked the beginning of an evolutionary journey, the ultimate destination of which remains unclear, after many twists and turns, although it is not likely to be reversed.

2

Exploring Outsourcing Space

Outsource, outsourced, outsourcer, *outsourcing*. "A community is known by the language it keeps," lexicographer John Algeo has written, "its words chronicle the times."[1] While the practice of outsourcing is in many ways as old as capitalism, referring as it does to basic "make or buy" decisions that effectively define the boundaries of the enterprise, the neologism itself forced its way into the industrial-relations lexicon of Anglo-American capitalism during the 1970s. This chapter embarks on the book's exploration of the worlds of offshore outsourcing by going to the source—in a literal, figurative, and ultimately political-economic sense. It begins by presenting a situated genealogy of the word/concept/strategy itself, before discussing the influential treatment of the outsourcing zeitgeist in the shape of Thomas Friedman's popular treatment of corporate globalization, *The World Is Flat*. The chapter then turns to those accounts that have positioned outsourcing, more methodically, in the context of transnational modes of economic restructuring, from the identification of the "new international division of labor" (NIDL) in the 1970s, through to contemporary work on global production networks and value chains. The chapter is concluded with an initial sketch of the outsourcing complex, and the birth of outsourcing as a managerial field, one that combines skill sets while also spanning industries, organizations, and countries. This liminality is one reason for the somewhat ambiguous and insecure status of outsourcing as a field of paraprofessional practice, one in which both expertise and value are repeatedly lost to the market.

Outsourcing, in Word and Deed

The first recorded reference to the word *outsourcing* came, quite appropriately, from an investigative report in the *New Yorker*, where it was portrayed as a

---

[1] Algeo, J. (1991) Introduction. In J. Algeo with A. S. Algeo, eds, *Fifty Years among the New Words: A dictionary of neologisms, 1941–1991*. New York: Cambridge University Press, 1–16, p. 1.

weapon of a globalizing managerial class bent on "colonizing the future." In 1974, the magazine's reporters at large in the world of the multinational corporations, Richard Barnet and Ronald Müller, delivered an extensive exposé on what they characterized, quite presciently, as the coming age of globalization, one marked by widening inequalities, unprecedented concentrations of corporate and financial power, ecological and social devastation, and the erosion of democratic institutions. The argument was that the rise of the "global factory," propelled by the accelerating foreign investments of major corporations since the late 1950s, was establishing a "new division of labor... around the world," threatening a "Latin-Americanization" of the U.S. job market.[2] Hatched in the boardrooms and banking headquarters of the United States, the plan to relocate jobs to low-wage "export platforms" like Taiwan and Singapore, which were beginning to move into higher value-added activities, was equated to a centrifugal force of global reach that was destined to undermine wages, conditions, and employment security. A new world was being made, with disturbing implications for the domestic economy of the United States, and for the country's working class in particular. "Foreign competition," on this telling, was literally that, indeed it was embodied as such. Representative Joseph Gaydos of Pennsylvania was quoted in the New Yorker story, who in a speech to the U.S. Congress in 1971 had vividly portrayed the new competitive threat:

> The unschooled girls of Taiwan can do just as well assembling complex TV components as the high-school graduates of New Jersey. The untrained workers of African or Asian nations can be taught to produce complex products, ranging from tiny transistors to giant turbines, as readily as the skilled workers of Pennsylvania or the West Coast. And the depressed inhabitants of the most squalid slums of the Far East can be taught to make specialty steel products just as well as the experienced workers of Pittsburgh.[3]

The strongholds of unionized labor, in particular, were now being confronted by "take it or leave it" bargaining positions, premised on the implicit or explicit threat of disinvestment in the form of the "runaway shop," a corporate scheme to move production and jobs overseas in order to tap cheap labor abroad while breaking unions at home. "Nothing is better calculated to weaken the bargaining power of labor," Barnet and Müller concluded, "than management's prerogative to divide and shift tasks at will on a global scale."[4] Sensing that they were living through an "apocalyptic age"—a time of stagflation, falling living standards, and a wave of factory closures that would later metastasize into "deindustrialization"—the New Yorker contributors emphasized

[2] Barnet and Müller (1974: 131, 139, 100).
[3] Quoted in Barnet and Müller (1974: 122).
[4] Barnet and Müller (1974: 131). See also Bluestone and Harrison (1982).

24

that a host of more subtle and rather less palpable changes were also afoot, courtesy of the corporate strategies for profit restoration and the dull compulsion of rising international competition. One of the "less drastic" tools at the disposal of corporate management, less drastic than plant closure and offshore relocation that is, was the new strategy of "what is called multiple worldwide sourcing— different plants in different countries producing the same component."[5]

This rudimentary form of international sourcing has been identified by lexicographers as the root of the contemporary meaning of the term. By the time that the word had made it into the principal dictionaries of new words, in the early 1980s, *out-sourcing* was already traveling with a bundle of generally negative connotations relating to international relocation, cost cutting, and deunionization:

> out-sourcing, *n*. in manufacturing, the practice of acquiring parts from non-union or foreign suppliers, especially as a cost-cutting measure.

The compilers of the *Barnhart Dictionary Companion*, from which this original definition comes, noted that by the early 1980s the term had become part of the standard vocabulary in commerce and industry, where it had promptly passed into a verb.[6] Renowned wordsmith William Safire would later observe that by the 1990s the term had plummeted to the status of a "national dirty word," commenting that "[w]hen a new verb makes it to a gerund so quickly, it's a sign that the word fills a linguistic need."[7] Outsourc*ing* was not only a fast-moving gerund—the present participle of a verb that is used as a noun—it had found its way into the populist arsenal of "attack gerunds," Safire complained, along with other Clinton-era signifiers of economic angst like *offshoring* and *downsizing*.[8]

It is quite appropriate that outsourcing expresses an action while also becoming a thing, and that negative or pejorative connotations typically attach to its signification of managerial assertiveness coupled with a sense of *loss*. In negotiations between the auto unions and Ford and GM in the early 1980s, outsourcing first acquired a truly public meaning, as the antithesis of "job security" and a synonym for "jobs shipped overseas," not as an abstract matter of the optimal organizational boundaries of this or that activity, but as a purposeful act of economic *displacement*. Outsourced jobs, in this (received)

---

[5] Barnet and Müller (1974: 156, 132).

[6] Barnhart, D. K. (1983) Changing English. *Barnhart Dictionary Companion* II(3): 80.

[7] Safire, W. (2004) On language: Outsource. *New York Times Magazine* March 21: 30.

[8] During the 1990s, the dirty-word status of outsourcing was affirmed as the strategy was elided with acts of unilateral restructuring on the part of major corporations. In 1996, for example, outsourcing was an especially divisive issue in a strike at General Motors, where the term hardly required any translation: according to Mullin (1996: 32), "'outsourcing' in this context meant knocking yet another raft of auto workers off GM's assembly lines." See also Safire, W. (1996) On language: Downsized. *New York Times Magazine* May 26: 12.

sense, were those jobs that were once performed "in-house," and which had been moved offsite or offshore as a deliberate managerial strategy.[9] Outsourcing had risen to prominence during the 1970s as part of a new, and notably more aggressive "language of capitalism," being applied in the subsequent decade both to lengthening supply chains for manufactured components and to the relocation of manufacturing *jobs*—an indication that employment itself was being modularized and commodified. Subsequently, the phenomenon would begin to sprawl into the service sector, into the world of white-collar work, and then more widely still into the political-economic and cultural imagination.[10] This is how the *Oxford Dictionary of New Words* sought to stabilize the meaning of outsourcing in the late 1990s:

> Outsourcing played a significant role in the drive towards greater cost effectiveness in the manufacturing world of the eighties. Increasing numbers of businesses chose to concentrate their resources on their primary activities, shutting down those secondary and support operations which could be acquired from outside sources. The phenomenon brought with it the need to refine the ordering and supply of components, and the subsequent influence of the Japanese system known as JUST-IN-TIME. As the decade advanced, *outsourcing* became a common concomitant of DOWNSIZING, and some concern about its effect on job security was voiced by manufacturing unions.
>
> During the nineties application of the term has spread beyond the supply of components to the purchase of specialist services, especially those requiring high levels of technological or computing expertise. This is perceived as allowing firms to take advantage of the very latest developments and expertise, offered at competitive rates.[11]

In the period since the 1980s, outsourcing had become an increasingly mainstream component of management theory and practice. Business gurus like Tom Peters had long been making the case for "leaner" managerial structures, encouraging firms to "stick with their knitting," those activities most closely aligned with the corporate mission, while the concept of "core competences" likewise suggested that companies divest themselves of functions, such as administrative processing and information technology, that might be better handled by specialist providers.[12] Countless models of the "flexible enterprise"

---

[9] Hence Merriam-Webster's definition from 1986: "outsourcing: the procurement by a corporation from outside and esp. foreign or nonunion suppliers of parts it formerly manufactured" (*12,000 Words: A supplement to Webster's third new international dictionary*, Springfield, MA, p. 142). See also Bluestone and Harrison (1982) and Peck (2002).

[10] Ayto, J. (1999) *Twentieth Century Words*. Oxford: Oxford University Press, p. 456.

[11] Knowles, E. with Elliot, J., eds. (1997) *The Oxford Dictionary of New Words*. Oxford: Oxford University Press, p. 227.

[12] Peters, T. and Waterman, R. H. (1982) *In Search of Excellence*. New York: Harper and Row; Prahalad, C. K. and Hamel, G. (1990) The core competence of the corporation. *Harvard Business Review* 68(3): 79–91.

have been similarly predicated on elevated levels of subcontracting and out-sourcing, reflecting the ascendancy of "postfordist" logics of vertical disintegra-tion, lean(er) production, and flexible specialization.[13]

There were some companies, like GE under the leadership of Jack Welch, that practically epitomized this mainstreaming of outsourcing, from an almost reactionary operational measure to an axiom of world-class managerial practice. By way of a strategy that the unions at GE had initially dubbed "farm out," the company had started early in "whittling away at the number of parts it manufacture[d] and buying in more from outside suppliers all over the world"; before long, what GE "refer[red] to as 'outsourcing' [had become] standard operating procedure for every manufacturer in America."[14] Welch loudly championed the strategy of aggressively and ceaselessly restructuring corporate operations, driven by the unforgiving rationality of shareholder value and premised on the philosophy of "boundaryless" change manage-ment. Along with Sam Walton of Wal-Mart—with his paradigm-moving model of cost suppression in retailing, via the aggressively lean management of extended supply chains—Welch would come to symbolize the 1990s cul-ture of U.S.-style corporate machismo and global triumphalism. Welch and Walton were lionized on Wall Street, even as their corporate strategies drove manufacturing capacity and blue-collar jobs offshore.[15]

The story of what had been the world's first computerized manufacturing facility—GE's Appliance Park in Louisville, Kentucky—has passed into out-sourcing lore. Established in the early 1950s on a site sufficiently large to warrant its own zip code, Appliance Park had a payroll of 23,000 workers by the early 1970s, but also a growing reputation for combustible industrial relations. What became known as "strike city" would have no place in Jack Welch's vision of the corporate future.[16] By the mid-1990s, Welch was requiring that the heads of each of his company's divisions draw up plans for

[13] See Atkinson, J. and Meager, N. (1986) *Changing Working Patterns: How companies achieve flexibility to meet new needs*. London: National Economic Development Office; Volberda, H. W. (1998) *Building the Flexible Firm*. Oxford: Oxford University Press; Kalleberg, A. L. (2001) Organizing flexibility: The flexible firm in a new century. *British Journal of Industrial Relations* 39(4): 479–504. On the geographical aspects and implications of flexible production/employment, see Scott (1988b) and Harrison (1994).

[14] O'Boyle, T. F. (1998) *At Any Cost: Jack Welch, General Electric, and the pursuit of profit*. New York: Vantage.

[15] On the Wal-Mart model and outsourcing, see Lichtenstein, N. ed. (2006) *Wal-Mart: The face of twenty-first-century capitalism*. New York: New Press; Lichtenstein, N. (2010) *The Retail Revolution: How Wal-Mart created a brave new world of business*. New York: Picador; Gereffi, G. and Christian, M. (2009) The impacts of Wal-Mart: The rise and consequences of the world's dominant retailer. *Annual Review of Sociology* 35(1): 573–91. On the spatial implications of "flexibilization," see Scott (1988a, 1988b) and Peck (1996).

[16] On recent developments at Appliance Park, relative to wider patterns of transformation in the U.S. manufacturing sector, see Conerly, B. (2015) Are American manufacturers reshoring? *Forbes* May 13, accessed at <http://www.forbes.com/sites/billconerly/2015/05/13/are-american-manufacturers-reshoring/>, January 11, 2016.

realizing rolling efficiency gains through outsourcing: "Ideally," he is reported to have said at the time, "you'd have every plant you own on a barge to move with currencies and changes in the economy."[17] Welch's first glimpse of the future had occurred some years earlier, when he was reportedly "dragged" along on a business trip to India by his senior vice president for international strategy, Paolo Fresco, initially to select a high-technology partner for GE medical systems. "Neutron Jack" would return from his Eastern awakening a secular evangelist for white-collar outsourcing, and for a new model of corporate development:

> We moved from thinking of globalization in terms of markets to thinking of it in terms of sourcing products and components—and finally tapping the intellectual capital of countries... I was optimistic about [India's] brainpower, but our use of it has far outpaced my wildest dreams... GE Capital moved its customer service centers to Delhi, and the results have been sensational [with] better quality, lower costs, better collection rates, and greater customer acceptance rates than our comparable operations in the United States and Europe. All the GE industrial businesses have followed GE Capital there... We moved the GE "back rooms" in the United States to the "front room" in India.[18]

A transnational business in "back office" operations had been born. In the space of a decade, the support center that GE Capital had established in New Delhi to anchor its fast-growing mortgage-refinancing business had been spun off in a $500 million private-equity deal as Genpact. Today, Genpact is one of the lead players in what is now known as the BPO industry, with operations in twenty-four countries, a global workforce of 68,000, and an annual turnover of more than $2 billion. Domiciled in Bermuda, Genpact boasts a "customer-centric" culture focused on continuous improvement, with a client list that reportedly includes more than one fifth of the Fortune Global 500.[19]

GE was not alone in moving aggressively into the "outsourcing space" in the 1990s. Soon, technology and information-technology services companies like EDS, Dell, IBM, Apple, and Hewlett-Packard, consulting outfits like Accenture and Deloitte, and financial-services firms like Citibank, AmEx, HSBC, and J. P. Morgan were to be found there too, along with a new breed of outsourcing conglomerates, many of them based in Asia, including Foxconn, Wipro, Tata, and Infosys.[20] Back in the United States, the collateral effects were soon being

---

[17] Quoted in Economist (2013) Welcome home. *Economist* January 19: 11; Kripalani, M. (2006) Spreading the gospel. *Business Week* March 6: 46; Fishman, C. (2012) The insourcing boom. *Atlantic Monthly* December: 45–52.

[18] Welch, J. F. (2003) *Jack: Straight from the gut*. New York: Warner Business Books.

[19] Industry Report Online (2014) Genpact: Generating intelligent business impact, accessed at <http://industryreportonline.com/genpact-generating-intelligent-business-impact/>, May 16, 2015.

[20] The Economist has claimed that "EDS... pretty much invented the outsourcing industry." (Economist (2013) Services: The next big thing. *Economist* January 19: 10–12.) While this may not be strictly true—there were many more hands involved—it does underline the pioneering role of

felt far beyond Appliance Park. In the 1990s era of corporate downsizing, the kinds of insecurities that had long been associated with blue-collar, assembly-line work were now being visited on white-collar, technical, and even professional workers.[21] And even if, for some years, fear of outsourcing would far exceed its material reach as a job-displacing "disruptive technology," not for the first time fear itself was generating political and cultural consequences. The especially anemic "jobless recovery" after the dot-com bust of the early 2000s only amplified these concerns, coinciding as it did with the rise of outsourcing from an avant-garde concept to an increasingly normalized business practice. Capturing this moment, an early 2003 cover story in *Business Week*—picturing a suit-wearing male office worker clinging desperately to the bottom rungs of a shipping pallet destined for foreign shores—blurted out the unsettling question begged by this new round of globalization, "Is your job next?"

> It's globalization's next wave—and one of the biggest trends reshaping the global economy. The first wave started two decades ago with the exodus of jobs making shoes, cheap electronics, and toys to developing countries. After that, simple service work, like processing credit-card receipts, and mind-numbing digital toil, like writing software code, began fleeing high-cost countries... *Now, all kinds of knowledge work can be done anywhere*... The rise of a globally integrated knowledge economy is a blessing for developing nations. What it means for the U.S. skilled labor force is less clear. At the least, many white-collar workers may be headed for a tough readjustment.[22]

The pioneers of outsourced work, it was reported, had spent a decade or more climbing the learning curve of what could be a technically, operationally, and culturally challenging process of global transformation. They were now ready to push to scale, and to roll out outsourced work systems across a new and more complex range of activities, from legal-document review to the reading of radiological charts. But the work was not indiscriminately going "anywhere"; it was being relocated to some very particular places. There would be transformation at both ends of the white-collar supply chain. Barely noticed at first, cities like Manila, New Delhi, Shanghai, and Budapest, along with "dozens more across the developing world [had] become the new back offices for Corporate America, Japan Inc., and Europe GmbH."[23]

---

transnationalizing technology-service companies in the early days of outsourcing. See also the discussion of Bain Capital's identity as a "pioneer of outsourcing" in Chapter 3.

[21] For a timely account, see Uchitelle (2007). Downsizing was not only exercising the minds of corporate gurus and "change managers," it was also reshaping economic policy options. See Boyett, J. H. and Boyett, J. T., eds. (2000) *The Guru Guide: The best ideas of the top management thinkers*. New York: Wiley; Pollin (2003); and Peck (2002).

[22] Engardio, P., Bernstein, A., Kriplani, M., Balfour, F., Grow, B., and Greene, J. (2003) Is your job next? *Business Week* February 3: 50–60, p. 52, emphasis added.

[23] Engardio, P., Bernstein, A., Kriplani, M., Balfour, F., Grow, B., and Greene, J. (2003) Is your job next? *Business Week* February 3: 50–60, pp. 51–2.

New Worlds of Globalized Work

If there is an urtext for the global outsourcing movement, it is without doubt Thomas Friedman's bestseller, *The World Is Flat*. Written as a revelatory tale of a new world not just to be, but actively in the making, Friedman's book arrived as a breathless dispatch from the business-class circuit where he has long plied his trade, a second instalment to that paean to free-market globalization, *The Lexus and the Olive Tree*.[24] Echoing the tone and tenor of its predecessor, *The World Is Flat* is animated by propulsive metaphors and "driving forces," yielding inexorably towards the earth-outcome of "global convergence." Friedman begins his story on a golf course in Bangalore, courtesy of a Discovery Times documentary assignment, where to his surprise he found himself surrounded by the gleaming office towers of U.S. technology and financial corporations and the no less impressive campuses of their Indian partners. The journalist had made his way to this Silicon Valley of the East on his "own Columbus-like journey of exploration" in order to learn rather than to expropriate, to understand not only why but *how* "the Indians I met were taking our work, why they had become such an important pool for the outsourcing of service and information technology work from America and other industrialized countries."[25]

Friedman mixes his take on post-Cold War geopolitics with a narrative of mutually reinforcing technological and organizational innovation, describing a new world opened up by savvy entrepreneurs, digital capabilities, and free-market business practices. His account of the "forces that flattened the world" begins with the fall of the Berlin Wall and the invention of the internet, moves through the development of enabling technologies like the development of workflow software and open-source collaboration, and on to the breakthrough moment of mundane contingency that was the global effort to fix the Y2K coding snafu, the so-called millennium bug. A practically universal coding error had threatened to crash not only millions of desktop machines but an equally countless number of computer-dependent organizations across the world—and there simply was not enough trained labor to fix the problem, onsite and in a timely manner. Fortunately, India would come to the rescue. (Fortunate in that this moment happened to coincide with the historical confluence of a cluster of innovations in supply-chain systems, long-distance management capabilities, and ICTs.) The Indian IT sector, with its vast reserves of technical labor and access to cheap and fast fiber-optic networks, consequently possessed the solution. Y2K recoding may have been the ultimate example of digital drudge work, but it stress-tested the capabilities of the

---

[24] Friedman T. L. (2000) *The Lexus and the Olive Tree*. New York: Farrar, Straus, and Giroux.
[25] Friedman (2005: 4–5).

emergent business of e-commerce, while initiating a new round of corporate relation building.

> The Indian IT industry got its footprint across the globe because of Y2K [and soon] a whole new driver of business emerged—e-commerce . . . India didn't benefit only from the dot-com boom; it benefited even more from the dot-com bust! That is the real irony. The boom laid the cable that connected India to the world, and the bust made the cost of using it virtually free and also vastly increased the number of American companies that would want to use that fiber-optic cable to outsource knowledge work to India. [Having done] a lot of very specific custom code maintenance to higher-value-added companies, [Indian contractors] started to develop their own products and transform themselves from maintenance to product companies, offering a range of software services and consulting. This took Indian companies much deeper inside American ones, and business-process outsourcing—letting Indians run your back room—went to a whole new level.[26]

The quick fix that was Y2K recoding duly illuminated the path towards a new techno-organizational fix for big corporations.[27] If the passage to India had been opened up by Jack Welch-style corporate foresight, the (post)industrial accident of the millennium bug created the conjunctural opportunity for the global debut of the outsourcing industry.

On Friedman's telling, this confluence of historic forces took globalization to another level too. If globalization 1.0 defined the period between Columbus' fateful voyage and some time around 1800 (the time when *countries* were globalizing), and the two centuries of globalization 2.0 saw the rise to prominence of the multinational corporation (the era of *companies* globalizing), then Friedman had arrived in the nick of time, and indeed just in the right place, to witness the birth of globalization 3.0, when thanks to a technologically leveled playing field, collaborative networking and multicultural empowerment would mark the ultimate evolutionary stage. The contemporary round of supercharged globalization, which would enable "*the sharing of knowledge and work—in real time, without regard to geography, distance, or, in the near future, even language,*" is being propelled by what Friedman calls a "triple convergence."[28] This began with the advent of web-based capacities, to be followed (after a period of social and organizational learning) by an array of productivity-enhancing "flanking technologies," business processes, and work habits, the advance guard of which was a new "cadre of managers,

---

[26] Friedman (2005: 109, 110, 112).

[27] The Y2K case is more than an apt journalistic illustration. Economic modeling exercises suggest that temporary shocks like the Y2K episode can indeed have permanent effects, initiating a step-change increase in the level of offshore outsourcing. See Ranjan, P. and Mitra, D. (2008) Temporary shocks and offshoring: The role of external economies and firm heterogeneity. *Journal of Development Economics* 87(1): 76–84.

[28] Friedman (2005: 176, emphasis in original).

innovators, business consultants, business schools, designers, CEOs," indeed all manner of horizontal collaborators; under the command of this networked elite would be a practically infinite supply of wage-earning footsoldiers, "the people of China, India, Russia, Eastern Europe, Latin America, and Central Asia [who after their] economies and political systems all opened up during the course of the 1990s . . . were increasingly free to join the free-market game."[29]

One need not buy Friedman's libertarian futurology, or for that matter his wide-eyed economics of beneficent global evolution, to recognize that many of the techno-corporate trends that he describes are quite real—he is a reporter after all—even if they are not opening a one-way path to free-market convergence. The truly historic "great doubling" of the global wage-labor workforce, following the waves of economic liberalization after 1989, has been real enough, and even if the competitive crowding is most intense at the lower reaches of the skills spectrum, it certainly has not been confined to that level.[30] And the lagged realization of productivity gains from new information, logistics, and communications technologies are surely real enough too, even if this is more like a moving challenge than a simple windfall or organizational fait accompli.[31] The world that he describes may not be flat, or so abruptly disconnected from longer histories of corporate restructuring, but it is a world that in a host of material and social ways has actually arrived.

This is why the UCLA economist Edward Leamer went to some length to cut through Friedman's exuberant metaphors in order to expose some of the underlying truths, being prompted by *The World Is Flat* to trace a long path via von Thünen, (Alfred) Weber, Lösch, and Hotelling, through the new economics of trust and untraded interdependencies, to an anything-but-stable contemporary geography of competitive opportunities and threats:

> The fear that seems to underlie much of Friedman's flat earth metaphor is that work is becoming commoditized and sold in global markets . . . It is mostly about the commoditization of work and the extension geographically of the contest for mundane work in manufacturing and services like sewing apparel and reading manuals at call centers over the phone and also not-so-mundane intellectual activities . . . The central issue is whether Americans are going to sell their products and services in a global "market" that completely determines wages and conditions, or are American jobs going to be protected by relationships and geography . . . Friedman's flat world hypothesis seems to be that there are or will be many

---

[29] Friedman (2005: 181).

[30] Freeman R. (2007) The great doubling: The challenge of the new global labor market. In J. Edwards, M. Crain, and A. L. Kalleberg, eds, *Ending Poverty in America*. New York: New Press, 55–65.

[31] See, notably, Brynjolfsson and McAfee (2012), Frey and Osborne (2013), Brynjolfsson (2014), and the further discussion in Chapter 6.

U.S. jobs that are contested by Chinese and Indians. This strikes me as rather far from reality. It is only the mundane codifiable tasks in tradables for which there are global markets. You'd be surprised how few of these remain in the United States.[32]

Leamer is surely correct to check Friedman's tendency to overreach, even as the economist marvels at what can be learned, methodologically speaking, from actually talking to the protagonists of such putative economic trans-formations,[33] but having dispatched the utopian vision of competitively induced horizontal collaboration in near-perfect global labor markets what is left behind is a much murkier world of tradeoffs, trends, and tendencies. Quite rightly skeptical of the effective reach of *actually* market-like conditions into globally dispersed labor markets, Leamer tends to ascribe the sources of "stickiness" or "friction" in the location of jobs and economic activities to the realm of "relationships." An insight that can be lost, however, beneath Friedman's corporate-libertarian rhetoric is that the bundle of social, technical, and organizational innovations that has accompanied and enabled the rise of transnational outsourcing has effectively stretched out and reconstructed these relationships. The coevolution of "onshore" and "offshore" employment systems, management regimes, communications technologies, and corporate (inter)relationships has established an historically new organizational platform, rendering the "threat" of outsourcing much more real and present. (It may not be universal and free, as Friedman is want to suggest, but the offshore outsourcing option is certainly widespread and cheap.) This has helped give rise to a new and enlarged category of *persistently contestable work*, even if in the terms of orthodox economic analysis transnational job markets are not really contestable on a daily basis. Instead, outsourced supply chains often resemble super-extended "internal" labor markets, in that corporate buyers disproportionately drive the system, even if they are not the employers of record for, say, Indian call centers or Chinese subcontractors.[34]

[32] Leamer (2007: 100, 101). See also Leamer, E. E. and Storper, M. (2001) *The Economic Geography of the Internet Age.* Cambridge, MA: National Bureau of Economic Research.

[33] "There is something we can learn from Friedman's methodology. He does an extraordinarily good job of creating ideas especially when you consider that he is not a card-carrying member of our guild... Economists create knowledge, or think they do, using an entirely different methodology that keeps them always very far from CEOs and any of the other actors in the drama of their study," Leamer (2007: 106) reflects, "Some economists noodle away at the blackboard or on pads of paper. We call them theorists. Other economists stare at computer screens downloading data from various web sites and organizing these data with econometric software packages. I am one of these."

[34] See Manwaring, T. (1984) The extended internal labour market. *Cambridge Journal of Economics* 8(2): 161–87, and the discussion in Peck (1996).

Divisions of Labor, Old and New

The idea of "stretched out" transnational labor systems has a long pedigree, going back at least as far as formative research on changing spatial divisions of labor, dating back to the new international division of labor, or NIDL, thesis of the 1970s.[35] The observed tendency of leading multinational corporations, based in Western Europe and the United States, to separate out and then relocate labor-intensive components of the production process to low-wage sites across Eastern Europe, Latin America, and East and Southeast Asia was associated with a fracturing of the modernist ontology that had divided the "industrialized" from the "developing" world, and the "core" economies from raw-materials suppliers.[36] Only in part was this move offshore by major manufacturing companies motivated by an objective of accessing overseas markets for final products; it had more to do with the elemental goal of profit restoration, in this case by tapping into low-cost labor reserves, often in officially designated export-processing zones, and by unilaterally withdrawing from social contracts and union deals accumulated in domestic, or "high-cost," locations.[37] As Gary Gereffi puts it, "international companies [were] slicing up their supply chains in search of low-cost and capable suppliers offshore."[38] In this way, the hierarchical structure of the multinational corporation found a spatial analogy in the unequal and asymmetrical relations between headquarters regions, research-and-development centers, back-office sites, and branch-plant locations. And as Doreen Massey emphasized,[39] this was always more than a simple process of spatial redistribution, "more than just new patterns, [or some] geographical re-shuffling of the same old pack of cards," because it entails the stretching out *and transformation* of social relations, indeed the establishment of "whole new sets of relations between activities in different places, new spatial patterns of social organisation, new dimensions of inequality and new relations of dominance and dependence."

[35] Hymer, S. (1972) The multinational corporation and the law of uneven development. In J. N. Bhagwati, ed., *Economics and World Order*. London: Collier-Macmillan, 113–40; Fröbel et al. (1980); Massey (1984); Lipietz, A. (1985) New tendencies in the international division of labour: Regimes of accumulation and modes of regulation. In A. J. Scott and M. Storper, eds, *Production, Work, Territory: The geographical anatomy of industrial capitalism*. Hemel Hempstead: George Allen and Unwin, 16–40; Schoenberger, E. (1988) Multinational corporations and the new international division of labor: A critical appraisal. *International Regional Science Review* 11(2): 105–19.

[36] According to Fröbel et al. (1980: 45), the advent of NIDL "(a) undermine[d] the traditional bisection of the world into a few industrialised countries on one hand, and a great majority of developing countries integrated into the world economy solely as raw material producers on the other, and (b) compel[led] the increasing subdivision of manufacturing processes into a number of partial operations at different industrial sites throughout the world."

[37] See Massey, D. (1978) Capital and locational change: The UK electrical engineering and electronics industries. *Review of Radical Political Economics* 10(3): 39–54; Lipietz, A. (1982) Toward global Fordism. *New Left Review* 132: 33–47.

[38] Gereffi (2014: 10).   [39] Massey (1984: 8).

The NIDL model had posited a relatively narrow and rudimentary set of transformed relationships between technical change (towards standardization and deskilling), organizational restructuring (towards vertical disintegration and cost-driven decentralization), and spatial transformation (towards "peripheral" locations in search of a cheaper and more compliant workforce). The drivers here were changes in the manufacturing sector, the decentralization of which provided the template for the NIDL model.[40] If the NIDL-era move to offshore locations was notable more for the signal that it sent than for its scale—since at least initially the relocations were selective and modest, even as they involved some very large brand-name companies—it gave an indication that the old binary order of the world economic system was beginning to break down. In place of the colonial rubric of first- and third-world national economies, engaged in (unequal) trade, a new ontology was coming into view, based on deepening interdependencies and globalizing *networks*, albeit in the context of continuing power asymmetries.[41]

The successor to NIDL, as an analytical framework commensurate with the scope, scale, and specificity of this evolving web of cross-border corporate structures and relations—is the family of global commodity chain, global value chain, and global production chain concepts, which together have sought grasp what has since come to be presented as "the world economy's backbone and central nervous system," those proliferating network forms that are "perhaps [its] predominant organizational feature."[42] Founded on a network ontology, these approaches are united in their concern to comprehend the complex global restructuring of corporate, organizational, technological, and employment systems, with an emphasis on the dynamic development of intra- and inter-firm relationships. Their contribution has been to chart at least four significant transformations in the reorganization of the global economy over recent decades.

First, at the most basic level, these investigations of evolving global networks have described a pattern of widening sectoral reach, increased sophistication, and deepening complexity. What started off with labor-intensive operations in a relatively small group of industries like consumer electronics, garment production, and automotive component assembly, would later spread to routine service work, including back-office processing, customer

---

[40] See the discussion in Poster and Yolmo (2016).

[41] The most effective rendering of this formulation is found in Peter Dicken's (2015) *Global Shift*. For a suggestive discussion of the contribution and limits of network optics, see Bair, J., Berndt, C., Boeckler, M., and Werner, M. (2013) Dis/articulating producers, markets, and regions: New directions in critical studies of commodity chains. *Environment and Planning A* 45(11): 2544–52.

[42] Cattaneo, O., Gereffi, G., and Staritz, C. (2010) Global value chains in a postcrisis world: Resilience, consolidation, and shifting end markets. In O. Cattaneo, G. Gereffi, and C. Staritz, eds, *Global Value Chains in a Postcrisis World: A development perspective*. Washington, DC: World Bank Publications, 3–20; Coe and Yeung (2015: 3). See also Dicken (2015).

support, and software-code writing, before reaching into knowledge-intensive and high value-added functions in fields such as accounting and finance, research and development, and medicine and pharmaceuticals.[43] Crucial in this respect has been the growing "service intensity" of transnational corporations, and indeed economies more generally, to borrow Saskia Sassen's terminology.[44] In the early stages of this pathfinding process of evolution, the offshoring strategies of international corporations were reciprocated (and incentivized) by the development of export-processing zones in lower-cost locations across Asia and Latin America; with time, a new generation of offshore suppliers would develop significant corporate capacities of their own, rising in some cases to positions of leadership in supply-chain platforms, which in turn has enabled the development of symbiotic and partnership-based relationships with (erstwhile) "lead firms" in North America and Western Europe.

These deepening interdependencies and complex connectivities bring significant implications for patterns of trade, for relative rates of growth and profitability, for local development prospects, and for corporate organizational structures, whether or not particular jobs or functions actually move offshore or stay put. While there has certainly been some "hollowing out" of employment and corporate structures in the advanced industrial nations, and while some rapidly developing countries have been able to transition from low-wage assembly work through "upgrading" strategies into higher-value work, Gary Gereffi explains that:

> Despite popular notions to the contrary, global outsourcing has not meant a whole-sale transfer of economic activity out of developed economies and into developing ones. A large and important set of activities have remained rooted, at least so far, in advanced economies, even as they have become tightly linked to activities located elsewhere. The cumulative effect is that cross-border linkages between economies and firms have grown more elaborate. Firms are less likely simply to make products and export them; they increasingly participate in highly complex cross-border arrangements that involve a wide array of partners, customers, and suppliers. Global outsourcing has given rise to a new set of structures in the world economy.[45]

---

[43] Gereffi (2006: 9–16) distinguishes four categories of offshored employment: assembly work using imported inputs in export-oriented sectors; basic manufacturing jobs involving "full package" production and buyer-oriented upgrading; more advanced forms of manufacturing work, often based on original design and brand-name capabilities, linked to supplier-oriented upgrading; and a range of services, including routine white-collar jobs, advanced professional work, and business-process outsourcing.

[44] See Sassen, S. (2008) Two stops in today's new global geographies: Shaping novel labor supplies and employment regimes. *American Behavioral Scientist* 25(3): 457–96. See also Poster and Yolmo (2016).

[45] Gereffi (2006: 2). See also Werner, M., Bair, J., and Fernández, V. R. (2014) Linking up to development? Global value chains and the making of a post-Washington consensus. *Development and Change* 45(6): 1219–47.

Second, the network perspective has encouraged analysts to think in a manner analogous to the way that many executives, suppliers, and indeed workers do; rather than conceiving of jobs and activities in terms of a notionally fixed location (within industries or countries), they are understood in "relational" terms, relative to their shifting positions in networks, chains, stretched-out hierarchies, and long-distance relationships. The "new set of structures" duly emerges as a connective infrastructure, around which jobs and activities are variously (re)positioned.

Dynamic capacities can therefore be ascribed to outsourcing networks *qua* networks—as an emergent property of networked systems, rather than (merely) some aggregate of the capacities of participating organizations, or a byproduct of reductions in trading and transaction costs. Outsourcing must not be reduced to an isolated make-or-buy calculation, involving one-time adjustments to the boundaries of the firm, but is better understood as an always moving, dynamic, and interdependent calculus. The "simple models of outsourcing" found in the orthodox economics literature reduces the phenomenon to a cost-reduction exercise (as falling costs of communication incentivize new markets for the "trade in tasks"), but these models do not account for the "hidden" costs of coordination, the dynamic interplay of actors and organizations across geographies, or the complex production and maintenance of network value added.[46] As the infrastructural capacities of these networks have deepened, the decision-making domain itself has become much more complex and multilayered. In the process, the cost-reduction imperatives that drove the first generation of offshore spatial fixes have been supplemented (although not supplanted) by an array of other considerations and tradeoffs relating to competitive flexibility, shared competences, and improved responsiveness (or "time to market"), along with a raft of accompanying organizational and technological fixes. Neil Coe and Henry Yeung have presented a neat summary of this trajectory of qualitative transformation: the "perennial drive" to reduce costs has found an expression in the offshoring of non-core competences (the spatial fix), which has been supplemented by a search for competitive advantage via superior forms of productive networking and flexibility (the organizational fix), coupled with an increased

---

[46] See Grossman, G. M. and Helpman, E. (2002) Outsourcing in a global economy. *NBER* working paper #8728. Cambridge, MA: National Bureau of Economic Research; Grossman, G. M. and Rossi-Hansberg, E. (2008) Trading tasks: A simple theory of offshoring. *American Economic Review* 98(5): 1978–97; Baldwin, R. and Robert-Nicoud, F. (2014) Trade-in-goods and trade-in-tasks: An integrating framework. *Journal of International Economics* 92(1): 51–62; Rodriguez-Clare, A. (2010) Offshoring in a Ricardian world. *American Economic Journal: Macroeconomics* 2(2): 227–58; Ebenstein, A., Harrison, A., McMillan, M., and Phillips, S. (2014) Estimating the impact of trade and offshoring on American workers using the Current Population Surveys. *Review of Economics and Statistics* 96(4): 581–95; Crinò, R. (2009) Offshoring, multinationals and labour market: A review of the empirical literature. *Journal of Economic Surveys* 23(2): 197–249. See also the discussion in Coe and Yeung (2015).

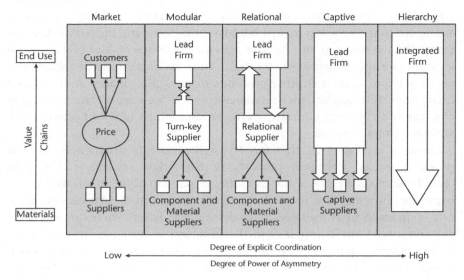

Figure 2.1 Five types of global value chain governance
Source: Gereffi et al. (2005), reprinted with permission of Taylor and Francis

emphasis on market-facing responsiveness by way of a host of organizational and technical innovations (the technological fix).[47] The outcome of this triple fix is a new set of coordinates for global trade, production, and services, which are dynamically interrelated and therefore in perpetual motion.

Third, the heuristic distinction that was made, early on, between "producer-driven" and "buyer-driven" chains, the former describing a situation in which power was largely vested in final-product manufacturers, like automobile companies, and the latter one in which control lay with non-manufacturing companies capitalizing on strong brands and market dominance, soon proved to be altogether too coarse. In its place has come widespread recognition of the growing variety and complexity of even ideal-typical network forms, each of which is associated with distinctive patterns (and challenges) of network governance (see Figure 2.1). As Gereffi has explained, the value of this typology is that it enables the analysts of global networks to see

> how the form of governance can change as an industry evolves and matures, and indeed how governance patterns within an industry can vary from one stage or level of the chain to another. For example, in the offshore services value chain, all five types of [network] governance structures identified in the typology coexist, but their role in upgrading varies according to the characteristics of suppliers in

---

[47] Coe and Yeung (2015: 6–8).

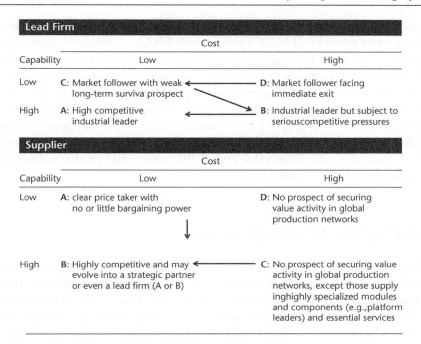

Figure 2.2 Matrix of cost-capability ratios in global production networks
Source: Yeung and Coe (2015). Copyright © Clark University, reprinted by permission of Taylor and Francis, <http://www.tandfonline.com> on behalf of Clark University

developing countries, the requirements of lead firms and the kinds of international professional standards utilized in these chains.[48]

Fourth, as global networks have proliferated and deepened in these and other ways, the once relatively inert categories of the offshore "supplier," "subcontractor," and "site" have been remade as loci of productive capabilities, developmental strategies, and active interests. What has been called globalization's "second unbundling," facilitated by the role of ICTs in "massively lower[ing] the cost of organising complex activities over distances," has opened up new development paths for regions or countries connecting to global networks not only as suppliers of cheap labor but as providers of a wide range of specialist inputs and services.[49] And of course, the calculus for lead firms and supply-chain

---

[48] Gereffi (2014: 14). See also Fernandez-Stark, K., Bamber, P., and Gereffi, G. (2011) The offshore services value chain: Upgrading trajectories in developing countries. *International Journal of Technological Learning, Innovation and Development* 4(1–3): 206–34.

[49] Baldwin, R. and Venables, A. J. (2013) Spiders and snakes: Offshoring and agglomeration in the global economy. *Journal of International Economics* 90(2): 245–54, p. 245; see also formulations in Gereffi (2014) and Dicken (2015). For a critical discussion of these issues, along with reflections on the rise of global networks as a development paradigm, see Werner, M., Bair, J., and Fernández, V. R. (2014) Linking up to development? Global value chains and the making of a post-Washington

organizations has been changing too. Henry Yeung and Neil Coe have visualized this in terms of cost-capability matrices, which yield a variety of market-cum-organizational strategies and trajectories (see Figure 2.2). On the one hand there are the low-cost suppliers of old, located in developing countries, occupying essentially subordinate positions within supply chains and performing routine assembly and assistance tasks for lead firms in Europe or North America. On the other, there is the new generation of "lead suppliers," which have secured strong market positions on the basis of economies of scale or specialist capabilities, and which engage in and shape value chains that are neither producer-driven nor buyer-driven in the original sense.

Exporting Jobs, Importing Insecurity

Offshore outsourcing has opened up new opportunities for economic development around the world, most conspicuously in the "global factory" that is China and in India, the "world's back office," but in many other locations too. In North America and Western Europe, on the other hand, these same developments have been enveloped in narratives of loss, inflamed from time to time by populist fearmongering about an imminent exodus of jobs offshore. While such claims were always exaggerated, the cumulative consequences of what has been a deep-rooted and continuing transformation of the global economy may prove in the long run to be similarly profound. The consequences for those on both ends of global outsourcing relationships have proved to be more complicated than was suggested by the forecasters of zero-sum migratory change, but they also seem certain to be more disruptive than the prophets of lift-all-the-boats global development have implied. "The rise of global outsourcing has triggered waves of consternation in advanced economies about job loss and the degradation of capabilities that could spell the disappearance of entire national industries," Gary Gereffi has observed, while pointing out that there are many that believe these concerns to be not only mistaken or exaggerated, but wrongheaded, with some trade advocates insisting instead that "global outsourcing should be embraced as a mechanism for economies to shift out of low-value activities and old industries, freeing up capital and human resources for higher-value activities and the development of newer industries and cutting-edge products."[50] The latter arguments may only be persuasive, however, to those fortunate enough to be on the right side

consensus. *Development and Change* 45(6): 1219–47. For the Philippines case, see Del Prado, F. L. E. (2015) The BPO challenge: Leveraging capabilities, creating opportunities. *PIDS Discussion Paper* No. 2015-36, Philippine Institute for Development Studies, Makati City, Philippines.

[50] Gereffi (2006: 2).

of the global redivision of labor, or who otherwise have the luxury of contemplating life in the orthodox economists' "long run." It is cold comfort for those workers and firms that have found themselves on the receiving end of this ascendant mode of global competition, the trade victims of the digital age. This said, the situation of "receiving" economies has hardly been unequivocally positive, either. Gereffi points out that:

> Global outsourcing has also triggered a debate about the benefits and costs of globalization for developing countries. Some claim that it has been extremely beneficial, while others argue that global outsourcing has led only to "immiserizing" growth and a "race to the bottom," as developing countries compete with one another to offer transnational companies the lowest operating costs...The recent emergence of China and India as important nodes of activity—or hubs—in global value chains has expanded the global labour force so significantly that globalization may bid down the living standards not only for unskilled work and primary products, but increasingly for skilled work and industrial products as well.[51]

The basic narrative established in the late 1970s and early 1980s, when the NIDL was really *new*, was centered on the technologically enabled fragmentation of production systems and the flight to low-cost locations. This has been repeatedly reworked and reiterated, all the way through to Friedman's third age of globalization. Less hyperbolic assessments of the global "redivision" of labor, however, have been more inclined to parse and qualify what often come across as predictions of inexorable and unidirectional change. First, a substantial proportion of even relatively standardized production has remained "onshore," in higher-cost countries, while a large share of relocations favored *other* high-cost locations, often for reasons of market access. Patterns of trade and foreign direct investment likewise tell a story of uneven integration that is still largely dominated by flows between the so-called advanced industrial economies, but with Asia rising to prominence alongside North America and Europe within what has become a multipolar economic system.[52] Second, although NIDL-like patterns were revealed across some corporate structures, especially in sectors like garment manufacturing and electronics assembly, countervailing tendencies have been documented as well. Flexibly specialized clusters, just-in-time delivery systems, the exploitation of untraded interdependencies at the regional scale, all testify to the strength (and, some would say, intensification) of agglomeration tendencies in the globalizing economic system.[53] And third, there has proved to be more variability (and creativity) in corporate restructuring programs than the

---

[51] Gereffi (2006: 2).   [52] Peter Dicken's (2015) *Global Shift* provides the definitive account.
[53] See, especially, Storper, M. (1997) *The Regional World*. New York: Guilford; Scott, A. J. (2001) *Global City-Regions*. Oxford: Oxford University Press.

rudimentary labor-cost reduction model suggested, including a wide range of in situ strategies like subcontracting arrangements, the development of two-tier and core-periphery employment systems, the deployment of contingent-labor strategies, and so on.[54]

Yet even as the transformations heralded by the NIDL model were not as absolute and irreversible as had been suggested by the early forecasts (and fears) of some, they were nevertheless harbingers of an ascendant *offshore consciousness*, prelude to an age in which competition in a host of more or less "exposed" segments of the labor market would be imagined—and to varying degrees, experienced—globally.[55] Erica Schoenberger has been one of those to emphasize that, from the start, there was a *politics* to the way in which popularized renderings of NIDL-like conditions sought and found an echo in changed public understandings of the causes and consequences of industrial restructuring, a discourse that generally

> underestimate[d] the extent to which the employment crisis in the advanced regions is also generated internally as a result of labor-saving technological change in production . . . combined with problems of aggregate demand growth and the lack of outlets for profitable investment and surplus capital. This omission reinforces the impression that employment gains in one location are made strictly at the expense of jobs in another, distracting attention from the further question of what forces inhibit the creation of enough jobs to go around. It also encourages workers in the industrial countries to view low-cost foreign labor as the primary threat to their well-being.[56]

Allusions to "foreign competition," and later to offshoring, evoked a nebulous *and external* threat, when these were in fact elements (or modular components, one might say) of the larger phenomena of corporate and labor-market restructuring. The (counter)point here is that the developments that are signaled by concepts like the NIDL, or subsequently, practices like global outsourcing should not be understood as (merely) discrete and transactional, but rather as moments in wider patterns of transformative change.

More specifically, the strategy of relocating blue-collar jobs to offshore locations emerged in the historical context, not coincidentally, of deindustrialization in the United States—the insecurity fomented by both the threat and the fact of runaway shops exerting downward pressures on wages and conditions in what would become known as the "rustbelt" regions of the

---

[54] See Sayer, R. A. (1985) Industry and space: A sympathetic critique of radical research. *Environment and Planning D: Society and Space* 3(1): 3–29; Schoenberger, E. (1988) Multinational corporations and the new international division of labor: A critical appraisal. *International Regional Science Review* 11(2): 105–19; Peck (1992, 1996).

[55] See the discussion in Urry (2014).

[56] Schoenberger, E. (1988) Multinational corporations and the new international division of labor: A critical appraisal. *International Regional Science Review* 11(2): 105–19, p. 116.

Midwest and northeast.[57] Arguably no less consequential, in this context, was the sustained migration of manufacturing capacity and employment to the "right to work" states of the south and southeast of the United States, which has only intensified in recent years, and which now represents the dynamic core of the country's lean production system, itself deeply integrated into global networks.[58] Furthermore, the subsequent offshoring of back-office work has also had an onshore precursor (or parallel) in the relocation of routine white-collar work from downtown to suburban locations beginning in the 1950s.[59] Against a background of robust service-sector growth, these latter developments did not appear to be, for the most part, politically disruptive. But after decades of flat or even negative real-earnings growth, to which U.S. households have responded by committing more and more working time to waged employment and by multiple job holding, the preconditions for *generalized* economic insecurity had been established.[60] Rising anxiety about the threat of downsizing, which went beyond the shop floor and back office and into middle management, became a public issue during the 1990s, only to be compounded by an amorphous, and apparently growing, "fear of outsourcing" in the period since, rising to the top of the political agenda in a succession of presidential campaigns.[61]

The near impossibility of properly quantifying the scale of the "offshoring" issue has not helped matters. Even if those involved were minded to do so, calculating the net effect on domestic headcounts of what are often complex and extended programs of task redesign, automation, decomposition, and recomposition would be extremely difficult. Outsourcing is an adaptive process, not a singular event in which fifty or 500 jobs are unambiguously "moved" from Indiana to India. Wary of negative publicity, the corporate architects of these programs prefer to keep the details to themselves. The major vendors of outsourcing services, and the overlapping network of consulting and advisory firms, much prefer discretion as well—not to mention

[57] For the classic account, see Bluestone and Harrison (1982). For a retrospective review, see Peck (2002).

[58] See Wright, G. (1986) *Old South, New South: Revolutions in the Southern economy since the Civil War*. New York: Basic Books; Moody, K. and Post, C. (2014) The politics of US labour: Paralysis and possibilities. In L. Panitch and G. Albo, eds, *Transforming Classes*. London: Merlin Press, 295–317; Peck (2016).

[59] See Nelson, K. (1985) Labor demand, labor supply and the suburbanization of low-wage office work. In A. J. Scott and M. Storper, eds, *Production, Work, Territory*. Boston, MA: Allen and Unwin, 149–71; England, K. V. L. (1993) Suburban pink collar ghettos: The spatial entrapment of women? *Annals of the Association of American Geographers* 83(2): 225–42. For historical context, see Hoos, I. R. (1961) *Automation in the Office*. Washington, DC: Public Affairs Press, 124–5. See also Chapter 6.

[60] See Uchitelle (2007); Mishel, L., Bivens, J., Gould, E., and Shierholz, H. (2013) *The State of Working America*, 12th edition. Ithaca, NY: Cornell University Press. See also <http://stateofworkingamerica.org/>.

[61] On public concerns over outsourcing and media representations of the outsourcing threat, see Chapter 3. See also Dobbs (2004) and Bhagwati et al. (2004).

their own understandable interests in contractual confidentiality in what is a fiercely competitive (and price-sensitive) business. Furthermore, the trade statistics and labor-market information systems of public agencies were not designed to capture such complex, cross-border flows, while perhaps it goes without saying that they have never had much of a handle on the measurement of conditions like stress and insecurity. As Timothy Sturgeon has pointed out, the resulting "vacuum...has helped to create a debate [around offshore outsourcing] that has been notable for its polarization and lack of nuance," a vacuum that has been filled by the (sometimes questionable) forecasts of consulting firms and a veritable deluge of thinly sourced speculation and editorial chatter.[62]

In a convergence decidedly less fortuitous than those celebrated by Thomas Friedman, these circumstances—of endemic information shortage, rising public anxiety, and political complacency—generated something like a near perfect public storm around offshore outsourcing during the Bush–Kerry presidential contest of 2004. It was N. Gregory Mankiw, George W. Bush's appointee as chair of the Council of Economic Advisors, who unwittingly exposed the profound disconnect between public attitudes, everyday business practice, and mainstream economic theory in his candid remark that, "Outsourcing is just a new way of doing international trade...the latest manifestation of the gains from trade that economists have talked about at least since Adam Smith...More things are tradable than in the past and that's a good thing."[63] This was the prominent economist's attempt to contextualize—indeed to defuse—a conspicuous assertion made in the newly released *Economic Report to the President* that outsourcing need not be considered inherently problematic since it was but "one facet of the increased trade services," a statement that provoked what Mankiw later described as a bout of "political hysteria."[64] The political timing could hardly have been worse: in a presidential campaign year, these revelations of business-as-usual behavior and normal-science neoclassical economics provided an irresistible opportunity to attack

[62] Sturgeon, T. J. (2006) *Services Offshoring Working Group Final Report*. Cambridge, MA: MIT Industrial Performance Center, p. 15. Sturgeon continues: "It is notable and quite unsettling that the most widely quoted estimates of the kind and number of jobs affected by services offshoring have come from the private sector. Whatever their actual quality, consulting firm estimates involve actions of current or potential clients, and therefore cannot be counted on to support public policy." See also Sturgeon, T. J. and Gereffi, G. (2009) Measuring success in the global economy: International trade, industrial upgrading and business function outsourcing in global value chains. *Transnational Corporations* 18(2): 1–35; Brown, C., Sturgeon, T. J., and Cole, C. (2014) The 2010 National Organizations Survey: Examining the relationships between job quality and the domestic and international sourcing of business functions by United States organizations. *IRLE* Working Paper No. 156-13, Institute for Research on Labor and Employment, Berkeley, CA.

[63] Quoted in Cassidy, J. (2004) Winners and losers: The truth about free trade. *New Yorker* August 2: 26–30.

[64] Mankiw and Swagel (2006: 1031).

the Bush White House for its apparent complicity with "Benedict Arnold CEOs [who] send American jobs overseas."[65]

This was the very same time that Thomas Friedman was researching his celebratory treatise, *The World Is Flat*, dissonant circumstances that gave the author a sense that he was living in a "parallel universe," since the dawning realities of the technological, organization, and employment revolution that were being disclosed to him, by prominent CEOs and Indian outsourcing companies, described a new reality that had all but arrived, yet no one was "telling the public or the politicians [perhaps because they were] too distracted, too focused on their own businesses, or too afraid."[66] What Friedman himself failed to appreciate was that the plans and projections of corporate visionaries, just like the hard-nosed rationality of orthodox economists, were seen by many to be part of the problem, rather than some new-age solution or (even) salvation. The less than reassuring message was that there would be painful dislocations and collateral damage, yes, but the bigger story was one of planetary progress, so the naysayers and protesters really ought to learn how to get with the (new) program.

This said, the scale of the disruptive change ahead was apparently such that it even caused Friedman momentarily to entertain some private doubts about his abiding faith in free trade, before concluding, *sans* ambiguity, that "Ricardo is right, Ricardo is right, Ricardo is right." The theory of comparative advantage—that every nation should specialize in the economic activities for which it has a cost advantage, yielding long-run mutual gains all around—is one that Friedman had earlier endorsed by quoting a memo sent to the staff of Reuters America by their boss, outsourcing evangelist David Schlesinger:

> Change is hard. Change is hardest on those caught by surprise [and] those who have difficulty changing... But change is natural; change is not new; change is important. The current debate about offshoring is dangerously hot. But the debate about work going to India, China and Mexico is actually no different from the debate once held about submarine work leaving New London [Connecticut, Schlesinger's home town] or shoe work leaving Massachusetts or textile work leaving North Carolina. Work gets done where it can be done most effectively and efficiently. That ultimately helps the New Londons, New Bedfords and New Yorks of this world even more than it helps the Bangalores and Shenzhens. It helps because it frees up people and capital to do different, more sophisticated work, and it helps because it gives an opportunity to produce the end product more cheaply,

---

[65] Quoted in Drezner, D. W. (2004) The outsourcing bogeyman. *Foreign Affairs* 83(3): 22–34, p. 31. Benedict Arnold (1741–1801), a general in the American revolutionary war, notoriously defected to the British side. In U.S. political discourse, his name has since been synonymous with betrayal. See Ducharme, L. J. and Fine, G. A. (1995) The construction of nonpersonhood and demonization: Commemorating the traitorous reputation of Benedict Arnold. *Social Forces* 73(4): 1309–31.

[66] Friedman (2005: 199–200).

benefiting customers even as it helps the corporation. It's certainly difficult for individuals to think about "their" work going away, being done thousands of miles away by someone earning thousands of dollars less a year. But it's time to think about the opportunity as well as the pain... Every person, just as every corporation, must tend to his or her own economic destiny, just as our parents and grandparents in the mills, shoe shops and factories did.[67]

Neither this corner-office version of a trust-me argument, nor its Ricardian predecessor, have ever seemed especially persuasive to those actually at risk of displacement. The latter might be more inclined to appreciate the sarcastic bite of Barnet and Müller's mid-1970s exposé of "multiple worldwide sourcing," in which the Ricardian logic of labor arbitrage was summarized as follows: "If illiterate Hong Kong children do what they do best (working on assembly lines ten hours a day for about thirty cents an hour) and Manhattan accountants make their unique contribution, everybody benefits."[68]

A generation later, ironically, many of those Manhattan accountants would find themselves directly exposed to the threat of offshore outsourcing. This is not to say that every accountant in Manhattan is about to be displaced by low-wage avatars toiling in windowless bunkers in Manila or Mumbai, but many have been, and those that remain are now seeing the terms of their employment radically transformed. As Edward Leamer puts it: "jobs may be contested by low-wage foreign workers but still stay right here [the principal outcome being] a deterioration of wages and working conditions in the United States, not a movement of jobs to low-wage countries."[69] To the extent that the arrival of outsourcing technologies—social, organizational, and digital—has extended the "theoretical" contestability of jobs across the oceans, then they will have effects that extend beyond any arithmetically verifiable cross-border movement of FTEs. The complex accounting of the "outcomes" of offshore outsourcing must therefore encompass jobs that do not move at all.

The largely theoretical promises of free-trade advocates that all the boats will eventually be lifted, on the other hand, sound especially hollow. As Harvard economist, Robert Z. Lawrence, a leading supporter of free-trade principles and policies, confessed in relation to the offshore outsourcing debate, "I still have faith that globalization will make us better off, but it's no more than faith."[70] Comparative advantage, it turns out, is more like a lore

---

[67] Friedman (2005: 226) and Schlesinger, quoted in Friedman (2005: 20–1).
[68] Barnet and Müller (1974: 132, 131). See also Barnet, R. J. and Müller, R. E. (1975) *Global Reach*. London: Jonathan Cape; Barnet, R. J. and Cavanagh, J. (1995) *Global Dreams*. New York: Touchstone.
[69] Leamer (2007: 117).
[70] Quoted in Engardio, P., Bernstein, A., Kriplani, M., Balfour, F., Grow, B., and Greene, J. (2003) Is your job next? *Business Week* February 3: 50–60, p. 57.

than a law. As Alain Lipietz, a long-time skeptic of free-trade arguments, once pointed out in the context of Reagan-era deindustrialization:

> [T]he cruellest irony for American industry [is that] having chosen for itself a strategy of low wages and low skill levels, it had no reason to keep on its own territory the heart of its productive apparatus, as was done by Japan and Germany. All US manufacturing is being drawn towards a Mexican workforce which is increasingly using European and Japanese machines... [U]nder the new rules of the game, it is Mexico that has the absolute advantage over the USA for semi-skilled labour in most sectors.[71]

Later, the passage of the North American Free Trade Agreement in 1994 would amplify the Mexican advantage but according to Friedman's version of events, the country was too complacent fully to capitalize on the opportunity, rapidly losing ground to China, especially after its accession to the World Trade Organization in 2001. On this telling, the Mexican "tortoise" was soon out-paced by the Chinese "hare," with its prodigious advantages not just in low-cost labor, but in "education, privatization, infrastructure, quality control, mid-level management, and the introduction of new technology."[72]

Friedman prefers to talk about the upside of the permanent revolution that is global outsourcing, rather than dwell on its costs or victims (a perspective that is echoed in value-chain discourses around upgrading). This causes him to bridle at the persistently negative connotations that attach to the term, the practice, and the "industry" of outsourcing. It is true, he acknowledges, that outsourcing got its start as a cost-saving measure—propelled by windfall gains from labor arbitrage—but global optimization is ultimately a noble cause, indeed a vector of economic progress. In this sense, "Outsourcing isn't just for Benedict Arnolds," Friedman protests, "It's also for idealists."

> Have no doubt, there are firms that do and will outsource good jobs just to save money and dispense it to shareholders or management. To think that this is not happening or will not happen is beyond naïve. But firms that are using outsourcing primarily as a tool to cut costs, not to enhance innovation and speed growth, are the minority, not the majority—and I would not want to own stock in any of them. The best companies are finding ways to leverage the best of what is in India with the best of what it is North Dakota with the best of what is in Los Angeles. In that sense, the word "outsourcing" should really be retired. The applicable word is really "sourcing."[73]

In some circles, no doubt, it would be convenient if the word outsourcing was ruled out, while all-purpose sourcing was in, but the travels of the original

---

[71] Lipitez, A. (1997) The post-Fordist world: Labour relations, international hierarchy and global ecology. *Review of International Political Economy* 4(1): 1–41, p. 29.
[72] Friedman (2005: 331, 335).   [73] Friedman (2005: 362).

word have proved difficult to regulate. Friedman's sometime colleague at the *Times*, William Safire, appears to have sympathized, but always tended to regard such efforts at semantic cleansing with detached amusement. Safire remarked that the short-lived industry neologism *intersourcing* may have more precisely signified the complex practice of blending and synergizing the work systems of clients and vendors, doing away with the outmoded connotations of putting *out*, although perhaps not with the problems of juvenile innuendo; meanwhile, technically correct terminology like global (or worldwide) sourcing just seemed to lack the kind of traction to displace an unloved word that had clearly stuck.[74] Like it or (much more likely) not, *outsourcing* was here to stay.

Outsourcing Expertise

If the practices and language of offshore outsourcing are here to stay, then so (in some form or another) is the outsourcing industry, or what is styled here, rather more expansively, as the outsourcing complex, the sprawling network of managers, technicians, and organizations that facilitate the business of global sourcing, that enable it *to work*. Still relatively young—whether understood as an industry, a profession, or an operational field—outsourcing has never been entirely comfortable in its own skin. Part of the problem may be a lack of status and respect in the corporate community of "sending" economies. Here, the outsourcer's basic mission is to clean up and contract out an untidy bundle of "second-tier" and non-core tasks, many of which are regarded by management as "messy," and to execute without creating a new set of problems, such as failures in customer service, system integrity, or communication. (Minimizing friction, almost striving not to be noticed, therefore becomes a paradoxical measure of success.) The work of outsourcing is perceived, even (and perhaps *especially*) by some business colleagues, to be the managerial equivalent of dirty work: they recognize that the effective management of outsourced contracts and relationships is necessary, but it is no longer seen to be heroic or glamorous, and unlikely to define the career goals of corporate high fliers. Meanwhile, the image of outsourcing outside the corporate world is often unequivocally negative, it being seen by many as a slightly squalid or barely ethical enterprise. Never mind that such blanket generalizations are inaccurate (or at the least unevenly accurate), and therefore to some degree also unfair, they nevertheless seem to inform durable perceptions of the practice and profession of offshoring. Outsourcers may have long given up on the idea of ever being understood, let alone appreciated, by the public, but the lack of professional recognition from their peers arguably grates even more.

---

[74] Safire, W. (2004) On language: Outsource. *New York Times Magazine* March 21: 30.

This may explain why the outsourcing industry has been repeatedly trying—but always apparently failing—to find a new name (and indeed identity) for itself, and why it seems keener than most to dress up its activities with euphemistic buzzwords and the latest business-school jargon. But the problem, according to leading industry analyst and commentator Phil Fersht, runs deeper than the fact "that 'outsourcing' is broken terminology," because ultimately there are many working on the inside who believe that theirs "isn't a real industry." Fersht goes as far as to call it "a sham":

> When God created "outsourcing," she/he/it clearly had a sense of humor. I mean, how do you encourage people who offloaded a chunk of their low-end processes offshore to get together and form an "industry"?... [T]he reality is, outsourcing "networks" are strange concoctions of individuals striving to feel part of a "community" that doesn't really exist.[75]

The public (relations) face of the outsourcing business is of course much more upbeat and positive, but Fersht's remarks come closer to capturing how those on the inside talk amongst themselves. This often maligned industry appears to be gripped by a certain malaise, lacking proper recognition on the outside and meaningful cohesion on the inside.

Since its emergence as a quasi-industry sometime in the 1990s, outsourcing has been an heterogeneous paraprofessional space populated by a diverse array of advisory firms, management consultants, brokers, intermediaries, enablers, contract lawyers, and service providers. Beyond the shared concern with outsourced processes and some overlapping skill sets, and perhaps a shared sense of private grievance, there is not much that unites this variegated network. It is an industry divided to its absent core by competition, in which brand-based and establishment hierarchies are not particularly strong, where even market leaders are vulnerable to undercutting on the next contract. There is some coming together at the level of deals and projects, and more rarely around longer-term partnerships or alliances, but not much more than that. Phil Fersht turns to the analogy of marriage, one that is often used in these circles,[76] to characterize the true nature of what after all are properly called outsourcing "engagements." Normally, these will be initiated by a contractually solemnized transaction (following a brief period of courtship

---

[75] Fersht, P. (2012) Why today's outsourcing industry is a sham. *Horses for Sources* blog, March 24, accessed at <http://www.horsesforsources.com/outsourcing-industry-sham_032512>, May 1, 2015, p. 1. Closely attuned to the competitive dynamics and prevailing mood of the outsourcing complex, the *Horses for Sources* blog, which is described as "the leading destination for unfettered collective insight, research and open debate of sourcing industry issues and developments," is characterized by an irreverent tone, mixing corporate realism, market research, and unrestrained advocacy of outsourcing-industry interests, sometimes with a libertarian inflection.

[76] Thomas Friedman (2005) did the same, equating the Y2K episode to a "first date," out of which a successful marriage would grow, in the shape of the sourcing industry.

and some consideration of alternative suitors), but beyond this moment of inception, outsourcing projects really have more to do with the management of complex, evolving, and invariably trying relationships: for corporate buyers of outsourced services, the experience can be rather like "purchasing a wedding dress—a one-time transaction followed by seven years of relationship struggles and future legal wrangles."[77]

The nature of these relationships, however, has also been changing, and quite fundamentally. After the early years of "lift and shift" outsourcing—the time when entire departments and job functions were being moved offshore through large-scale, Jack Welch-style maneuvers—engagements have almost inevitably become more complex, more challenging. The "days of lump-sum outsourcing deals and blunt offshore labor arbitrage are gone," Ben Worthen has explained, as companies have learned that outsourced problems often remain problems, and that maintaining quality and integrity with subcontracted processes and supply-chain partners is no less important than driving down bottom-line costs.[78] Since what some portray as the "wild west" days of outsourcing, corporate buyers have become more sophisticated, but much more demanding too. Cost-control concerns have hardly gone away, but now they are accompanied by an elaborate range of measures intended to shape and sustain the subsequent "relationship," from exacting performance contracts to partnership arrangements around technology sharing and systems development. Outsourcing contracts—the equivalent of prenuptial agreements—routinely run into hundreds of pages these days, and many will be revised almost continuously. Meanwhile, the vendors of outsourcing services have constructed prodigious capacities as well, both reflecting and anticipating these shifting demands from corporate clients. At the top of the pile are those blue-chip vendors with worldwide capacities, with their own centers of excellence and deep reserves of managerial talent and technical knowhow, a new generation of "suppliers [that] are expected to be bigger, more capable and strategically located to access large markets."[79] The outsourcing industry has matured as its markets have expanded, but the expectations of corporate clients have been increasing as well, perhaps even more quickly.

Out of this combination of friction and symbiosis, new forms of managerial and technical expertise have emerged, but the targets are always moving. Phil Fersht continues:

[77] Fersht, P. (2012) Why today's outsourcing industry is a sham. *Horses for Sources* blog, March 24, accessed at http://www.horsesforsources.com/outsourcing-industry-sham_032512, May 1, 2015, p. 1.

[78] Worthen, B. (2007) What *The World Is Flat* means to IT outsourcing, *CIO Magazine* May 1, accessed at <http://www.cio.com/article/2439122/outsourcing/what-the-world-is-flat-means-to-it-outsourcing.html>, August 1, 2015.

[79] Gereffi (2014: 15). See also Sako, M. (2006) Outsourcing and offshoring: Implications for productivity of business services. *Oxford Review of Economic Policy* 22(4): 499–512.

Most of tomorrow's deals are not going to involve major staff transitions from buyer to provider... [such] engagements are on the wane as most of the bloated buyers have been progressively trimming their fat in recent years. Moreover, most of the providers today have the capacity they need to service their clients and will only entertain major "lifts and shifts" of employees if these deals are strategic to their [own] growth ambitions, and involve the transition of *both* domain expertise and technology assets... So isn't it high time we stopped convincing ourselves there really is an outsourcing industry? If you base your entire career living in a perpetual outsourcing transaction-cycle involving hordes of staff transfers and staff re-badging, then, fair enough—YOU *REALLY ARE* AN OUTSOURCING PROFESSIONAL. However, if you want to focus your career on improving processes, finding new and creative ways to improve companies' productivity and growth, and leverage today's availability of global talent into the bargain, aren't you probably what we are calling a GLOBAL BUSINESS SERVICES PRO?[80]

This (clearly frustrated) desire for reinvention, indeed for new forms of recognition, is a recurrent one in the industry still generally known by the moniker of outsourcing.[81] In practice, the transactional and the transformational moments of the outsourcing process are inextricably entangled, including in the occupational identities of those in the outsourcing profession. The ongoing work of "orchestrat[ing] global operations" has necessitated the mobilization of the pseudo-industry that is outsourcing, along with a transnational managerial complex comprising "shared service specialists, outsourcing governance pros, finance and procurement executives, business analysts, customer service managers, IT leaders, systems architects and functional leads," which as Fersht points out extends to generalist players like the "Big-5 consultants who focus on anything from outsourcing to tax advice and service providers who'd do anything to remove the term 'outsourcing' from the Oxford English and Webster dictionaries."[82]

Another industry insider, Jack Buffington, placed the management-consulting companies right at the top of his list of the "opportunists of outsourcing," although this arguably understates (or at least misstates) their role.[83] It is certainly the case that management consultants were instrumental in formulating and testing operational concepts of offshore outsourcing, alongside complementary and coevolving strategies like reengineering and supply-chain

---

[80] Fersht, P. (2012) Why today's outsourcing industry is a sham. *Horses for Sources* blog, March 24, accessed at <http://www.horsesforsources.com/outsourcing-industry-sham_032512>, May 1, 2015, pp. 1–2, emphasis original.

[81] The causes and consequences of these necessary fantasies of professional reinvention are examined further in Chapter 4.

[82] Fersht, P. (2012) Why today's outsourcing industry is a sham. *Horses for Sources* blog, March 24, accessed at http://www.horsesforsources.com/outsourcing-industry-sham_032512, May 1, 2015, p. 2.

[83] Buffington (2007: 35). See also O'Mahoney and Markham (2013).

management, and a phallanx of consultants would subsequently take on central roles in the design, execution, and evaluation of outsourcing projects, with some crossing over to join newly formed career tracks as advisors, analysts, IT applications, and contracts specialists, while others worked in more strategic ways, at the fuzzy outsourcing/consulting interface, on the propagation of "best practices," on the promotion of techno-organizational projects for corporate transformation, and on "thought-leadership" around next-wave models. Management consultants, in this sense, have not only been the gurus of outsourcing, they have taken on some of the grunt work as well, and they have had a hand in most of the functions in between.[84]

The history of management-consultancy business itself, in fact, cannot be told without reference to "long waves" of corporate philosophy and practice, the most recent of which has been defined by outsourcing and the associated challenges of designing and delivering "globalized" business processes. The origins of the consulting profession are traced to the widespread adoption of scientific management and the rise of cost accounting in the early twentieth century, after which came the drive to reorganize around the norm of the multidivisional or "m-form" firm after the Second World War, followed after the 1970s by countervailing trends for vertical disintegration, corporate unbundling, and the "reinvention" and privatization of government services; and since the 1990s by downsizing and rightsizing, value-chain engineering, knowledge-based business processes, and various forms of sourcing.[85] Matthias Kipping suggestively summarizes this episodic evolution in three waves. The first was defined by scientific management, with its emphasis on workplace "efficiency experts"; next, questions of organization and strategy came to the fore, focused on issues of corporate structure and competitive environments; and in the latest wave, beginning in the 1990s, the consulting sector has been reorganized, once again, this time around the nexus of information technologies, human resources, and global networks.[86]

---

[84] On management gurus, and the production and circulation of fads and fashions, see Micklethwait, J. and Wooldridge, A. (1997) *The Witch Doctors: Making sense of the management gurus*. New York: Times Business; Jackson, B. (2001) *Management Gurus and Management Fashions*. London: Routledge; Collins, D. (2000) *Management Fads and Buzzwords: Critical-practical perspectives*. London: Routledge.

[85] See, especially, Kipping (2002) and McKenna (2006). On various facets of the management-consulting sector's historical evolution, see United Nations Conference on Trade and Development, Programme on Transnational Corporations (1993) *Management Consulting: A survey of the industry and its largest firms*. New York: United Nations; Saint-Martin, D, (2000) *Building the New Managerialist State*. Oxford: Oxford University Press; Clark, T. and Fincham, R., eds. (2002) *Critical Consulting: New perspectives on the management advice industry*. Oxford: Blackwell; Kipping, M. and Engwall, L., eds. (2002) *Management Consulting: Emergence and dynamics of a knowledge industry*. Oxford: Oxford University Press; and Armbrüster (2006); O'Mahoney and Markham (2013).

[86] See Kipping (2002: 37–8). The repeating pattern has been that "the evolution of the consulting industry and of its pre-eminent firms [have been] closely linked to the development

For more than a century, the management-consulting industry has been playing a major role in capitalizing upon, mediating, translating, and recursively shaping the "downstream" consequences of disruptive events, transformative technologies, regulatory reforms, and management theories. This is sometimes trivialized as a merely predatory function, based on the exploitation of corporate uncertainty-cum-insecurity and the development of secondary markets built on the shaky foundations of managerial fads and fashions,[87] but this understates the pervasiveness and creativity of consultants' "liminal" interventions in managerial practice, and their creative and generative roles in the articulation and roll out of new organizational forms, techniques, and methodologies.[88]

Management consultants were present at the birth of outsourcing and they have been active players in every stage of its subsequent development. Outsourcing markets are strategically critical for the management-consulting industry (writ large) today, not just as a revenue generator and profit center, but also as a locus for successive waves of strategy development, organizational experimentation, codification, and best-practice learning. Outsourcing is an important practice field for most of the top consulting houses and generalist providers, some of which define corporate divisions around outsourcing (or one of its synonyms). For some years, Accenture advertised its wares under the strapline of *consulting • technolology • outsourcing*, before itself succumbing to the temptation of euphemistic redescription.[89] Capgemini boasts a workforce of more than 15,000 "outsourcing professionals," selling a range of services under the proprietary name of *Rightshore®*, its global delivery model.[90] In some form or another, outsourcing is a primary value

---

of managerial practice and ideology" (Kipping, 2002: 29). Across this unevenly developed history, McKenna (2006: 14) observes that cost accounting, perhaps above all else, has been the recurrent concern, since in one form or another, "Consultants . . . prosper on the razor's edge of the managerial/transaction-cost calculus." This is clearly true of the current conjuncture between consulting and outsourcing.

[87] See the discussion in Sorge, A. and van Witteloostuijn, A. (2004) The (non)sense of organizational change: An essay about universal management hypes, sick consultancy metaphors, and healthy organization theories. *Organization Studies* 25(7): 1205–31.

[88] See Sturdy, A. (1997) The consultancy process: An insecure business. *Journal of Management Studies* 34(3): 389–413; Fincham, R. and Evans, M. (1999) The consultants' offensive: Reengineering—from fad to technique. *New Technology, Work and Employment* 14(1): 32–44; Clegg, S. R., Kornberger, M., and Rhodes, C. (2004) Noise, parasites and translation: Theory and practice in management consulting. *Management Learning* 35(1): 31–44; Armbrüster, T. and Glückler, J. (2007) Organizational change and the economics of management consulting: A response to Sorge and van Witteloostuijn. *Organizational Studies* 28(12): 1873–85; Whittle, A. (2006) The paradoxical repertoires of management consultancy. *Journal of Organizational Change Management* 19(4): 424–36.

[89] See Hallard, K. (2014) Out and proud. *Sourcing Focus* blog, April 17, accessed at <http://www.sourcingfocus.com/site/blogentry/out_and_proud/>, August 5, 2015.

[90] See https://www.capgemini.com/rightshore>, and Vault (2007) *Vault Guide to the Top 50 Management and Strategy Consulting Firms 2008*. New York: Vault.

generator for countless other consulting firms and hybrid service providers. The small library of executive manuals for the management of outsourced operations will typically recommend the recruitment of consultants to assist with the design, oversight, and evaluation of outsourcing projects;[91] many of these being written by consultants themselves.[92] Annually updated field guides to the latest hotspots on the outsourcing investment landscape, priced for the business market, such as Tholons' *Top 100 Outsourcing Destinations*, have become familiar "products" amongst the consulting and advisory firms.[93]

In material terms, the rise of the outsourcing market was registered in a significant surge in consulting-industry revenues from the mid-1990s,[94] after which the boundaries between what has been described as the "world's newest profession" and the even newer profession that has been developing around the outsourcing complex would become increasingly blurred.[95] The two sectors effectively became co-evolutionary, and ever since have been difficult to separate in any clear-cut way. As a late 1990s survey of the consultancy sector in the *Economist* concluded:

> It is hard to know just how big the management consultancy business is … The narrowest definition includes only McKinsey and a handful of other strategy firms; the broadest definition takes in large chunks of the outsourcing business, particularly anything to do with installing and integrating computer systems … [The] boundary between offering advice and managing systems is blurring. The strategic firms no longer just put forward bright ideas, but offer to implement them as well. Conversely, many information-technology and outsourcing firms are employing a swelling army of consultants.[96]

This process of fusion has been barely two decades in the making, however. The most authoritative source on the management-consulting business, the International Labour Office's *Guide to the Profession*, contained no mention of outsourcing even as recently as its 1996 edition, but by the early 2000s

---

[91] See, for example, Power, M. J., Desouza, K. C., and Bonifazi, C. (2006) *The Outsourcing Handbook*. London: Kogan Page. Alternatively, follow Stephanie Overby's tutorial, *The ABCs of Outsourcing*, which was developed by the organization of chief information officers as an online resource containing "everything you need to know to avoid the pitfalls of outsourcing," June 8, 2007, accessed at <http://www.cio.com/article/2438784/outsourcing/the-abcs-of-outsourcing.html>, August 1, 2015.

[92] See Vashistha, A. and Vashistha, A. (2005) *The Offshore Nation: The rise of services globalization*. New Dehli: Tata McGraw-Hill; Greaver, M. F. (1999) *Strategic Outsourcing: A structured approach to outsourcing decisions and initiatives*. New York: AMACOM; Brown, D. and Wilson, S. (2005) *The Black Book of Outsourcing*. Hoboken, NJ: Wiley; Koulopoulos, T. M. and Roloff, T. (2006) *Smartsourcing: Driving innovation and growth through outsourcing*. Avon, MA: Platinum Press; and Corbett (2004).

[93] Tholons (2015) *2016 Top 100 Outsourcing Destinations*. New York: Tholons. See Figure 1.1.

[94] See Armbrüster (2006, figure 2.1).

[95] The phrase belongs to McKenna's (2006) unmatched account of the history, and economic sociology, of management consulting.

[96] Wooldridge, A. (1997) Trimming the fat: A survey of management consultancy. *Economist* March 22: S1–S22, p. S3.

recognized outsourcing as a structurally significant field of practice that was already "transforming the shape of the consulting sector."[97]

Itself increasingly unbounded, the management-consultancy industry has played a multifaceted, enabling, and in many ways catalytic role in the formation and evolution of the outsourcing complex, the existence of which speaks to the technical, managerial, cultural, and organizational challenges of making long-distance sourcing really *work* for client companies, not just as a cost-saving measure but as a permanent feature of the ongoing process of corporate transformation. Those working on the inside of global sourcing operations will often refer to their "industry" as little more than a badge of convenience, recognition that they are engaged with others in the manufacture and sale of the same basic product—outsourced labor. In terms of corporate and professional identities, however, the outsourcing complex exhibits a center that barely holds, subject as it is to alternating currents of normative codification and associative ambivalence. It might be considered to resemble, in this and other respects, the consulting business itself, as well as the temporary staffing "industry" (albeit with lower status than the former, and higher or equivalent status to the latter). All three are business-to-business activities, wide in reach but quite diffuse in form, that ply their respective trades across the full spectrum of industries and services. All three are defined, too, by their work as organizational intermediaries, relationship managers, boundary players, operating in some respects like an outside supplier and in other respects like an in-house collaborator. And all three tend to work (much more than they would wish) in fiercely competitive, price-oriented markets, in which power asymmetries tend to favor corporate buyers, within which they accumulate—and trade on—specialist knowhow and practice-based expertise acquired across a multiplicity of engagements, much of which routinely "leaks" beyond the boundaries of the firm. Relative to the ideal-type models of market, hierarchical, and network organization, these are rather unstable hybrids: they are assembled as network organizations, bundling functions and working across boundaries of various kinds; they find their business "inside" the fragmenting and flattening hierarchies of corporate clients; and they are persistently exposed to, and disciplined by, market forces.

As a far-from-typical economic formation, the outsourcing complex has been a nexus for all manner of innovations, the incubator of experimental forms of expertise and improvised practice, and an enabler of new configurations of distantiated employment. In this respect, it can be seen to play a bridging or "infrastructural" role, as a facilitator of methods and mechanisms of cross-border restructuring that were otherwise unrealizable. Analogous to

---

[97] Kubr, M. (2002) *Management Consulting: A guide to the profession*, 4th edition. Geneva: International Labour Office, p. 29.

the way in which a mature and expansive network of temporary-labor agencies has enabled forms of contingent employment that for the individual firm were previously unfeasible (such as tapping into highly specialist skills for short periods, managing large-scale fluctuations in labor utilization on a continuing basis, or commodifying supervision activities along with contracted-out employment functions), global-sourcing infrastructures likewise render newly possible *and profitable* innovative forms of job-task fragmentation, recombination, and relocation, executed over long distances. Exploring how these infrastructures operate, and with what consequences, is the wider task of this book. While the nub of these questions concerns the production of new rationalities, practices, capacities, and forms of expertise, central to the ensuing argument is that these are much more than narrow questions of economics, conventionally understood. Rather, they pose a host of much wider questions that reach deeply into the domains of cultural political economy, economic sociology, and economic geography, among other fields. In this respect, it is a matter of more than passing concern that the outsourcing business has operated, practically since birth, amid a miasma of political negativity. These are more than "background" conditions, but shape in a constitutive sense how the outsourcing complex operates and how it represents itself to the world. For this reason, before delving into the diffuse heart of the outsourcing complex in Chapter 4, the book next turns to the troubled politics of outsourcing. It looks at the phenomenon of offshore work from "onshore," from the perspective of which "[o]utsourcing creates an invisible workforce that can be paid a fraction of wages in the US," Poster and Yolmo point out, "while also decoupled from that country's employment laws, policies, and benefits."[98] Under these conditions, it should be no surprise that offshoring has emerged as a uniquely negative and threatening political issue.

---

[98] Poster and Yolmo (2016: 585).

3

Outsourcing Politics

Offshore outsourcing may have become normalized as a corporate practice, yet its conditions of existence and future prospects seem anything but settled or certain. Rather than a marker of a one-time fix or stable new paradigm, the globalizing world of outsourcing is characterized by ongoing roil and transformative change. This can be seen in the persistently high rates of project failure and contract turnover in outsourcing engagements, in the moves from first-tier to second- and third-tier cities in India and elsewhere, and in the drift toward nearer-shore locations, for instance. So much is to be expected of an historically emergent business practice, it might be said, one that was first developed as an experimental strategy and which necessarily entails various degrees of organizational risk and learning. But offshore outsourcing is about much more than an evolving search for technically or organizationally optimal solutions; it has been a politicized and controversial activity from the beginning, and remains so, in ways that are far more significant and consequential than political chatter on the sidelines. In important respects, offshore outsourcing has been constitutively politicized, in that the generally negative political optics of the activity—at least in "sending" countries—materially impact the practice itself, its status, its presentation, and even calculations of its "cost." In the United States, especially, offshoring remains a dependable attack term, especially in presidential election seasons, where it has become a recurring excuse for populist grandstanding and name calling. Here, outsourcing has become a byword for economic insecurity and competitive stress, the rhetorical antithesis to homegrown and middle-class sustaining "American jobs." It has come to define the space of an enduring political and economic problem, although one notably light on practical, tractable, and deliverable policy *solutions*.

Even though the world of outsourcing is a turbulent one, there are few serious observers who believe that its dynamics are likely to be reversed. Yet there is a host of serious questions concerning the measurement, monitoring, management, and effective regulation of this activity, and regarding trade, taxation, and employment policy, that remain open or unresolved. At the

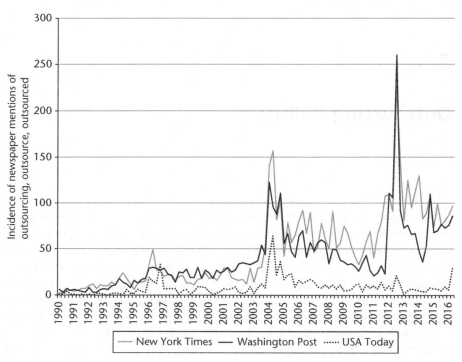

Figure 3.1 Outsourcing as political keyword, 1990–2016
Source: author's calculations from Factiva

same time, there appears to be precious little scope for sober assessment, considering policymaking, or even informed political debate, when the issue remains so hot as to be almost untouchable, except for the discussion of (often symbolic) policies nominally aimed at its suppression. Public anxieties about offshore outsourcing in the United States have been cynically whipped up, repeatedly, in the service of partisan advantage. "Offshoring" has become firmly lodged in the public imagination as an outsized threat to jobs and livelihoods, disproportionate to the widespread but measured expansion of the corporate practice to date, although perhaps more proportional to its *potential* impact.[1] Meanwhile, in the United States, spasmodic pulses of "outsourcing talk" have tended to track—and be sharply amplified by—the presidential electoral calendar (see Figure 3.1). Channeling deep currents of economic anxiety, the "outsourcing threat" has generated significant amounts of (political)

[1] For polling data, see German Marshall Fund (2007) *Perspectives on Trade and Poverty Reduction.* Washington, DC: GMF; Public Citizen (2015) *U.S. Polling Shows Strong Opposition to More of the Same U.S. Trade Deals from Independents, Republicans and Democrats Alike.* Washington, DC: Public Citizen. See also Uchitelle (2007) and Blinder (2009).

heat, if remarkable little in the way of (policy) light. Fear and misinformation have flourished in the resulting vacuum.

Before venturing, as subsequent chapters will do, into some of the inner worlds and corporate recesses of offshore outsourcing, this chapter takes a look at the issue from the outside, as it were, in the space of public discourse. Hostility to outsourcing first made the political headlines in the Bush versus Kerry contest of 2004, but there was an unseemly reprise in 2012, when offshoring slurs and accusations were hurled in both directions by the Obama and Romney campaigns, straining the capacity (and independence) of the fact-checking organizations, in a context in which the "facts" of cross-border outsourcing remain almost uniquely opaque and contestable. If nothing else, though, the remarkable superficiality of the rhetorical war between the Democrats and Republicans, and the shared detachment of the major-party policy platforms from these fundamental issues of trade and employment, serves to call attention to a marked disjuncture—between a largely symbolic debate characterized on all sides by varying degrees of evasiveness, cynicism, and hypocrisy, and what properly ought to be a substantive issue of concern for both the public and for policymakers. Election-season attempts to hurriedly assess the "facts" relating to trends in corporate restructuring, the adoption of "lean" staffing models, and the utilization of outsourcing also call attention to the remarkable elusiveness, if not illusiveness, of these facts, occluded as they are by corporate secrecy and political sensitivity, in addition to some serious challenges of a technical and interpretative nature.

The prominent economist Alan Blinder has made the argument that offshore outsourcing might mark the beginning of a "great dislocation" in the United States, comparable to the historical moments of industrialization and deindustrialization, and quite possibly "a nasty transition, lasting for decades."[2] Rather than squaring up to these issues, however, resort to populist posturing has been accompanied by a parallel degradation of economic-policy discourse, as performative displays of ostensible commitment to "American jobs" have filled the void created by what is in effect a silent bipartisan pact—the abrogation of political responsibility for domestic employment conditions, together with a near consensual embrace of ongoing trade liberalization coupled with light-touch corporate regulation and largely hands-off approaches to labor-market policy. Rather than begin with some corporate "essence" of, or primal motivation for, offshore outsourcing, the approach in this chapter is to work from the outside in, journeying between the muddy waters of political rhetoric and pristine (re)statements of neoclassical economic theory, and between foreboding visions of the "offshore threat" and glimpses of the actually existing phenomenon itself.

---

[2] Blinder (2009: 28).

Trading Blows

There was a line in the 2004 edition of the *Economic Report of the President* that read, "When a good or service is produced more cheaply abroad, it makes more sense to import it than to make or provide it domestically."[3] This had been written (and was initially read by some) as an uncontroversial reiteration of economic orthodoxy, but in the context of a presidential election year the statement was interpreted by others as a symbol of the Bush Administration's indifference to the economic plight of middle-class Americans and its laissez-faire attitude towards corporate behavior. Soon, the issue of offshore outsourcing was all over the front pages. Harvard economist N. Gregory Mankiw, the Bush-appointed chair of the Council of Economic Advisers at the time, demonstrated an uncanny ability to dig more deeply into a hole of his own making when in a press conference he described offshore outsourcing as "probably a plus for the economy in the long run," in a misguided attempt to tamp down the controversy around a report that had also raised the question—technically valid, perhaps, but nevertheless politically tin-eared—of whether fast-food "assembly" work should be reclassified as manufacturing.[4] A few weeks later, a consulting firm's estimate that offshoring could cost the U.S. economy approaching 4 million jobs by 2015 further fanned the flames.[5] The ensuing controversy put the Bush Administration on the defensive, exposing as it did a vulnerable political flank, given the especially anemic "jobless recovery" that had followed the 2001 recession. It also gifted the Democrats' presidential candidate, Senator John Kerry, with what would become a stump-speech staple, notably in the swing states of the Rust Belt, about the need to rein in the irresponsible behavior of those "Benedict Arnold CEOs." The challenger's implication was that offshoring amounted to a kind of economic treachery, with which the business-friendly Bush Administration was complicit.[6]

Never mind that Kerry had himself long been an enthusiastic supporter of the North American Free Trade Agreement and other trade liberalization initiatives, the opportunistic embrace of an anti-outsourcing stance combined populist appeal with political traction, tapping into public concerns about job insecurity and global competition while highlighting the Bush Administration's apparent detachment from "main-street" issues of economic policy.

[3] United States Government Printing Office (2004) *Economic Report of the President*. Washington, DC: USGPO, p. 229.
[4] *Wall Street Journal* (2004) Mankiw lays furor to loss in translation. *Wall Street Journal* February 18, A2; Johnston, D. C. (2004) In the new economics: Fast-food factories? *New York Times* February 20, C2; Andrews, E. L. (2004) Economics adviser learns the principles of politics. *New York Times* February 26, C4.
[5] See McCarthy, J. C. (2004) *Near-Term Growth of Offshoring Accelerating*. Cambridge, MA: Forrester Research.
[6] Quoted in Drezner, D. W. (2004) The outsourcing bogeyman. *Foreign Affairs* 83(3): 22–34, p. 31.

Labor unions, of course, were amongst the original opponents of outsourcing, even before there was recognized terminology for the practice, and the issue continued to play well with Democratic primary campaign audiences. But venting against offshoring would also become a rallying cry of the populist right, not least as the central plank in the sustained campaign for economic nationalism championed by Lou Dobbs, at the time a news anchor at CNN, later to move to the Fox Business Network. "The ultimate message in outsourcing is this," Dodd thundered, "America be damned... It's all about the lowest cost."[7]

Polling data consistently revealed that the American public roundly rejected Mankiw's positive and apparently complacent assessment of outsourcing, which had effectively become equated with the position of the Bush Administration, although the restive electorate remained unconvinced that the policies of either of the major parties were equal to the task of properly addressing the worrying phenomenon.[8] Sixty-eight percent of American voters opposed outsourcing, which was seen to be synonymous with the movement of jobs overseas, according to a typical poll at the time; more surprisingly, a similar proportion of business investors even conceded that the practice was bad for the country.[9] Kerry had struck a chord by playing to these concerns, knowing full well that the major party platforms were closely aligned on the questions of (free) trade and corporate regulation, even if the Democrats were more open to interventionist measures on job training and tax reform. These small differences in policy would be drowned out by loud disagreements at the level of rhetoric. In a period of protracted and mounting economic insecurity, outsourcing was perceived as something approaching an existential threat.

If the 2004 presidential election campaign positioned outsourcing as a highly charged political issue, establishing mainstream currency for the term (in the pejorative register), the incremental ascendancy of the actual business practice continued, almost uninterrupted, albeit discreetly. Across the fast-growing industry-cum-profession of outsourcing—whose appropriately low key but tenacious trade association, the International Association of Outsourcing Professionals, had been formed in the wake of this torrid period of politicization, in 2005—discretion became the watchword. "While

[7] Quoted in McCarthy, M. (2005) Dobbs fires away against outsourcing. *USA Today* February 23, B3. See also Dobbs (2004).

[8] Substantive policy debates around offshore outsourcing, in fact, had barely been engaged by this time, beyond some consideration of short-term measures. See Lohr, S. (2004) Debate over exporting jobs raises questions on policies. *New York Times* February 23, C1; Anderson, S., Cavanagh, J., Madrick, J., and Henwood, D. (2004) Toward a progressive view on outsourcing. *Nation* March 22, 22–6.

[9] Data at Angus Reid Public Opinion (2004) Americans reject job outsourcing. *Angus Reid* April 10, accessed at <http://www.angus-reid.com/polls/24826/americans_reject_job_outsourcing/>, June 5, 2014; Jacobe, D. (2004) Do investors support outsourcing? *GPNS Commentary* April 27, accessed at <http://www.gallup.com/poll/11506/investors-support-outsourcing.aspx>, June 5, 2014.

companies have become quieter about their plans," an article in the *Wall Street Journal* disclosed in the aftermath of the Benedict Arnold furor, "the pace of outsourcing continues to increase as businesses seek to use lower-cost labor overseas."[10] A *Business Week* cover story that positioned outsourcing as both economically inevitable, *à la* Thomas Friedman, and integral to a new wave of "transformational" corporate management, spoke to the normalization of the practice, even if once again it was to provoke dissenting responses from the public.[11] "Global economic competition and the outsourcing of American jobs" remained the top concern of U.S. voters in a 2006 poll, above the Iraq War and even further ahead of "illegal immigration."[12] Meanwhile, Lou Dobbs' televised tirades against outsourcing continued.[13]

For a time, though, it seemed like the sting might have been taken out of the outsourcing issue. The "change" election of 2008 was preoccupied by a different legacy of Bush years, the enormous costs of two prolonged and unpopular wars, only to be dominated in its final act by the financial emergency that was the Wall Street crash.[14] Outsourcing did not seem to define or divide the presidential candidates, even though it remained an underlying source of socioeconomic concern. A German Marshall Fund study published in the run up to the 2008 election found that 61 percent of Americans believed that outsourcing was the leading cause of job loss in the country, way ahead of factors like corporate restructuring (29 percent), technological innovation (16 percent), and trade (12 percent).[15] A few months later, a Harris poll found that 76 percent of Americans were concerned that "outsourcing, that is jobs going overseas" would affect them personally.[16] But if these concerns failed to find a direct outlet in the 2008 campaign, they would be vented anew in the Obama/Romney contest of 2012.

Hostilities broke out, in fact, in the unruly Republican primaries, almost a year before the November 2012 general election. The eventual nominee, Mitt Romney, was running on his business credentials, rather than his record as the relatively centrist Governor of Massachusetts (ostensibly, a strategy intended to distance the candidate from earlier, moderate positions on healthcare and abortion deemed out of step with the party's rightward-lurching base). Before

---

[10] Drucker, J. and Solomon, J. (2004) Outsourcing booms, although quietly amid political heat. *Wall Street Journal* October 18, B1.

[11] Engardio (2006). See also Friedman (2005); Phillips (2012).

[12] Angus Reid Public Opinion (2006) Outsourcing of jobs is top concern in U.S., March 22, accessed at <http://www.angus-reid.com/polls/11462/outsourcing_of_jobs_is_top_concern_in_us/>, May 7, 2013.

[13] Dobbs, L. (2007) *War on the Middle Class*. New York: Penguin.

[14] Abramowitz, A. I. (2008) *The 2008 Elections*. New York: Pearson.

[15] German Marshall Fund (2007) *Perspectives on Trade and Poverty Reduction*. Washington, DC: GMF.

[16] Baron, D. (2008) *More than half of Democrats and Independents feel the economy will get worse in 2008*, Harris Poll #3. Rochester, NY: Harris Interactive.

politics, Romney had built Bain Capital into one of the country's top private-equity firms, earning him a reputation as a formidable "turnaround specialist." But to the surprise of many (not least the candidate himself), Romney was to fall under sustained attack as a "vulture capitalist" from leading members of his own party—supposedly a more reliable friend to the business community—most notably from Governor Rick Perry of Texas and former Speaker of the U.S. House of Representatives, Newt Gingrich.[17] Romney eventually prevailed in the protracted and turbulent Republican primaries, only to be (quite predictably) assailed in the same terms during the general election campaign, as the Obama camp moved to redefine the challenger on the basis a fortune allegedly made through ruthless corporate restructuring.

For some time, Obama's campaign team had been sitting on "oppo," or opposition research, directly implicating Romney and Bain Capital with offshore outsourcing, which by this time had become the economic policy equivalent of a sex scandal. The Bain file included prominent examples of target firms being aggressively restructured through a combination of asset stripping, domestic layoffs, and offshoring, as well as politically embarrassing evidence of "[Bain-]sponsored workshops [designed] to help companies learn how to outsource."[18] The Democrats' plan had been to assail Romney when the maximum moment of political opportunity presented itself, but this was hastily rescheduled when an investigative journalist at the *Washington Post* scooped the story.[19] The Obama campaign capitalized on this independent confirmation by trumpeting graphic details of Romney's "record" of corporate purging and overseas outsourcing (see Figure 3.2), and by branding the Republican candidate, in a memorable series of attack ads, as the "outsourcer-in-chief." Apparently, Obama himself had been hesitant to launch these sharply negative campaign ads,[20] but they were soon in heavy rotation in swing-state media markets. Overdubbed with Romney's tuneless rendition of "America the Beautiful," which the Republican nominee had taken to singing at campaign stops as an ill-judged attempt to appear less wooden, the outsourcer-in-chief campaign commercials juxtaposed images of shuttered American factories and empty offices with headlines linking Bain-controlled companies to outsourcing projects in China, Mexico, and India. They closed, in case anyone might have missed the point about this new model of financialized restructuring, with shots of Swiss banks and Cayman Islands tax havens.

[17] Financial Times (2012) The bane of Bain. *Financial Times* January 13, 10; Weisman, J. (2012) Republicans asked to bash Obama, not one another. *New York Times* January 13, A14.

[18] Alter, J. (2013) *The Center Holds: Obama and his enemies.* New York: Simon and Schuster, p. 261.

[19] Hamburger, T. (2012) Bain's firms sent jobs overseas. *Washington Post* June 22, A13.

[20] Alter, J. (2013) *The Center Holds: Obama and his enemies.* New York: Simon and Schuster.

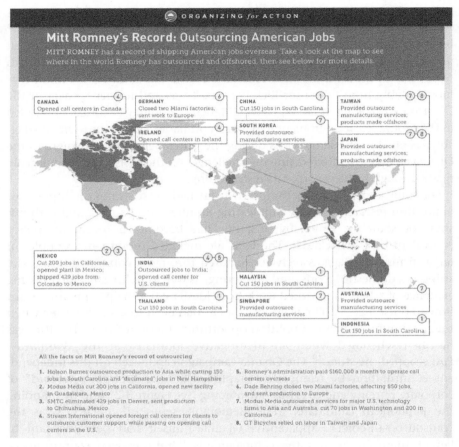

Figure 3.2 The Obama campaign offensive, "Romney's record"
Source: <http://www.barackobama.com>

Even if the near term scale of the "outsourcing threat" to the U.S. economy (and electorate) was being exaggerated and exploited for political advantage, the threat was certainly a serious one for Romney. Polling data confirmed that voters of all stripes remained deeply fearful of outsourcing, and not surprisingly very much opposed to the practice (see Table 3.1). Unwilling to publicly defend his own record, or for that matter what had become ordinary business practice, Romney sought to navigate around this electorally treacherous terrain by blurring, deflecting, and defusing the issue, while some of his allies mounted a counterattack predicated on almost the same terms: the Republican National Committee (RNC) quickly launched a website, ObamaOutsourced.com, featuring an interactive map of jobs allegedly shipped abroad under the federal stimulus program—the Obama Administration's signature economic policy, if

Table 3.1. Outsourcing anxieties: offshoring as a threat to the U.S. economy

Do you agree or disagree that outsourcing of production and manufacturing work to foreign countries is a reason the U.S. economy is struggling and more people aren't being hired?	%
By income	
Under $30,000 per year	78
$30,000–$50,000	89
$50,000–$75,000	86
Over $75,000	93
By occupation	
Blue collar	83
White collar	89
Professional/managerial	95
Retired	76
By party affiliation	
Democrat	84
Republican	90

Source: WSJ/NBC News poll, September 2010; Murray, S. and Belkin, D. (2010) Americans sour on trade. *Wall Street Journal* October 2, A1. Margin of error + or − 3.5 percentage points

hardly a chosen one—including solar-panel production and electric-car manufacturing "sent to" China (see Figure 3.3); Americans for Prosperity, one of the most powerful conservative advocacy groups, bankrolled by the Koch Brothers, launched a series of ads accusing the Obama Administration of sending $2.3 billion of tax credits, along with "American jobs," overseas; and it was left to RNC chair Reince Priebus to declare the President himself to be the *"real outsourcer-in-chief."*[21] Prominent conservative think tanks like the Heritage Foundation joined the attack on the Democrats' so-called "exercise in Venture Socialism," castigating the (liberal) media for ignoring programmatic outsourcing (suitably redefined) on the part of the Obama Administration, which was alleged to have "(1) outsourced stimulus monies to create jobs in foreign nations, (2) outsourced U.S. foreign policy to [the] U.N. and (3) outsourced our kids and grandkids financial future to pay for his unprecedented spending binge."[22]

---

[21] Shear, M. D. (2012) Conservative web site points to Obama as "real" outsourcer-in-chief. *New York Times Caucus* blog, accessed at <http://thecaucus.blogs.nytimes.com/2012/07/10/republican-web-site-points-to-obama-as-real-outsourcer-in-chief/>, March 14, 2014; Vespa, M. (2012) Obama is the REAL outsourcer-in-chief. *Conservative Daily News*, July 10, accessed at <http://www.conservativedailynews.com/2012/07/obama-is-the-real-outsourcer-in-chief/>, March 14, 2014.

[22] Darling, B. (2012) Obama's outsourcing of jobs, foreign policy, and debt. *Commentary*, Heritage Foundation, July 16, accessed at <http://www.heritage.org/research/commentary/2012/07/obamas-outsourcing-of-jobs-foreign-policy-and-debt>, March 15, 2014.

OBAMANOMICS OUTSOURCED

The Truth About How Obama Shipped The Recovery Overseas

CLICK HERE TO FOLLOW THE JOBS AT
WWW.OBAMANOMICSOUTSOURCED.COM

Figure 3.3 The Republican counter, "Obamanomics outsourced"
Source: <http://www.gop.com>

In the course of the presidential campaign, these shrill claims and counter-claims would reverberate across the news channels and the political blogs, between the two campaigns and their politically aligned Super PACs,[23] drawing in not only the most influential commentators and satirists but also the expanding network of fact-checking organizations. At a time of lingering economic uncertainty and high unemployment, the resulting cacophony apparently even registered with the newly identified electoral subject of the 2012 season, the "low-information voter," but all but the most fastidiously prepared would have struggled to separate the underlying facts from their often hysterical (misre)presentation. A barrage of sporadic truths, frequent half-truths, and outright untruths would accompany the efforts of the two campaigns to besmirch the other by association with "one of the great economic sins" of the times, with actions that had "accelerated the exodus of American jobs to foreign countries," as the *New York Times* put it.[24] By hurling accusations, rather than dealing with substantive questions of corporate practice and economic

---

[23] Super PACs are a variant of the political action committees, or PACs, that have long been a feature of the U.S. political system; they are permitted to engage in unlimited political spending as long as this is not formally "coordinated" with the campaigns.

[24] Shear, M. D. and Oppel, R. A. (2012) Obama and Romney trade shots, a few possibly accurate, on outsourcing. *New York Times* July 11, A17.

policy, the *Times* went on, Romney and Obama had "all but stuck their fingers in their ears while continuing with their outsourcing attacks."

Parsing Words, Checking Facts

The Romney campaign reportedly "went ballistic" on hearing word of the *Washington Post* outsourcing exposé, which documented in some detail the involvement of Bain companies in what was plainly portrayed as the "offshoring" of jobs to low-cost locations.[25] On the basis of evidence from Securities and Exchange Commission filings, the *Post* linked Romney to a series of firms that Bain had restructured and which placed the candidate and his company—in a phrase that would resound through to the presidential debates—amongst the "pioneers of outsourcing." Tom Hamburger of the *Post* wrote that,

> During the nearly 15 years that Romney was actively involved in running Bain...it owned companies that were pioneers in the practice of shipping work from the United States to overseas call centers and factories making computer components... While economists debate whether the massive outsourcing of American jobs over the last generation was inevitable, Romney in recent months has lamented the toll it's taken on the U.S. economy. He has repeatedly pledged he would protect American employment by getting tough on China. "They've been able to put American businesses out of business and kill American jobs," he told workers at a Toledo fence factory in February. "If I'm president of the United States, that's going to end."[26]

Bain Capital, which Romney had founded in 1984 as a spinoff from the management-consulting firm, Bain and Company, had undeniably been a pioneer in the private-equity business. A creature of the liberalizing corporate environment of the Reagan years, Bain Capital had generated large pools of (practically unregulated) private funds for the purpose of leveraged buyouts. Back in the 1980s, the new business of taking stakes in, restructuring, and then "flipping" undervalued companies—sometimes in the service of reinvigoration and rebirth, but in other cases on a downward path to break-up and bankruptcy—had been "a place for mavericks and outsiders," as the *Economist* once observed; but it would later come to define what the magazine liked to think of as the "sharp end of capitalism," its financial backers and corporate leaders including some of the "most talented members of the business, political and cultural establishment," from former president George H. W. Bush to

---

[25] Krugman, P. (2012) Off and out with Mitt Romney. *New York Times* July 6, A23; Pexton, P. B. (2012) Mitt Romney demands a retraction. *Washington Post* July 1, A19.
[26] Hamburger, T. (2012) Bain's firms sent jobs overseas. *Washington Post* June 22, A13.

U2's Bono.[27] But while the private-equity industry preferred to imagine itself as a source of creative dynamism, "saving" troubled companies and identifying new sources of value, others portrayed its asset-stripping behavior as predatory.

As one of the "new kings of capitalism," to borrow the *Economist*'s effusive phrase, Romney was at the center of this world, and at Bain he was no sleeping partner. As Hamburger concluded his investigation, "Until Romney left Bain Capital in 1999, he ran it with a proprietor's zeal and attention to detail, earning a reputation for smart, hands-on management."[28] Nevertheless, the Romney campaign demanded an immediate retraction of the *Post*'s allegations, complaining that,

> This is a fundamentally flawed story that does not differentiate between domestic outsourcing versus offshoring nor versus work done overseas to support U.S. exports. Mitt Romney spent 25 years in the real world economy so he understands why jobs come and they go. As president, he will implement policies that make it easier and more attractive for companies to create jobs here at home. President Obama's attacks on profit and job creators make it less attractive to create jobs in the U.S.[29]

This resort to semantic distinctions satisfied almost nobody. The *Post* stood by its story. Meanwhile, the well-documented connection between the Republican candidate and outsourcing would prove to be a gift that kept on giving for the Obama campaign. New waves of attack ads soon followed. A typical example, *Revealed*, declared: "The *Washington Post* has just revealed that Romney's companies were pioneers in shipping U.S. jobs overseas, investing in firms that specialized in relocating jobs done by American workers to new facilities in low-wage countries like China and India," posing the question to voters, "Does Iowa really want an outsourcer-in-chief in the White House?"[30]

Linking Romney to the unsavory practice of outsourcing put in question not only his policy program, but his business credentials and personal ethics too. The Obama campaign presented offshoring as the very essence of the "Romney model," while a later round of campaign commercials sought to put the President squarely and literally on the other side of the issue, as an enabler of *insourcing*:

[27] Economist (2004) The new kings of capitalism. *Economist* November 25, S1–16, pp. S3, S1.

[28] Hamburger, T. (2012) Bain's firms sent jobs overseas. *Washington Post* June 22, A13.

[29] Andrea Saul, Romney campaign press secretary, quoted in Burns, A. (2012) Romney campaign: "outsourcing" does not equal "offshoring." *Politico* Burns and Haberman blog, June 22, accessed at <http://www.politico.com/blogs/burns-haberman/2012/06/romney-campaign-outsourcing-does-not-equal-offshoring-127021.html>, May 9, 2014.

[30] Nicholas, P. (2012) Obama TV ads attack Romney on outsourcing. *Wall Street Journal*, Washington Wire, June 26, accessed at <http://blogs.wsj.com/washwire/2012/06/26/obama-tv-ads-attack-romney-on-outsourcing/>, March 14, 2014.

What a president believes matters. Mitt Romney's companies were pioneers in outsourcing U.S. jobs to low-wage countries. He supports tax breaks for companies that ship jobs overseas. President Obama believes in insourcing. He fought to save the U.S. auto industry and favors tax cuts for companies that bring jobs home.[31]

The alternating accusations of the two campaigns would keep fact-checking organizations busy during most of the summer. But the fact checkers too were soon sucked into a debate that they had been attempting to referee from the sidelines. The ensuing controversy ultimately defined at least one of the candidates, while also generating new clouds of obfuscation.

Obama campaign ads that branded Romney as a "corporate raider," citing the derogatory phrase originally used by Reuters in this context (but later retracted, under pressure), were judged to be "a stretch" by the *Post*'s resident fact checker, Glenn Kessler, on the basis of the finely parsed distinction that Bain had not been engaged in hostile takeovers of publicly listed companies, to which the epithet is usually attached, but instead targeted privately owned firms for acquisition and restructuring. Kessler also questioned the accuracy of the claim that Romney had authorized the outsourcing of state functions while governor of Massachusetts, a charge later deemed to be "overblown," in light of what turned out to be a tortuous history of a project to outsource the servicing of the food-stamp program to India. (The operation was later outsourced to Utah.) These ads earned the Obama campaign the damning grade of four Pinocchios on the *Post*'s trustworthiness scale, just short of a "Whopper."[32] However, the newspaper also acknowledged that it had been placed in "a bit of a strange position," since both campaigns had "seized on a news report in *The Post*, and both [were] describing it inaccurately for their own political purposes."[33] Splitting yet more semantic hairs, Kessler concluded that Bain was perhaps not literally a "pioneer" of outsourcing, although the company was "prescient" in taking early advantage of what would become a widespread business practice. Crucially, Kessler also raised questions about the exact timing of the outsourcing maneuvers initiated by Bain-associated companies, asserting that "Romney stopped managing Bain in 1999, so much of [the] movement overseas took place after he left the firm."[34] These and other

[31] Obama campaign ad, quoted on National Public Radio, *It's all politics*, July 5, 2012.
[32] Kessler (2012) 4 Pinocchios for Obama's newest anti-Romney ad. *Washington Post*, The Fact Checker, June 21, accessed at <http://www.washingtonpost.com/blogs/fact-checker/post/4-pinocchios-for-obamas-newest-anti-romney-ad/2012/06/20/gJQAGux6qV_blog.html>, May 5, 2013.
[33] Kessler, G. (2012) Obama's new attacks on Romney and outsourcing. *Washington Post*, The Fact Checker, June 21, accessed at <http://www.washingtonpost.com/blogs/fact-checker/post/obamas-new-attacks-on-romney-and-outsourcing/2012/06/29/gJQA5FbbCW_blog.html>, May 5, 2013, p. 1.
[34] Kessler, G. (2012) Obama's new attacks on Romney and outsourcing. *Washington Post*, The Fact Checker, June 21, accessed at <http://www.washingtonpost.com/blogs/fact-checker/post/obamas-new-attacks-on-romney-and-outsourcing/2012/06/29/gJQA5FbbCW_blog.html>, May 5, 2013, p. 2.

investigations would therefore speak to both the timing and the scale of the offshore outsourcing movement, as well as Bain's position within it.

FactCheck cautioned the President's campaign for "overreaching" on its claims concerning Romney's personal involvement in "shipping jobs overseas," while confirming that there was "no question that Bain invested in some companies that helped other companies outsource work and that some of that work went overseas."[35] PolitiFact rated this charge against Romney "half true" on its Truth-o-Meter™ in recognition of the fact that Bain was less of an outsourcing pioneer than a mere "part of the herd," in the words of MIT's Timothy Sturgeon. Even if some of the documented cases of outsourcing took place some months after Romney took a leave of absence to manage preparations for the Winter Olympics in Salt Lake City, PolitiFact doubted whether the Republican candidate could realistically "divorce himself from the strategies that made Bain profitable."[36]

Denial and distancing, however, had become the means for mounting what was a defensive strategy. Suddenly, the small-print details of the timing (and nature) of Romney's "secondment" to Salt Lake came to assume central importance. This was robustly tackled by the Obama campaign in a six-page letter to all of the major fact-checking and news organizations, citing scattered documentary evidence that Romney had remained formally at the helm of Bain Capital for at least two additional years. For its part, FactCheck stood by its claim that Romney had absented himself from day-to-day management at Bain, pointing out that proof to the contrary would expose the Republican candidate to felony charges for misrepresentation on federally mandated financial disclosure forms.[37] Within days, however, investigative reporting by *Mother Jones* magazine and by journalists at the *Boston Globe* did indeed tie Romney to Bain's ongoing activities, well into 2002 and therefore into the red zone of several of the extant allegations concerning outsourcing (mis)behavior, to which were now added questions about improper financial reporting.[38]

---

[35] FactCheck (2012) Obama's "outsourcer" overreach. *FactCheck* July 2, accessed at <http://factcheck.org/2012/06/obamas-outsourcer-overreach/>, May 5, 2013.

[36] PolitiFact (2012) Were Romney's companies "pioneers in outsourcing?" *Tampa Bay Times* July 3, accessed at <http://www.politifact.com/truth-o-meter/statements/2012/jul/13/barack-obama/were-romneys-companies-pioneers-outsourcing/>, May 5, 2013, p. 2.

[37] FactCheck (2012) FactCheck to Obama camp: your complaint is all wet. *FactCheck* July 2, accessed at <http://factcheck.org/2012/07/factcheck-to-obama-camp-your-complaint-is-all-wet/>, May 6, 2013.

[38] See Borchers, C. and Rowland, C. (2012) Romney stayed longer at Bain. *Boston Globe* July 12, A1; Corn, D. (2012) Romney invested millions in Chinese firm that profited on US outsourcing. *Mother Jones* July 11, accessed at <http://www.motherjones.com/politics/2012/07/bain-capital-mitt-romney-outsourcing-china-global-tech>, May 5, 2013; Murphy, E. (2012) Mitt Romney's Bain Capital timeline. *Mother Jones* July 16, accessed at <http://www.motherjones.com/mojo/2012/07/mitt-romney-bain-capital-timeline>, May 12, 2013; Serwer, A. (2012) What we know about Romney and Bain, explained. *Mother Jones* July 13, accessed at <http://www.motherjones.com/mojo/2012/07/what-we-know-about-romney-and-bain-explainer>, May 5, 2013.

Romney's six-figure salary was paid by Bain Capital throughout the period in question, courtesy of his singular role as the company's "sole stockholder, chairman of the board, chief executive officer, and president."[39] While these waters were to remain somewhat muddy, it must be recognized that the evidence implicating Romney in "crimes" of outsourcing—which, in effect, is how these overseas ventures were portrayed by *both* campaigns—had by this point exceeded the circumstantial. The larger truth behind the Romney denials, of course, was that outsourcing was (and remains) a completely unexceptional business practice. Bain was "part of the herd." Being *seen* as such had become, by implication, profoundly problematic both for a publicly visible company and for a political candidate—hence the lengths to which Romney's aides went to try to distance the businessman-turned-politician from the scene of this alleged offense.

A protracted war of words, when these words included *outsourcing*, evidently favored the Obama campaign. The subsequent less than clarification—that Romney had been on a "leave of absence" from Bain, later formalized as a "retroactive retirement" (in a private agreement signed in 2002), as he prepared to run for the Massachusetts governorship—only seemed to confirm suspicions that this was a world of less than plain dealing, if not routine corporate subterfuge. Even if he was putting in sixteen-hour days at Salt Lake, the fact that through to 2002 Romney retained 100 percent ownership and formal managerial control of Bain Capital undermined the credibility of the claim that he lacked knowledge of, *or indeed responsibility for*, its key business decisions and the strategic parameters of the company's operational behavior. As Obama would later comment,

> My understanding is that Mr. Romney attested to the SEC, multiple times, that he was the chairman, CEO and president of Bain Capital and I think most Americans figure if you are the chairman, CEO and president of a company that you are responsible for what that company does.[40]

This extended episode of mud slinging and name calling had not only raised searching questions about the stability of the "facts" that were subject to such meticulous checking by media organizations, it had drawn the fact checkers themselves into dialogue and disputation with both campaigns. What few facts there were about outsourcing became, in the process, even more contested and destabilized. As David Corn later pointed out, Republican allegations concerning the "outsourcing" of green jobs via the federal stimulus program may have

---

[39] SEC, quoted in Borchers, C. and Rowland, C. (2012) Romney stayed longer at Bain. *Boston Globe* July 12, A1.

[40] Barack Obama, interviewed on *ABC7 News*, Washington, DC, July 13, accessed at <http://www.wjla.com/articles/2012/07/president-obama-says-romney-should-answer-bain-capital-questions-77842.html>, May 28, 2014.

Table 3.2. Truth-o-Meter™ ratings of presidential campaigns

Rating of campaign statements (%)	Obama	Romney
True	22	15
Mostly true	23	16
Half true	27	28
Mostly false	12	16
False	14	16
Pants on fire	2	9

Source: PolitiFact.com

been the most cynical and egregious, but the Obama camp repeatedly stretched its own versions of the truth. The White House may have been able to claim a hollow victory in the Truth-o-Meter™ stakes, as Table 3.2 reveals, yet this was a notably shallow and cynical debate characterized not by black-and-white distinctions or mutual clarification, but by a descent into the grayscales of "truthiness," to borrow Stephen Colbert's ironically turned phrase.

Attacking Capitalism?

Romney's denunciations of outsourcing may have seemed to be politically expedient, but they were widely derided by his supporters in the business community, many of whom would have preferred to hear a more full-throated defense of the corporate logics and practices that Bain Capital epitomized. The candidate who had for so long struggled to ignite the passions of his own party's base had been forced, during the course of an extended primary campaign, to repudiate much of his own pragmatically moderate record, embracing hardline positions on issues like immigration and entitlement reform, while at the same time exhuming an unreconstructed version of supply-side economics predicated on aggressive, rolling tax cuts. In the practiced language of contemporary conservativism, the rationale of such measures is that they liberate and incentivize society's "job creators." Romney's triangulations, denials, and euphemistic gyrations around the issue of outsourcing, however, were drawing unwanted attention to the contradictions of this narrative. Some in the business community were urging the candidate to get a grip of the issue, and himself, and then move on. Bloomberg columnist Caroline Baum, for one, upbraided the Republican nominee for fencing around the outsourcing question, boldly proffering "five ways Romney can own 'outsourcer-in-chief.'"

Facts aren't the issue here. Image is. Romney needs to seize the day and start wearing his outsourcing stripes as a badge of honor instead of accusing Obama of the same...Obama managed to spend 12 years as part of the University of Chicago Law School faculty without ever learning how an economy works. This is an area where you have a clear comparative advantage, Mitt. Use it, to explain why outsourcing isn't a dirty word, or lose it in November.[41]

Baum recommended that Romney should press the business case for outsourcing and private equity as accelerators of creative destruction (since net job gains across the economy as a whole would surely eventually outweigh company-specific losses); that he should overcome his learned timidity and proclaim, without apology, the righteousness of the economic "laws" of free trade and comparative advantage; and that he should leverage his own comparative advantage over Obama, his knowledge of business realities, by explaining how the embrace of innovation, efficiency, and new technology would in the long run raise living standards, drive down prices, and generate better-paying jobs. "Never mind that academic studies have found private equity's effect on employment to be mixed," Baum casually counseled. Romney was urged to take a leaf from Diana Farrell's widely discussed study for the McKinsey Global Institute—surely "right up [the] alley" of the analytical candidate—which had discovered that "offshoring creates wealth for everybody except those who lose their jobs in the short run."[42]

Contributors to the *Financial Times* likewise came to the defense of the much maligned outsourcers, as hardworking heirs to the free-trade cause, affirming the irrefutable logic of continuing global integration. The newspaper's management correspondent, Andrew Hill, acknowledged that it was always tempting for politicians to take the easy path, pandering to a jittery public by simplistically laying the blame for economic ills at the door of "fat fingered technicians in Bangalore or Hyderabad," although he acknowledged that corporations still had public-relations work to do if they were to "get past the stigma of outsourcing."[43] The *Financial Times* later devoted an editorial to the outsourcing controversy, imploring Romney to resist the urge of stooping

---

[41] Baum, C. (2012) Five ways Romney can own "outsourcer-in-chief." *Bloomberg.com* July 11, accessed at <http://www.bloomberg.com/news/2012-07-11/five-ways-romney-can-own-outsourcer-in-chief-.html>, May 14, 2013, p. 1. See Farrell (2006) for a McKinsey-flavored defense not only of outsourcing but of its offshore variant too.

[42] Farrell was the Global Head of McKinsey's Center for Government before joining Obama's White House team as Deputy Assistant to the President on economic policy (and Deputy Director of the National Economic Council under Larry Summers), where she served from 2009 to 2011. She left the Administration to become the founding president and CEO of the JPMorgan Chase Institute. See also Baum, C. (2012) Five ways Romney can own "outsourcer-in-chief." *Bloomberg.com* July 11, accessed at <http://www.bloomberg.com/news/2012-07-11/five-ways-romney-can-own-outsourcer-in-chief-.html>, May 14, 2013, p. 1; McKinsey Global Institute (2003) *Offshoring: Is it a win–win game?* San Francisco, CA: McKinsey Global Institute. For a wider discussion of the private equity business, see Applebaum, A. and Batt, R. (2014) *Private Equity at Work: When Wall Street Manages Main Street*. New York: Russell Sage Foundation.

[43] Hill, A. (2012) Time to get past the stigma of offshoring. *Financial Times* July 10, A16.

to populist mercantilism and, instead, to teach the public a lesson in economics, "mak[ing] the case for globalisation."

> Mr Romney's biggest error is to pretend Bain had nothing to do with outsourcing... Some of the most notable acts of offshoring by Bain-controlled companies took place after 1999 when Mr Romney moved to Utah to resuscitate the 2002 Winter Olympics. By insisting on 1999 as the cut-off point for his tenure at Bain, Mr Romney has made two missteps. First... he continued as chairman, chief executive and sole owner of Bain Capital until 2002 [and] the fact his name is included on 62 separate Bain filings to the SEC after 1999 is uncomfortable...
>
> More seriously, by drawing the line at 1999, Mr Romney has made it clear he disowns any subsequent Bain investment involving offshoring... Mr Romney is embarrassed by any hint of offshoring. A candidate can run but he cannot hide. If Mr Romney had painted a target on his back that said "shipping jobs overseas" he could not have helped his opponent more.
>
> Unless Mr Romney embraces the logic of the global economy he will be condemned to the losing side of a mercantilist argument. If offshoring is a bad thing... so by extension is globalisation. By accepting this logic, Mr Romney betrays his integrity and the basis of his agenda... It is an argument worth owning. Alas his campaign has embraced the reverse by accusing Mr Obama of being "outsourcer-in-chief."[44]

Others opted for a yet more robust response. In an op-ed for *Forbes* magazine, Harry Binswanger thundered that "fear of outsourcing" reflected not only "economic nonsense and moral blindness," but worse still, an "anti-profit attitude [that was intrinsically] un-American," a refuge for political tribalists and economic racists, and perhaps worst of all, a violation of the Law of Comparative Advantage.[45] Less hysterical tones were struck by the worldly voice of the free-market establishment, the *Economist*, where the Lexington column longed for some respite from what had become an unedifying election campaign, characterized by "half-truths and low blows."

> Democrats... hint that bosses like Mr Romney... willingly ship jobs abroad because they put profits before people. Mr Obama says America "can choose" a future with less outsourcing. His solutions include curbing tax breaks for firms that send jobs overseas and launching trade complaints against China... Aiming low, Obama campaign managers note that Mr Romney still holds investments in China, as if that alone signals bad faith.[46]

Soon, however, the *Economist*'s favored candidate was aiming just as low, as Romney stepped up his own rhetoric against China in the second of the

---

[44] Financial Times (2012) Mitt Romney must face his Bain past. *Financial Times* July 17, 8.

[45] Binswanger, H. (2012) Obama and Romney are wrong: Outsourcing is America at its best. *Forbes*, July 26, accessed at <http://www.forbes.com/sites/realspin/2012/07/26/obama-and-romney-are-wrong-outsourcing-is-america-at-its-best/>, May 9, 2014.

[46] Economist (2012) There goes the neighbourhood. *Economist* September 22, 42.

presidential debates, in what the *China Daily* ridiculed as a comprehensively negative and nationalistic discussion of economic policy. Reflecting the extent to which the outsourcing issue was making new allies, as well as adversaries, this organ of the Chinese Communist Party ironically turned to the libertarian Cato Institute for the reassurance that "outsourcing is inevitable," as well as to the free-trade advocate Jagdish Bhagwati, who had warned that "the Obama administration has clearly shown that it's open to protectionism," accusing the President of "sound[ing] like Lou Dobbs."[47]

From the left, David Moberg had earlier expressed the forlorn hope that, following the outsourcing furore, "the stage [might be] set for a serious, substantive debate about how the current model of American capitalism works—and how it fails."[48] It was not to be. Writing from the conservative center, David Brooks had likewise gamely attempted to inaugurate what he dubbed "the capitalism debate" from his influential position at the *New York Times*. Presuming to divine the ideology behind the Obama campaign's outsourcer-in-chief ads, Brooks indicted the market-friendly, trade-liberalizing president for duplicity, arguing with some justification that this amounted to "attack[ing] modern capitalism as it now exists."

> You blame the system for the economy. You do this with double ferocity [because] your opponent happens to be the embodiment of that system... [The Obama] campaign has begun a series of attacks on the things people don't like about modern capitalism. They don't like the way unsuccessful firms go bust... They don't like C.E.O. salaries... They don't like financial shenanigans... They don't like outsourcing and offshoring... The accuracy of the [Obama campaign's outsourcing-in-chief] ad has been questioned by the various fact-checking outfits. That need not detain us... What matters is the ideology behind the ad: the assumption that Bain... should not have invested in companies that hired workers abroad; the assumption that hiring Mexican or Indian workers is unpatriotic; the assumption that no worthy person would do what most global business leaders have been doing for the past half-century... This ad—and the rhetoric the campaign is using around it—challenges the entire logic of capitalism as it has existed over several decades. It's part of a comprehensive attack on the economic system Romney personifies.
>
> This shift of focus has been audacious. Over the years of his presidency, Obama has not been a critic of globalization. There's no real evidence that, when he's off

---

[47] Weihua, C. (2012) Obama and Romney indulge in debate accusations. *China Daily* October 18, accessed at <http://europe.chinadaily.com.cn/china/2012-10/18/content_15825804.htm>, May 12, 2013, p. 3. Bhagwati's view of the offshoring kerfuffle during the 2004 presidential election campaign was that N. Gregory Mankiw had merely been giving voice to a "simple truth" of economics in articulating the long-run benefits of outsourcing. See Bhagwati, J. (2004) Why your job isn't moving to Bangalore. *New York Times* February 15, 11.

[48] Moberg, D. (2012) The Bain legacy. *In These Times* September, 14–17, p. 14. See also Anderson, S., Cavanagh, J., Madrick, J., and Hood, D. (2004) Toward a progressive view on outsourcing. *Nation* March 22, 22–6.

the campaign trail, he has any problem with outsourcing and offshoring... But, politically, this aggressive tactic has worked.[49]

Brooks implored his readers to sympathize with Romney, who were invited to believe that he was "not a heroic entrepreneur [but a humble] efficiency expert," engaged in the business of "tak[ing] companies that were mediocre and sclerotic and [making] them efficient and dynamic," according to the (politically neutral) principles of "rigor and productivity," but an honest operator who had been unfairly reduced to a "punching bag" by opportunist critics of the capitalist system. What was needed, he rather donnishly insisted, was a "discussion over the existing forms of capitalism: Anglo-American capitalism, Continental European Capitalism, Chinese State Capitalism and so on."[50]

But life, Brooks complained, had apparently begun to imitate art—or at least satire: "The two candidates this year are like Stephen Colbert, really smart people who are making a living pretending they're idiots."[51] An intelligent and fair-minded assessment, he had earlier observed (in the process of disputing another Obama campaign ad), would recognize that even if "[p]rivate equity firms are not lovable, [they have] forced a renaissance that revived American capitalism," in effect as an accelerant of the (necessary) process of creative destruction through which "jobs are lost in old operations [and jobs] are created in new, promising operations."[52] Romney's sin was to epitomize, or perhaps merely be a cipher for, the "logic of capitalism as it has existed for several decades" in the United States.[53] In fact, Brooks went as far as to suggest that *gratitude* was due to those "[f]inanciers, private equity firms and bare-knuckled corporate executives" that had transformed the corporate world of the 1970s, "bloated, sluggish and losing ground to competitors in Japan and beyond," into the vibrant economy of today, one that was altogether "leaner, quicker and more efficient."[54]

---

[49] Brooks, D. (2012) The capitalism debate. *New York Times* July 17, A25.

[50] For her part, Brooks' Opinionator sparring partner Gail Collins readily acknowledged, "I agree with you that until about five minutes ago, outsourcing jobs overseas wasn't high on the president's worry list." But this did not appease Brooks, who lapsed into a one-sided reading of his own, "Obama's ad is cynicism on stilts. Companies that outsource jobs become more competitive. They grow faster and then end up hiring more people at home. Outsourcing increases employment levels. Outsourcing increases productivity. It also decreases the prices consumers pay for stuff. Obama knows all this. He's just paying the economic nationalism card for his own gain" (Brooks, D. and Collins, G. (2012) The debate we should be having. *New York Times* Opinionator blog, July 18, accessed at <http://opinionator.blogs.nytimes.com/2012/07/18/the-debate-we-should-be-having/>, July 14, 2012, p. 3).

[51] Brooks, D. and Collins, G. (2012) The debate we should be having. *New York Times* Opinionator blog, July 18, accessed at <http://opinionator.blogs.nytimes.com/2012/07/18/the-debate-we-should-be-having/>, July 14, 2012, p. 1.

[52] Brooks, D. (2012) How change happens. *New York Times* May 22, A27.

[53] Brooks, D. (2012) The capitalism debate. *New York Times* July 17, A25.

[54] Brooks, D. (2012) How change happens. *New York Times* May 22, A27.

Nobel-prize winning economist and *New York Times* columnist, Paul Krugman, for his part, defended the overall legitimacy, if not all of the precise details, of the Obama campaign's anti-outsourcing ads on the grounds these were entirely conventional practices in the private-equity world and beyond.[55]

> Just to be clear, outsourcing is only one source of the huge disconnect between a tiny elite and ordinary American workers, a disconnect that has been growing for more than 30 years. And Bain, in turn, was only one player in the growth of outsourcing. So Mitt Romney didn't personally, single-handedly, destroy the middle-class society we used to have. He was, however, an enthusiastic and very well remunerated participant in the process of destruction; if Bain got involved with your company, one way or another, the odds were pretty good that even if your job survived you ended up with lower pay and diminished benefits.[56]

Krugman went on to question the veracity of Romney's claims to the mantle of "job creator." Not only did the Republican candidate's record at Bain provide no verifiable material basis for such a moniker, the remarkable shallowness of the economic-policy program that his campaign had been promoting—relying on deep, across-the-board tax cuts and new rounds of corporate deregulation—invited an unthinking "return to Bushonomics." For all Romney's talk of job creation, Krugman insisted, he "doesn't have a plan; he's just faking it."[57] The fakery extended to an effective denial of corporate reality, ironically from a candidate styling himself as a corporate realist, in the shape of rhetorical appeals to (idealized) small-business values and the work of "job creators."[58]

Although "[c]reating jobs . . . wasn't the aim of Bain or other private-equity firms, which measure success by returns produced for investors," as Mark Maremont acknowledged in the *Wall Street Journal*, Romney himself had confused this issue, too, by attempting to take credit, courtesy of his pre-Salt Lake activities at Bain Capital, for the creation of more than 100,000 jobs.[59]

---

[55] Krugman demurred from the "outsourcer-in-chief" slur in connection with Romney, although possibly also because he had previously used this same epithet in a critique of the Bush Administration's military privatization policies (Krugman, P. (2006) Outsourcer in chief. *New York Times* December 11, A27).

[56] Krugman, P. (2012) Off and out with Mitt Romney. *New York Times* July 6, A23.

[57] Krugman, P. (2012) Snow job on jobs. *New York Times* October 18, A31.

[58] This led Krugman to resort to mockery: "Romney, who started as a business consultant and then moved into the heady world of private equity, insists on portraying himself as a plucky small businessman. I am not making this up. In [the last presidential] debate, he declared, 'I came through small business. I understand how hard it is to start a small business.' In his speech at the Republican convention, he declared, 'When I was 37, I helped start a small company.' Ahem. It's true that when Bain Capital started, it had only a handful of employees. But it had $37 million in funds, raised from sources that included wealthy Europeans investing through Panamanian shell companies and Central American oligarchs living in Miami while death squads associated with their families ravaged their home nations. Hey, doesn't every plucky little start-up have access to that kind of financing?" (Krugman, P. (2012) Snow job on jobs. *New York Times* October 18, A31).

[59] Maremont, M. (2012) Tally of job creation by Bain proves vexing. *Wall Street Journal* July 11, A4.

The provenance of these numbers was to remain a mystery to the fact checkers of the *Wall Street Journal*, who concluded that any proper verification attempt was ultimately "futile," since different rule-of-thumb methods for counting the net employment impact of Bain's work with the office-supplies giant Staples, for example, yielded results as divergent as 250 and 43,000. Inside knowledge would have hardly helped, either. As Romney's former Bain Capital colleague, Ed Conard—whose early-retirement book project secured the author a certain notoriety as one of the country's most enthusiastic defenders of the greed-is-good ethos—carelessly remarked, "no-one has been able to go back and count up all the employees from this date to that date, because no-one really has those old records."[60] This was not simply a matter, however, of Bain's secretive (or minimalist) bookkeeping.

Relatively little is known, systematically at least, about the actual impacts of private-equity firms on aggregate patterns of job creation, since much of this activity is effectively shielded from public scrutiny. The general perception is that such "buyout shops have always been associated with job losses," including employment "lost overseas," as a *Business Week* survey once put it,[61] even if the accompanying rationalization may ultimately "save" the target company, or lead to job creation in other parts of the operation. The most comprehensive attempts to calculate the net effects of private-equity buyouts have discovered that the sector's employment record is best described as mixed, combining as it does job losses at target firms (relative to control-group companies) with compensatory expansions in other locations.[62]

Nevertheless, few would deny that private-equity firms are associated with aggressive strategies for organizational and employment restructuring, with a repertoire that includes outsourcing, pay and benefit cuts, and the strict application of performance-based approaches to human-resources management, or "hard HRM."[63] Bain Capital, as one of the "big five" in the United States, has been an arch exponent of these practices, indeed something of an

---

[60] Interviewed at Bluey, R. and Stewart, B. (2012) Author Ed Conard talks Bain Capital, economics and Obama's record, *The Foundry*, Heritage Foundation, accessed at <http://blog. heritage.org/2012/06/28/author-ed-conard-talks-bain-capital-economics-and-obamas-record/>. Facing softball questions in the Heritage Foundation's Green Room, Conard—who was at Bain Capital for fourteen years, running the New York office—brushed off the critiques of the company as merely symptomatic of "attacks on business generally . . . it's kind of old-fashioned union organizing in a sense . . . Obviously, they cherry-pick examples, but the vast majority of Bain Capital's investments were successful."

[61] Thornton, E. (2006) Gluttons at the gate. *Business Week*, October 30, 58–66, p. 64.

[62] Davis, S. J., Haltiwanger, J. C., Jarmin, R. S., Lerner, J., and Miranda, J. (2012) Private equity and employment. *NBER Working Paper* 17399, National Bureau of Economic Research, Cambridge, MA; Applebaum, A. and Batt, R. (2014) *Private Equity at Work: When Wall Street manages Main Street*. New York: Russell Sage Foundation.

[63] Folkman, P., Froud, J., Williams, K., and Johal, S. (2009) Private equity: Levered on capital or labour? *Journal of Industrial Relations* 51(4): 517–27.

actual pioneer in the business of "how to succeed . . . without adding value."[64] This is not an accidental circumstance. In fact, the rationale of the private-equity business has been aptly summarized as one of "value capture," involving a combination of intensified restructuring and debt loading in the cause of "value extraction, particularly for the benefit of the few who are positioned as private equity principals or managers in the operating businesses."[65] The private-equity model not only compresses the process of creative destruction, it also concentrates subsequent financial returns into the hands of a spectacularly fortunate few, many of whom are rewarded with what have been described in the *Financial Times* as "life-changing amounts of money."[66]

It certainly changed Mitt Romney's life. And it is surely indisputable that Bain Capital never functioned "to build businesses; [rather] it bought and sold them," as Paul Krugman argued, and it did so in the ultimate service of value extraction, not job creation. Some survived, often in a leaner form, and then thrived; others were downsized and stripped of assets; some were broken up and driven into bankruptcy.[67] At the time, and applying a corporate calculus rather than a political one, the overall job-creation record was really beside the point: employment numbers were not deemed to be of sufficient importance even to track, as Ed Conard later confirmed. And whether or not it is semantically correct to have labeled Bain Capital a "pioneer of outsourcing," its target companies were all aggressively restructured and many of them routinely deployed the commonplace practice of outsourcing; some even got into the business of outsourcing themselves. Neither net employment effects, nor the location of subsequent employment, were ever really the issue. The private-equity business, true to its position in the corporate vanguard, has never been distracted by such matters; it is about the capture and extraction of value.

Imperfect Information

For the Democrats, denunciations of outsourcing have periodically served as a form of cathartic therapy in an age of economic insecurity—never mind the mismatch between ritualistic pledges to protect American jobs at campaign rallies (always an applause line), and the pragmatic realities of governing from the third-way center, which since Bill Clinton have been defined by an

---

[64] Moberg, D. (2012) How to succeed in business without adding value. *In These Times* September, 16–17, p. 16; SEIU (2007) *Behind the Buyouts*. Washington, DC: Service Employees International Union.

[65] Froud, J. and Williams, K. (2007) Private equity and the culture of value extraction. *New Political Economy* 12(3): 405–20, p. 407.

[66] Roberts, D. (2006) Hyper-capitalism. *Financial Times* May 2, 20.

[67] Krugman, P. (2012) Off and out with Mitt Romney. *New York Times* July 6, A23.

accommodation with Wall Street, by a pro-globalization stance, by the embrace of welfare reform and employability policies, and timidity on (or indifference toward) questions of union rights, social redistribution, and more forthright forms of economic-policy intervention.[68] There was some muted grumbling from the labor movement and its allies on the left that Obama's record in office contradicted his anti-outsourcing rhetoric,[69] since along with most of the party leadership the President remained an advocate of free trade, flexible labor markets, and light-touch corporate regulation, while the Obama Administration's efforts in the key area of job creation had barely exceeded occasional visits to the bully pulpit. These concerns went beyond the accusation that Obama had succumbed to the generalized post-crisis condition of "learned helplessness" on the issues of jobs and employment; his economic advisory team was stacked, from the start, with Wall Streeters, corporate realists, and advocates of merely nudging regulation.[70]

Barely remarked upon, the senior economic staff of the White House had included Diana Farrell, formerly of McKinsey consultants and a prominent cheerleader for outsourcing whose unvarnished views on the subject had previously been recommended, by Bloomberg's Caroline Baum, to Mitt Romney.[71] If Farrell's considered view, in her pre-political life, had been that offshore outsourcing was a win–win proposition, in that elusive economic long run, the Obama campaign's reading of the electoral tealeaves supported a very different conclusion. Railing publicly against the evils of outsourcing, however, meant that the President was at least talking about jobs, while conveniently defining his opponent in negative terms. And even modest proposals, like tax breaks for "insourcers," a rhetorically appealing if vaguely defined addition to the public-policy conversation, allowed Obama to appear more proactive than the intervention-averse Republicans. This looked like a winning electoral strategy, for all its flimsiness in substantive terms. Yet at the

---

[68] See Pollin (2003), Peck (2010), and the discussion in Pollin, R. (2004) Deepening divides in the U.S. economy, 2004: Jobless recovery and the return of fiscal deficits. *Working Paper* No. 82, Political Economy Research Institute, University of Massachusetts, Amherst.

[69] Hamburger, T., Leonnig, C. D., and Goldfarb, Z. A. (2012) Obama struggles to make headway on outsourcing. *Washington Post* July 10, A1.

[70] On "learned helplessness" on the jobs issue, see Krugman, P. (2011) Against learned helplessness. *New York Times* May 29, A19. On the Obama Administration's record on employment issues and labor policy, see Theodore, N. (2016) Unions in the Obama era: Laboring under false pretenses? In J. DeFilippis, ed. *Urban Policy in the Time of Obama*. Minneapolis, MN: University of Minnesota Press. On Obama's economic policy advisors, see Peck (2010). For Obama's own reflections on his Administration's economic record, see Sorkin, A. R. (2016) What Obama really thinks about his economic legacy. *New York Times Magazine* April 28, accessed at <http://www.nytimes.com/2016/04/28/magazine/what-obama-really-thinks-about-his-economic-legacy.html>, May 12, 2016.

[71] Baum, C. (2012) Five ways Romney can own "outsourcer-in-chief." *Bloomberg.com* July 11, accessed at <http://www.bloomberg.com/news/2012-07-11/five-ways-romney-can-own-outsourcer-in-chief-.html>, May 14, 2013.

same time it reeked of pure political calculation, enabled by an understandable degree of anxiety and confusion amongst the general public. As a reporter for *USA Today* protested:

> Neither Mitt Romney nor President Obama opposes offshoring. So why do they pretend to? The answer is simple: because Americans tell pollsters they dislike the idea of American companies moving jobs overseas. But just like the politicians, the average American doesn't really believe what he or she says about offshoring, either ... We Americans tell pollsters offshoring is a big cause of high unemployment, then we hang up our Chinese-made phones and go shopping.[72]

True perhaps, but the political optics generally favored the Obama Administration, which duly seized the opportunity to rebadge a White House business summit as an "insourcing forum." Surrounded by a hand-picked group of "investors in America," the President remarked that, "You've heard of outsourcing. Well, these companies are insourcing."[73] The photo opportunity was accompanied by a presidential report on the "new, promising trend of 'insourcing,'" interpreted liberally to refer to "bringing activities and jobs back to the U.S. or choosing to invest in the U.S. instead of overseas."[74] Notably, neither the report, nor the event, included any new policy measures.

Meanwhile, in the world capital of insourcing, India, the twists and turns of the U.S. presidential campaign were being watched with a mix of bemusement and irritation: both of the presidential candidates were chided in the local press for being "economical with the truth"—and more specifically for dodging the inconvenient reality "that America's over-indulgent lifestyle and expectations, combined with pressure on corporate bottom lines ... has forced the migration of jobs."[75] But from this perspective, the Obama Administration's turn to populist and protectionist rhetoric was more unnerving than the antics of an electoral challenger. Many Indian commentators had been prepared to take on face value that the President's high-profile visit to the

---

[72] Cline, A. (2012) Both presidential candidates love sending jobs overseas. *USA Today* August 8, 7A.

[73] Barack Obama, Remarks by the President on insourcing American jobs, January 11, 2012, White House, Office of the Press Secretary, accessed at <https://www.whitehouse.gov/the-press-office/2012/01/11/remarks-president-insourcing-american-jobs>, August 1, 2016.

[74] Office of the President (2012) *Investing in America*. Washington, DC: Office of the President, 3. In his 2012 State of the Union address, the President had insisted that "we will not go back to an economy weakened by outsourcing, bad debt, and phony financial profits," floating a tax-reform package designed to penalize companies intent on "moving jobs and profits overseas ... It is time to stop rewarding businesses that ship jobs overseas, and start rewarding companies that create jobs right here in America" (Barack Obama, Remarks by the President in State of the Union Address, January 24, 2012, White House, Office of the Press Secretary, accessed at <https://www.whitehouse.gov/the-press-office/2012/01/24/remarks-president-state-union-address>, December 2, 2014).

[75] Rajghatta, C. (2012) The hook of jobs—Barack Obama, Mitt Romney spar over outsourcing. *Times of India* October 18, accessed at <http://articles.timesofindia.indiatimes.com/2012-10-18/us/34554605_1_president-obama-mitt-romney-barack-obama>, May 13, 2014, p. 1.

country, in November 2010 and two years before this most recent election-season kerfuffle, marked an historic turning point in economic relations between the two countries, based on the recognition of mutual trading interests. As Obama had responded at the time to a reporter's question in New Dehli, "I don't think you've heard me make outsourcing a bogeyman during the course of my visit. In fact, I explicitly said in my address in Mumbai to the Business Council that I think both countries are operating on some stereotypes that have outlived their usefulness."[76] This had been a message that the Indian sourcing firms, long troubled by these "stereotypes," were relieved to hear:

> Anti-offshoring sentiment in the U.S.... has been rampant for years. However, the protectionist (and in cases even jingoistic and xenophobic) tide seemed to turn, at least at the highest level of the U.S. government, during President Obama's [November 2010] visit to India. The President, changing his messaging from previous years, presented his view of offshoring as part of international trade... The reality is that offshoring and nearshoring—to China, the Philippines, Egypt, South America, Canada, Mexico, or anywhere, even India, which has been singled out as the ultimate "villain," with offshoring often equated to being "Banga-lored"—will not go away. Nor should it... [G]lobal sourcing is an irreversible phenomenon. While [it] will continue to evolve, services will never go back *in-toto* to high cost onshore locations.[77]

In his first term in office, Obama the free-trading, pro-market pragmatist showed little desire to disrupt the established corporate practice of outsourcing, but in the heated environment of the 2012 presidential campaign, Obama would opportunistically find political value in those old stereotypes. Seasoned observers from the corporate outsourcing sector probably expected nothing different from a Democratic president. Somewhat more difficult to take, however, was the peculiar spectacle of Mitt Romney denouncing a mainstream business practice while ostensibly running on his record as a corporate leader.

One can only imagine what Harvard economist N. Gregory Mankiw made of this. Mankiw, of course, had taken much of the flak in the original outsourcing

---

[76] Remarks by President Obama and Prime Minister Singh in Joint Press Conference in New Delhi, India, November 8, Hyderabad House, White House, Office of the Press Secretary, accessed at <https://www.whitehouse.gov/the-press-office/2010/11/08/remarks-president-obama-and-prime-minister-singh-joint-press-conference->, May 12, 2004. As a senior figure in the U.S. outsourcing industry explained, in exasperated tones, of these disconnects: "In the U.S. it's very hard for me to turn on any news channel... and not see some politician or some union group... pointing at the evils of outsourcing and the jobs that are being destroyed... But even one of our most liberal presidents in recent history, *at least when traveling outside the U.S.*, is able to acknowledge that this is a much more complex [situation] than the simple creation or destruction of jobs" (Senior executive, outsourcing advisory firm, Cartagena, Colombia, interview by author, May 2011).

[77] Jain, V. (2010) Outsourcing, Ohio, Obama and offshoring. *Sherpas in Blue* blog, Everest Group, November 18, accessed at <http://www.everestgrp.com/2010-11-outsourcing-ohio-obama-and-offshoring-sherpas-in-blue-shirts-3130.html>, May 12, 2014.

storm of 2004—the regrettable practice acquiring the label "ouch-sourcing" in the communications department of the Bush White House. In his prominent role as the chair of the Council of Economic Advisers, Mankiw had been pilloried at the time not only as a "cold-hearted apologist for corporate outsourcing [but also as] an Ivy league academic who [knew] too little of the real world."[78] In a score-settling account of this frenzied period, Mankiw took swipes at Democratic Party-aligned economists, like Paul Krugman and Larry Summers, who had betrayed the principles of their training by remaining strategically silent during the outsourcing wars, but also went on to complain about journalistic debasement, about the cynicism and hypocrisy of the political classes, and even about the gullibility of the "broad public, most of whom have never taken a single course in economics."[79] A few years later, during campaign 2012, not only had Mitt Romney—whose Harvard MBA surely included several courses in economics—failed to articulate an economic case for outsourcing, he had, in the words of Yale business economist, Nayan Chanda "sought to avoid responsibility for his firm's entirely sound business decision by distancing himself" from the practice.[80] Romney would surely have been receiving rather different counsel, in private at least, from the senior economic advisor to his campaign . . . one N. Gregory Mankiw?

Mankiw's public position, prior to the 2012 campaign, had been that a robust restatement of free-trade principles was the least (and indeed only responsible) thing that a card-carrying economist could do, while conceding that "[o]ffshore outsourcing poses a communications challenge for economists."[81] After joining the Romney 2012 team, he was to become uncharacteristically circumspect, if not strategically silent, on the topic of outsourcing, which was once again a headline issue, but not one on which this economic advisor to a would-be president would now comment on publicly. Certainly no shrinking violet, Mankiw nevertheless maintained a pattern of almost daily blog posts on a wide range of (other) topics.[82]

Beyond the media glare of presidential campaign seasons, Mankiw holds to the professionally consistent position that offshore outsourcing is a broadly beneficial process. Well aware that "[o]utsourcing will create winners and losers, and the pain of dislocation will be real for workers and their families," Mankiw subscribes to the view of most mainstream trade economists, that the

---

[78] Andrews, E. L. (2004) Economics adviser learns the principles of politics. *New York Times* February 26, C4.

[79] Mankiw and Swagel (2006: 1040).

[80] Chanda, N. (2012) Flight of capitalism. *Businessworld* July 23, accessed at <http://yaleglobal.yale.edu/content/flight-capitalism>, July 31, 2016, p. 1.

[81] Mankiw and Swagel (2006: 1054) conclude that, "There is no doubt . . . that discontent arising from outsourcing will be an issue for politicians and economists alike for the foreseeable future."

[82] Mankiw's blog, *Random Observations for Students of Economics*, has been rated the number one choice of the U.S. economics profession.

negative job impacts are marginal *relative to* the size and rate of churn in the U.S. economy, and that, in any case, these will be outweighed, in the notorious long run, by the overall benefits of increased trade and by job creation in less trade-exposed segments of the labor market.[83] Echoing the professional consensus, Mankiw maintains that "the empirical evidence suggests that the hysteria over offshore outsourcing is far out of proportion to its actual impact," while acknowledging that the "information gap" that exists is available for ongoing exploitation by populist politicians and "the likes of Mr. Dobbs."[84] Orthodox economists, it would seem, are instead prone to fill the same "information gap" with their own assumptions, presented as Principles of Free Trade, or even more robustly, as the *Law* of Comparative Advantage. On the other hand, Mankiw's Harvard students seem to be well aware that the scientized and depoliticized presentation of these economic laws does not represent an accurate guide to their character or consequences.[85]

Wearing his columnist's hat, Paul Krugman was one of those who joined the chorus of criticism concerning Mitt Romney's outsourcing record, dubbing the candidate a "captain of deindustrialization."[86] Krugman the economist, however, is more inclined to hold faith with the founding assumptions of his profession. In defense of free-trade orthodoxy, Krugman maintains that these "assumptions . . . are justified by the whole fabric of economic understanding but are not at all obvious to non-economists."[87] (The orthodox model assumes the following of less than plausible conditions: that labor is perfectly mobile within national job markets, that full employment prevails at both ends of the trading relationship, and that there are no balance of trade imbalances.) "Teaching the model, to docile students, is one thing," Krugman continued, when these had already been fed a steady diet of neoclassical economics, but explaining it "to an adult, especially one who already has opinions about the subject" was quite another matter. In fact, these non-economists might have good reason to be troubled by the results of many of the attempts that have been made to fill this information gap more empirically.

Based on detailed work-content data for the U.S., economists Brad Jensen and Lori Kletzer scored occupations on an index of "offshorability," finding that up to 38 million jobs are exposed, in principle, to this form of global

[83] Mankiw and Swagel (2006: 1055). See also Bhagwati et al. (2004); Lawrence, R. Z. (2009) Comments. In B. M. Friedman, ed., *Offshoring of American Jobs*. Cambridge, MA: MIT Press, 91–100.

[84] Mankiw and Swagel (2006: 1054, 1041). See Dobbs (2004).

[85] Mankiw was the target of a student protest, linked to the Occupy campaign, against what was portrayed as "inherent bias" in his Econ 10 class at Harvard. See Concerned Students of Economics 10 (2011) An open letter to Greg Mankiw. *Harvard Political Review* November 2, accessed at <http://harvardpolitics.com/harvard/an-open-letter-to-greg-mankiw/>, June 13, 2014.

[86] Krugman, P. (2012) Off and out with Mitt Romney. *New York Times* July 6, A23.

[87] Krugman, P. (1996) Ricardo's difficult idea. *The official Paul Krugman web page*, accessed at <http://web.mit.edu/krugman/www/ricardo.htm>, June 12, 2013, p. 5.

competition.[88] The most and least vulnerable occupations, according to this index, are listed in Table 3.3. Even if these estimates define the outer (theoretical) bounds of the disruptive reach of offshoring, they imply that "many service workers will have to join manufacturing production workers in learning to live with job insecurity," suggesting also that, over time, domestic employment will tend to skew towards the kind of personal-service jobs that typically recruit "the least formally educated and have lower median annual earnings."[89] This reinforces the findings of an earlier study of the scale of the offshoring threat by Alan Blinder and Alan Krueger: with the parameters set to "aggressive," they conclude that up to 40 million U.S. jobs were vulnerable to long-distance relocation.[90] The leading trade economist, Robert Z. Lawrence, deems these calculations "superficially persuasive," but frets that this may be an instance of too much information: "I am concerned that [Blinder, in publicizing his offshoring estimates] could engender unnecessary alarm and provoke the very protectionist responses that he says he'd like to avoid."[91] (Before taking his temporary vow of silence on the issue of outsourcing, as a Romney campaign advisor, Greg Mankiw shared this view, complaining that Blinder's alarmist message might lead politicians to contemplate ill-judged policy interventions, violating free-trade principles.)[92] Likewise loyal to the orthodox worldview, Lawrence similarly remains "unconvinced that the scale and the pain is going to be greater than we are already familiar with [because it would be] spread out over a long time."[93] This apparently complacent claim rested on a troubling historical analogy: because the current share of offshorable jobs is broadly comparable with the proportion of Americans working in the manufacturing sector in 1970, then any future dislocation need not exceed that associated with the fallout of deindustrialization in subsequent decades. The country, presumably, has become acclimatized to this level of pain.

Blinder, for one, does not think so. In comparison with the impact of deindustrialization—which was socially and spatially concentrated, even if it was "spread out" over time—the gathering wave of outsourcing threatens

---

[88] See Jensen and Kletzer (2010).

[89] Kletzer, L. G. (2009) Comments. In B. M. Friedman, ed., *Offshoring of American Jobs*. Cambridge, MA: MIT Press, 82–91, pp. 90, 89.

[90] Blinder and Krueger (2008).

[91] Lawrence, R. Z. (2009) Comments. In B. M. Friedman, ed., *Offshoring of American Jobs*. Cambridge, MA: MIT Press, 91–100, p. 92.

[92] Mankiw, N. G. (2007) Blinder on offshoring. *Greg Mankiw's blog*, May 5, accessed at <http://gregmankiw.blogspot.ca/2007/05/blinder-on-offshoring.html>, May 21, 2014. Acknowledging the likelihood of short-term pain, Mankiw expected this to pass "[o]ver the course of a generation," and did not "expect future transitions [associated with job displacement due to offshoring] to be macroeconomically different than past transitions."

[93] Lawrence, R. Z. (2009) Comments. In B. M. Friedman, ed., *Offshoring of American Jobs*. Cambridge, MA: MIT Press, 91–100, pp. 95, 93.

Table 3.3. Most and least offshorable occupations

Offshorability ranking		Employment	Annual mean wage ($)	+/− all occupation wage
1	Mathematical technicians	1,060	50,910	+
2	Biochemists and biophysicists	25,160	87,640	+
3	Statisticians	23,770	77,280	+
4	Title examiners, abstractors, and searchers	49,760	44,850	−
5	Credit authorizers, checkers, and clerks	51,240	35,790	−
6	Weighers, measurers, checkers, and samplers, recordkeeping	68,090	29,270	−
7	Data-entry keyers	211,200	29,010	−
8	Accountants and auditors	1,085,150	70,130	+
9	Medical transcriptionists	76,570	34,050	−
10	Actuaries	19,590	103,000	+
11	Market research analysts and marketing specialists	318,190	67,130	+
12	Astronomers	2,080	101,630	+
13	Bookkeeping, accounting, and auditing clerks	1,643,470	36,120	−
14	Mechanical drafters	64,090	52,150	+
15	Economists	14,270	100,270	+
16	Mathematicians	2,980	101,320	+
17	Sociologists	2,830	79,460	+
18	Operations research analysts	65,030	78,840	+
19	Survey researchers	17,060	47,740	+
20	Credit analysts	59,140	69,640	+
438	Bartenders	512,230	21,550	−
439	Craft artists	4,810	32,270	−
440	Lifeguards, ski patrol, and other recreational protective service workers	123,140	20,850	−
441	Dancers	11,240	n/a	
442	Choreographers	10,870	44,160	−
443	Animal trainers	10,530	30,510	−
444	Self-enrichment education, teachers	169,200	41,070	−
445	Childcare workers	631,240	21,320	−
446	Models	2,760	27,830	−
447	Preschool teachers, except special education	349,430	30,150	−
448	Fitness trainers and aerobics instructors	231,500	36,150	−
449	Surgical technologists	94,490	42,460	−
450	Crossing guards	68,520	25,880	−
451	Massage therapists	63,810	39,920	−
452	Gaming dealers	88,370	21,930	−
453	Actors	60,830	n/a	
454	Manicurists and pedicurists	56,270	21,760	−
455	Hairdressers, hairstylists, and cosmetologists	357,030	26,460	−
456	Flight attendants	87,190	41,720	−
457	Barbers	10,430	28,050	−
	All occupations	128,278,550	45,230	

Source: author's calculations from Bureau of Labor Statistics, *Occupational Employment Statistics Survey*; offshorability ranking after Jensen and Kletzer (2010) reach deep into the white-collar services, right up to the managerial and professional level; it could leave behind a "new class of trade victims," many of them drawn from the already beleaguered middle of the socioeconomic spectrum, with potentially massive social, economic, and political consequences.[94] Confronted by these potentially seismic conditions, Blinder's recommendation was for a three-pronged policy response. There must be redoubled efforts to assist and retrain displaced workers; targeted educational reforms will be needed to prepare students for non-offshorable occupations, such as those in the personal services or trades; and it will be necessary to establish some kind of strategic support for activities in which the United States can expect to maintain a comparative advantage (currently, sectors like finance, higher education, and entertainment, although Blinder is notably squeamish about "picking winners" for the future). On the face of it, these measures—even if a politician had the courage to propose them, and even if (then) they had a chance of being enacted—are plainly insufficient to the scale of the task. Orthodox economists predisposed to the principle of first doing no (regulatory) harm have belittled them as "plain-vanilla remedies," while even those comfortable with more purposive governmental interventions, like Harvard's Richard Freeman, assess them as "surprisingly modest."[95]

On the obvious disconnect between these small-bore policy proposals and the "big deal" of outsourcing, Blinder's somewhat evasive response speaks to the limits of third-way economic policy. More as an apology than an explanation, he rather self-consciously asked how an economic advisor to Thomas Jefferson could have been expected to respond, had the foresight somehow been available in 1802 to predict that the share of the U.S. workforce employed on farms was to fall from 84 percent to 2 percent over the next 200 years. "The great man looks worried, and asks: 'And what will the other 82 percent do?' You couldn't have answered," he put it to an audience of leading economists at a Harvard outsourcing seminar, "but neither could anyone else."[96] Perhaps there

---

[94] Blinder (2009: 41–2).

[95] Irwin, D. A. (2009) Comments. In B. M. Friedman, ed., *Offshoring of American Jobs*. Cambridge, MA: MIT Press, 71–82, p. 78; Freeman, R. B. (2009) Comments. In B. M. Friedman, ed., *Offshoring of American Jobs*. Cambridge, MA: MIT Press, 61–71, p. 68. On the issue of the timidity of Blinder's policy proposals, at least, Freeman has something in common with his Harvard colleague, Greg Mankiw. In his blog, Mankiw reported that at "a dinner at the Harvard Faculty Club...Ben Friedman [had] asked Alan [Blinder] a good question: Now that Alan has had this epiphany about offshoring, does he favor economic policies any different than he favored a decade ago? Alan thought about the question for a moment and then said no. I found that answer reassuring. My fear is that many politicians reading Alan's work on offshore outsourcing will not come to the same conclusion" (Mankiw, N. G. (2007) Blinder on offshoring. *Greg Mankiw's blog*, May 5, accessed at <http://gregmankiw.blogspot.ca/2007/05/blinder-on-offshoring.html>, May 21, 2014). For a discussion of left positions on outsourcing—which in their own way are relatively modest—see Anderson, S., Cavanagh, J., Madrick, J., and Hood, D. (2004) Toward a progressive view on outsourcing. *Nation* March 22, 22–6.

[96] Blinder (2009: 50).

really has been no improvement in the predictive power of economics over the past 200 years, but it is becoming increasingly clear that a labor market thoroughly restructured by offshore outsourcing will look very different to the current one. The view of (more) orthodox economists, even if the details cannot be known in advance, is that the long-term trend is toward an ever higher equilibrium state, once the frictions of the transition itself have been overcome, "[o]ver the course of a generation," as Greg Mankiw puts it.[97] On the other hand, if the Blinder-Krueger and Jensen-Kletzer studies are any guide, enduring havens of employment security will be found in face-to-face service occupations like childcare and preschool education, hairdressing, dance instruction, bartending, and animal training, while the most vulnerable to this twenty-first-century form of trade exposure will include not only accountants, data-entry keyers, surgical technicians, and credit analysts, but also mathematicians, sociologists, and . . . economists.

Outsourcing Policy?

Perhaps hard-boiled truths of any stripe are destined to remain elusive, especially in the feverish context of election-season politics, but the nature and consequences of this episodic discourse itself perhaps warrant a more disconcerting diagnosis: that substantive debate around the means and ends of economic policy in the context of rising job insecurity and deepening global integration—ostensibly a matter of utmost priority for both the general public and for the leadership class—has been all but displaced from the political arena. It is as if the responsibility for the meaningful deliberation of economic policy has itself been outsourced. Two major outbreaks of political hostilities around offshore outsourcing, in 2004 and 2012 presidential campaigns, seem to have done little to elevate the issue to the level of serious policy debate. Meanwhile, the 2016 presidential election campaign may not have become bogged down in the o-word in quite the same way, but smoldering anxieties and unresolved tensions around trade, wages, and employment clearly motivated voters on both the right and the left—to the point of threatening to unhinge some parts of the neoliberal policy consensus that unites the "establishment" sections of both major parties.[98] Repeatedly, the political

---

[97] Mankiw, N. G. (2007) Blinder on offshoring. *Greg Mankiw's blog*, May 5, accessed at <http://gregmankiw.blogspot.ca/2007/05/blinder-on-offshoring.html>, May 21, 2014.

[98] Donald Trump's erratic campaign squarely challenged the Republican Party's position on free trade, sacrosanct since the Reagan years, which none of his primary challengers were able (or prepared) to defend. Bernie Sanders' insurgent campaign was also a repudiation of the Democratic Party's centrist line on trade, finance capitalism, employment, and inequality, forcing Hillary Clinton to recalibrate her more mainstream positions, at least on the campaign trail.

conversation has lurched between populist pandering, born of political opportunism, on the one hand, and theoretically induced complacency, born of abstract economic principle, on the other. Curiously, this marks out offshore outsourcing as something like a no-go area for policymaking discussion—a new kind of third-rail issue, distinctive to the globalization era, perhaps?—while at the same time the reach and range of the actually existing practice continue almost noiselessly to expand, largely shielded from public view as a matter of *corporate* policy.

Perhaps it is idealistic to fault Barack Obama for having pressed home his tactical advantage over Mitt Romney in 2012 on the outsourcing issue, but the fact remains that there is little integrity in his party's position, for all the triangulations of the Clintons. In the end, Romney's calculated self-editing extended to the erasure of his own business credentials, while the voting public's palpable fear of "shipping jobs overseas" meant that there seemed to be no politically viable way out of the outsourcing trap. The epitome of the Republican Party's business-establishment wing, Romney's gyrations provided a prelude of sorts to Donald Trump's nationalist and nativist campaign of 2016.[99] While it has become commonplace to portray public anxieties around offshoring as exaggerated, the fact that the eventual scale of the phenomenon might be commensurate, ultimately, with the post-1970s experience of deindustrialization suggests otherwise. And the economists' sanguine argument that there will be winners as well as losers from outsourcing, but net gain for (almost) all in the long run, is likely to be of little consolation to those on the wrong side of this emerging division of labor—the new generation of potential trade victims currently working in a broad and growing array of back-office occupations, many of whom will have already had workplace encounters with outsourcing.

What is perhaps most striking, in retrospect, about the outbreaks of outsourcing fever in the presidential elections of 2004 and 2012 is how thoroughly inconclusive these were. The transparently symbolic politics of offshoring have done little or nothing to fill the policy vacuum: it may seem on the surface that the candidates are talking about jobs and trade, but there is a shared disinclination to attend forcefully to these issues when in office. Instead, cranking up the election-season volume to the point of distortion smacks of cynical political calculation, for the underlying policy debates have been as vacuous as the theatrical rhetoric itself. Neither the business-rationalist style of neoliberalism

---

[99] Breaking with the free-trade doctrine, Trump is characterized by the *Economist* as a "conviction protectionist," one that not so much made but found a path to the Republican Party's presidential nomination by way of appeals to nativism and economic populism—a path that the magazine feared, with or without a Trump presidency, that others aspiring to leadership positions in the party might subsequently seek to emulate. See Economist (2016) Trump's triumph. *Economist* May 7, 6.

practiced by Romney (and Bush before him; if Trump can be considered an aberration), nor its more ameliorative third-way variant, as favored by the Clintons and Obama (and Kerry before them), engage seriously with the issue of offshore outsourcing; in fact, they all tend to defer to, while at the same time triangulating around, such "global realities." The largely laissez-faire attitude toward employment insecurity and dislocation that is a recurrent feature of both varieties of market-oriented politics deems that these have not been appropriate matters for intervention in the business-as-usual periods between elections. If the episodic and noisy denunciations of outsourcing from presidential candidates tell us anything, it is that these are strategically significant silences.

Unless a candidate for political office in the United States should make the mistake of stepping on one of the outsourcing landmines, the conclusion that many have drawn from the bruising encounters of 2004 and 2012 is that it is best to steer well clear. And when the issue arises, blasts of populist rhetoric seem to provide sufficient cover. After she had shaken off the troublesome challenge of Bernie Sanders from the left, Hillary Clinton's carefully calibrated line has hewed much closer to the positions of Kerry and Obama before her, favoring trade liberalization as a default position, but promising to roll back the tax breaks secured by corporations caught in the act of exporting "American jobs."[100] Meanwhile, Donald Trump's brazen and quixotic campaign overwhelmed the capacities of fact-checking organizations on all fronts, if not making a mockery of the very idea of facts. In other respects, Trump's flamboyantly inconsistent posturing took the hypocrisy of anti-offshoring rhetoric to its (il)logical conclusion: while his own companies continued to send work offshore, Trump vowed to "end outsourcing" if elected president,[101] in effect building a wall around the American labor market to match those imagined to keep the terrorists, refugees, and immigrants at bay.

---

[100] See Camia, C. (2014) Hillary Clinton clarifies comments on job creation, *USA Today OnPolitics* blog, October 27, <http://onpolitics.usatoday.com/2014/10/27/hillary-clinton-businesses-job-creation/>, December 1, 2015.

[101] Predictably, Trump's public position on outsourcing combines outright opposition with a soundbite solution: "I'm sick of always reading about outsourcing. Why aren't we talking about 'onshoring?' We need to bring manufacturing jobs back home where they belong" (Trump, D. J. (2011) *Time to Get Tough*. Washington, DC: Regnery, p. 37). See also Perry, M. J. (2015) Donald Trump's hypocrisy on trade: He outsources and invests globally, but doesn't want Ford to do the same? *AEIdeas blog*, August 17, accessed at <https://www.aei.org/publication/donald-trumps-hypocrisy-on-trade-he-outsources-and-invests-globally-but-doesnt-want-ford-to-do-the-same/>, December 1, 2015; Windsor, L. (2015) Donald Trump will end outsourcing if president. *Huffington Post* blog, May 18, <http://www.huffingtonpost.com/lauren-windsor/donald-trump-will-end-outsourcing-if-president_b_7307426.html>, September 12, 2015.

4

Into the Outsourcing Complex

The editorialist and media commentator Michael Kinsley at first questioned that there could even be an International Association of Outsourcing Professionals. Writing in the *Los Angeles Times*, he observed that outsourcing had "become such a dirty word that it's hard to believe there could actually be" such an organization. "What next?" Kinsley asked, "The Society of Professional Child Molesters?" Writing from the liberal center, Kinsley's more subtle point was that what he portrayed as "outsourcing's bad rap" had more to do with political calculation, on all sides, than with any realistic assessment of the economics of this notoriously difficult proposition. Moreover, the public could hardly be faulted for having a less than comprehensive grasp of the issue. The reasons for the public distaste of outsourcing were obvious, since:

> People lose their jobs when companies transfer parts of their operations overseas. But most economists believe in the theory of free trade, which holds that a nation cannot prosper by denying its citizens the benefit of cheap foreign labor. It's a hard sell because the victims are concentrated and easy to identify, while the benefit is diffused through the whole economy. That's why so many politicians pay obeisance to free trade in the abstract but oppose it in the particular.[1]

A convenient scapegoat, outsourcing has duly become, according to the *Economist*, "the aspect of globalization that workers in the developed world dislike and fear the most."[2] Never mind Kinsley's point that "most economists believe in the theory of free trade," workers fearful of losing their jobs and livelihoods have in practice been unmoved by abstract arguments about the benefits of long-run competitive adjustment. And very few politicians have been up to the "hard sell" of dealing squarely with the phenomenon of offshoring, with most tending to forego detailed policy discussion for the

---

[1] Kinsley, M. (2012) Outsourcing's bad rap. *Los Angeles Times* July 12, accessed at <http://articles.latimes.com/2012/jul/12/opinion/la-oe-kinsley-outsourcing-20120712>, May 1, 2013.
[2] Economist (2013) Outsourcing and offshoring: The story so far. *Economist* January 19, S5.

easy path of straightforward denunciation. In a parallel fashion to those corporations that opt to take the low-cost, low-wage route to profit maximization via offshore outsourcing, the political class rarely overcomes the temptation of the "the easy out."[3] Its cadre of economic advisors have hardly helped matters, most of which is recruited from a profession that, as a matter of framing and indeed faith, is committed to the free-trade doctrine.[4] Conventionally trained economists have been ill equipped to deal with the negative political optics that surround discussions of offshoring, dissent that they tend to put down to public ignorance rather than actually existing job insecurity, or for that matter to limitations in the theory itself. As Paul Krugman has complained, "the problem free traders face is not that their theory has dropped them into Wonderland, but that political pragmatism [places them] on the wrong side of the looking glass."[5]

The managers and paraprofessionals that ply their trade in the outsourcing "industry" find themselves living and working on the wrong side of this looking glass. They have grown accustomed to operating inside an envelope of political negativity, while at the same time wrestling with stubborn organizational challenges for which they rarely receive much credit, even from their superiors, let alone empathy. Protesting that they are not only unfairly maligned but thoroughly misunderstood, outsourcers will periodically bridle at this doghouse status, when they are on the wrong end of sustained campaigns of political bashing, even as they (must) reject the suggestion that theirs is a tainted mandate. The outsourcing industry's most widely used professional codebook squarely acknowledges the concern, "particularly when it comes to offshore outsourcing, about the community and political backlash over lost jobs," but rather obliquely advises that outsourcing engagements should be managed within the bounds of "political correctness."[6]

Talking amongst themselves, however, outsourcers will often breach these boundaries. When Obama was styling himself as the "Insourcing President," for example, this was the response of a prominent figure behind the U.S.-based industry blog, *Horses for Sources*, the global subscription list of which runs into the tens of thousands:

---

[3] Buffington (2007).
[4] For critiques of the free-trade doctrine and the culture of orthodox economics, see Sheppard, E. (2005) Constructing free trade: From Manchester boosterism to global management. *Transactions of the Institute of British Geographers* 30(2): 151–72; Irwin, D. A. (1996) *Against the Tide: An intellectual history of free trade*. Princeton, NJ: Princeton University Press. See also Sheppard, E. (2016) *Limits to Globalization: The disruptive geographies of capitalist development*. Oxford: Oxford University Press.
[5] Krugman, P. (1997) What should trade negotiators negotiate about? *Journal of Economic Literature* 35(1): 113–20, p. 114; see also Boudreaux, D. (2012) Mercantilist myths persist. *Cafe Hayek* July 12, accessed at <http://cafehayek.com/2012/07/mercantilist-myths-persist.html>, May 12, 2013.
[6] IAOP *Outsourcing Professional Body of Knowledge* (2010: 20, 62).

What [Obama] is glossing over is the fact that 97% of US organizations today, with over $1 billion in revenue, are already outsourcing some piece of their business or IT operations and—in most cases—some degree of overseas labor is used by the service provider. What he needs to focus in on is *why* service providers use overseas labor: because it is cheaper, and there is a lot more of it available...

US labor costs are far too high and the country is not currently blessed with millions of people... who are prepared to take on lower level white collar jobs at $25–40K per annum... [The problem is that] the US education system isn't producing hordes of graduates... that can compete with the Indian factory model. [This is why the] unemployed aren't filling the jobs that are being "shipped overseas"...

Organizations outsource because it makes them more competitive and it pleases their shareholders. If Obama truly wants to be the "Insourcing President," then he has to figure out how to make the US labor force *competitive* with the rest of the world... "Outsourcing" is a symptom of America's continuously spiraling cost of living and lack of available talent, which is the real cause.[7]

Setting aside the fact that the advocacy of such a domestic policy, based on low-wage adjustment, would be economically unpalatable even if it were politically saleable, the outsourcers' protests clearly speak to an accumulated sense of grievance, if not exasperation. These were, the blog post concluded, "dangerous times for the 'outsourcing' industry," which having been "caught in the crossfire" of political attacks from all directions might even be encountering an existential threat. At the very least, the repeated smears were aggravating what has been a longstanding identity crisis across this ostensibly essential but singularly unloved industry.

A few weeks later, Horses for Sources (HfS) Research, the outsourcing advisory company that hosts the *Horses for Sources* blog, decided to poll its worldwide membership network with the not wholly tongue-in-cheek question, "is it time to dump the term outsourcing?" Complementing the straight-talking, irreverent style of the blog, the survey featured an image of a gravestone marked with the self-pitying epitaph, "Always misunderstood" (see Figure 4.1).[8] Released to coincide with a major business-process outsourcing tradeshow in Gurgaon, India, the survey results revealed an industry sufficiently restive to propose the abolition of its own name, by a margin of 2:1. As usual, however, there was no consensus on the choice of euphemistic alternatives that HfS had offered, although the innocuous "business-process services," "global business services," and "managed services" scored better than most. Earlier that year, a high-level gathering

---

[7] Fersht, P. (2012) Caught in the xeno-bamia crossfire, these are dangerous times for the "outsourcing" industry. *Horses for Sources* blog July 15, accessed at <http://www.horsesforsources.com/xenobamia_071512>, June 1, 2013, pp. 1–2, original emphasis.

[8] HfS (2012) It's time for YOUR vote... should we drop the word "outsourcing"? *Horses for Sources* blog July 28, accessed at <http://www.horsesforsources.com/vote-drop-outsourcing_072712>, June 13, 2013, p. 1.

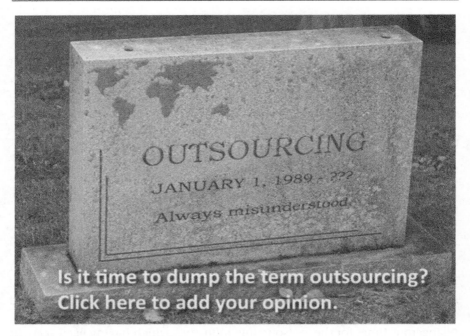

Figure 4.1 Outsourcing, R.I.P.?
Source: *Horses for Sources* blog. Reproduced with permission of HfS Research

of key players convened to assess the prospects of "the industry known as 'outsourcing,'" drawn from both the vending and buying sides of the business, had concluded, in a similarly ambivalent vein, that the o-word had become irretrievably "synonymous with greedy corporations exploiting low-cost labor [at the expense of] higher-paying jobs," despite the fact that the business practice was "now mainstream."[9] HfS would subsequently assert, however, that the industry's problems could not entirely be put down to malevolent forces on the outside. There were confusions and even delusions much closer to home too:

> There is far too much "believe our own bullshit" going on and this industry needs to change how it is perceived before it can effectively "rebrand." People in the industry are complaining that the ignorant masses confuse "outsourcing" with "offshoring" [but] isn't the vast majority of [the business] dependent on offshore labor to make the economics work? We should probably just call it "offshore outsourcing" to be even more accurate (eek!).[10]

---

[9] HfS Research (2012: 17).

[10] HfS (2012) An industry with no name? The outsourcing industry votes out the "O" word but can't think of an alternative…*Horses for Sources* blog September 7, accessed at <http://www.horsesforsources.com/o-word-no-alternative_090712>, June 6, 2013, p. 1.

For all its cosmopolitan connections, there is a somewhat alienated, cocoon-like quality to the social world occupied by the outsourcing industry. Here, this self-styled "industry with no name" has been busy making a parallel universe of its very own, not least through a host of organizational initiatives, communication platforms, and networking events dedicated to the cause of constructing an outsourcing "community."

There has certainly been plenty of work to do. Not only does outsourcing exist on the borderlands of managerial practice—between organizations, often between "cultures," and at the margins of established industries and professions—it has also been estranged, since birth, from the politically hostile world outside. A measure of camaraderie results from this shared sense of alienation, but the community made by outsourcing is in its own way extremely heterogeneous, and rather sharply divided in terms of loyalties and identities too. It comprises the vendors of technical, organizational, and human-resources services (comprising an array of service-delivery providers, contract-management, and technology firms), as well as the buyers of these services (a congeries of corporate executives with diverse backgrounds in human resources, IT, purchasing, logistics, finance, and so forth), plus a large cohort of third-party relationship managers, consultants, advisors, and facilitators.

So how should this "outsourcing space" be properly characterized? Its inhabitants will often refer to their "industry," but in practice there is little resemblance to a conventional industrial sector, as defined by its product. The endlessly repackaged and rebundled products, services, and functions of the outsourcing industry include the offshore sourcing of labor and expertise, the integration of new systems and technologies, the delivery of consulting services and projects of organizational transformation, the management of complex operations, and quite a lot more. Rather than discrete products or services, these are often customized configurations of hybrid and boundary-spanning activities that in practice morph and meld into an array of other industries, organizations, occupations, and systems. Virtually all of the underlying activities, or tasks, that are targets for offshore outsourcing have to be "routinizable" in some way, in order that they can be disembedded from host companies and their internal systems in a manner amenable to long-distance relocation, but these may reach into fields as diverse as legal and payroll services, software development, administrative processing, security monitoring, IT maintenance, human-resources functions, and so on—all of which connects outsourcing providers to field-specific practices, organizations, problems, and sources of expertise. The resulting degree of sectoral segmentation and specialization, in fact, practically mirrors the diversity of the economy as a whole. Furthermore, on the demand side of the outsourcing relationship, few corporate buyers of these services—for all their effective power over competitive dynamics, organizational norms, and daily practices in the sector itself—would consider themselves to be primarily "in" (or indeed of) the industry known as outsourcing. Befitting their position at the top of what are invariably very much *buyer-driven* supply chains, those representing corporate clients prefer to see themselves as "above" the industry, and some might even find the label demeaning. Corporate buyers may purchase from the outsourcing industry, and their functions are often deeply integrated with it, but they do not necessarily *belong* to it.

If the diverse assemblage of activities associated with offshore outsourcing is difficult to shoehorn into conventional understandings of "industry," might this instead be defined as a new field of practice, or profession? There are certainly ongoing efforts to professionalize the managerial work of outsourcing, but in many respects these have been little more than germinal. The International Association of Outsourcing Professionals (IAOP) itself recognizes that outsourcing has yet to achieve "maturity" as a profession, in its own surveys continuing to ask the question, "To what extent is outsourcing considered a profession at all?"[11] This might be seen, however, as an emergent paraprofession, founded upon still-to-be-realized ambitions, in which there is ongoing work to stabilize codes and practices, and to authorize common standards and forms of expertise in the face of sharp competitive divisions and entrenched status deficits. A work in progress, professionalization has far greater appeal on the provider (or vendor) side, with those selling outsourcing solutions, and with a peripatetic class of full-time "outsourcing advisors," than it does amongst corporate buyers, whose principal allegiances and sources of identity often lie elsewhere. IAOP surveys have discovered that, within buyer companies, "outsourcing is still not viewed as a long-term career choice," with most spending time in this role as part of an internal career move.[12] As the organization's Jag Dalal explains,

> It's difficult for outsourcing to be accepted as a profession because it's not a singular discipline in any company—except at provider organizations. This is very unlike disciplines like finance or HR, where there's a clear set of competencies attached to the profession. What's more, outsourcing overlaps with procurement and sourcing activities at many companies, and so it isn't recognized as an independent skill set. To be recognized as a career path, outsourcing will need to define itself as a function, and will need clear skills for training and certification.[13]

There is also a highly blurred boundary between the (lower reaches of the) management consultancy business and the paraprofession that is outsourcing, sharing as they do a project-oriented ethos, expertise in trading across (as opposed to simply within) organizations, and a somewhat liminal identity. In practice,

---

[11] IAOP (2015: 7) defines outsourcing professionals as "the customers, providers and advisors who are the designers, facilitators and implementers of outsourced solutions."
[12] IAOP (2015: 9).   [13] Quoted in IAOP (2015: 9).

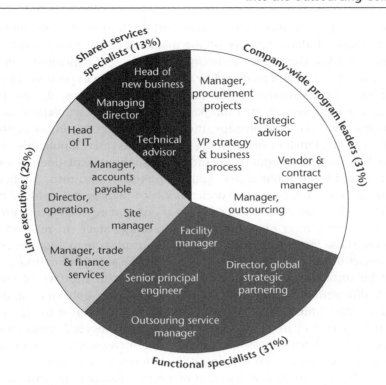

Figure 4.2 Distribution of outsourcing professionals
Source: author's rendering, derived from IAOP (2010)

though, consultants are as a tribe considerably more secure in their professional status, tending to look (down) on the "plain vanilla" work of outsourcing, at least after the design and deal-making stages are over, as a rather taxing space of operational middle management.[14] As a result, the occupational class, or discipline, provisionally defined by the label, "outsourcing professional" is extremely diverse, including managers possessing cross-functional skills of different kinds, consultants and advisors, and specialists in information technology, human relations, operations, and more (see Figure 4.2). The hard-to-classify work of the outsourcing professional resembles an "inter-discipline," in this respect.

A quasi-industry and an aspirant profession, the global outsourcing trade also exhibits some of the features of a market, although again far from a conventional one. While in significant respects this is a transactional domain, characterized by rigorous cost pressures and often fierce price-based competition, it is also a socially structured space, governed by implicit contracts,

[14] Senior partner, technology service provider, Singapore; consulting services manager, global technology firm, Kuala Lumpur; interviews by author, April 2011.

embedded relations, and emergent conventions. Bearing little resemblance to the neoclassical ideal, the outsourcing market is deeply structured by asymmetrical relationships and socio-organizational entanglements, many of which are managed and mediated by third parties. The imperatives of competition and commoditization are certainly endemic, if not constitutive, but this is also a space governed, far from perfectly, by socially regularized and contractually regulated relationships, themselves subject to almost continuous reconstruction. Offshore outsourcing is a site of pervasive ambiguities, born of blurred organizational boundaries and responsibilities, experimental divisions of labor, and (re)distributed risks and incentives; this, in turn, is reflected in emergent (and often contested) domains like co-management, shared competencies, and strategic partnerships. Even if outsourcing buyers and providers sometimes encounter one another, at the tender stage, in relatively open markets, those involved routinely equate their subsequent engagements not to transactions per se but to something more like a difficult marriage, which must be sustained, socially and organizationally, in the face of enduring power differentials, conflicts of interest, controlling behaviors, and cross-cultural communication problems. Complicating matters further, there are also third parties in many of these marriages—the lawyers, consultants, and advisors who act not only as matchmakers but, increasingly, serve in ongoing capacities as professional counselors or "relationship managers."

Rather than presume that, for want of a better placeholding term, the "outsourcing complex" can be interpreted through a preexisting analytical template, this chapter ventures into the world of global sourcing in a more exploratory fashion, seeking insights into its sociology and psychology, into its projects of organizational and discursive stabilization, and into the workings of its cultural economy. In preliminary terms, the outsourcing complex is understood as a multi-dimensional and heterogeneous socioeconomic formation: it has some of the characteristics of an industry, but its reach exceeds that; it possesses many of the features of a profession, but remains rather less than that; and it resembles a "market" in some respects, but hardly of the textbook type. The chapter takes seriously the ways that outsourcers talk about, and amongst, themselves, particularly at their conferences, workshops, and "summits," seeking to understand their world through its vernacular discourse and practice. It also delves into the ways in which those on the front lines have been grappling with the testing work of managing and living with offshored relationships. The chapter is concluded with some observations on the yearning for positive (self-)transformation that continues to animate, as well as frustrate, the managers of outsourcing projects. This is about more than a desire to migrate to a new organizational paradigm, with more value-adding and less competitive instability. It is also about a search for recognition and respect, and attempt to secure a status upgrade while shedding the reputational blight that long dogged this field of managerial practice. For many that work here, though, it still feels like a Cinderella undertaking.

Where Dreams Come True?

As the home (and in some respects the refuge) for outsourcing professionals, IAOP has fashioned a relatively comfortable existence for itself on the other side of the looking glass. As if to acknowledge its otherworldly positionality, a favored location for the organization's signature event, the Outsourcing World Summit®, is the Disney World resort in Orlando, Florida. At the first of these meetings, in 1998, 150 of the (true) pioneers of outsourcing had found their way to the Downtown Disney hotel for two days of networking. The annual event will now attract around 800 delegates from forty or more countries. When the industry is under sustained attack in the media, as it was during the 2012 presidential election season, this took on the function of a corporate sanctuary, at least temporarily, if not an exercise in escapism. Hosted at Disney's Contemporary Resort, just down the road from the Magic Kingdom®, this edition of the meeting was promoted as an opportunity to look beyond the travails of the moment, to imagine "Outsourcing beyond the horizon." Not for the first time, the outsourcing industry was striving to imagine itself a better place.

The Disney World summit comprised a busy four-day program, including seven "educational tracks," a sequence of how-to practicum sessions, and a host of networking luncheons and parties, all preceded by a now customary golf tournament. A crowded exhibition hall, repurposed for the occasion as the "global services mall," displayed some of the diversity of the outsourcing complex: row upon row of service providers, consulting and advisory firms, legal specialists, and IT contractors, interspersed with stands promoting up-and-coming locations like the Bogotá free-trade district and the would-be insourcing capital of Missouri. Many of those milling around in the global services mall were wearing name tags adorned with ribbons designating their status as corporate sponsors, founder members, or delegates to one of IAOP's advisory boards. Since almost nobody else will, this is a community that likes to congratulate itself, at least in such more private moments.

Flirting with self-parody, an annual crop of inductees to the Outsourcing Leadership Hall of Fame is one of the featured events at each summit, coinciding with a gala luncheon. This is a mark of recognition for the movers and shakers amongst the new generation of global service providers; true believers from buy-side corporations like General Motors, Unilever, BP, Rio Tinto, and Procter and Gamble are sometimes recognized, too, although this is an achievement that few are likely to trumpet back home (see Table 4.1). More

Table 4.1. Inductees to the Outsourcing Hall of Fame, 2006–16

2016	Greg Kirchhoefer	Partner	Kirkland and Ellis
	William P. Metz	Senior Director, IT Sourcing and Vendor Management	Walmart
	Christopher Stancombe	Chief Operating Officer	Capgemini Business Services
2015	Scott Singer	Head of Global Business Services	Rio Tinto
	Michael F. Corbett	Chairman	IAOP
	Adrian Quayle	Managing Partner	Avasant
2014	Leslie P. Willcocks	Professor	London School of Economics
	Mary C. Lacity	Professor	University of Missouri-St. Louis
	Michael J. Salvino	Group Chief Executive, BPO	Accenture
	Jagdish Dalal	Chief Advisor, Thought Leadership	IAOP
2013	Dana S. Deasy	Group Chief Information Officer	BP
	John K. Halvey	Group Executive VP and General Counsel	NYSE Euronext
	Morton H. Meyerson	Former Chair, President, and CEO	Perot Systems
2012	Wendell O. Jones	Chief Executive	Society for Information Management
	Thomas Meador	President and CEO	Michigan Avenue Real Estate
	Marco Stefanini	Global CEO	Stefanini IT
2011	Blanca Treviño	President and CEO	Softtek
	William F. Concannon	President, Global Corporate Services	CBRE
	Sandy Ogg	Former Chief Human Resource Officer	Unilever
2010	Joshua R. Jewett	Senior VP-IT and Procurement	Family Dollar Stores
	Dimitry A. Loschinin	President and CEO	Luxoft
	Dewang Mehta	(Posthumous) Past President	NASSCOM
2009	Oliver T. Bussman	Chief Information Officer	SAP AG
	Michael S. Mensik	Partner	Baker and McKenzie LLC
	Liu Jiren	Chairman and CEO	Neusoft Corporation
	Amirsham A. Aziz	Former President and CEO	Maybank
	Lynn Blodgett	President and CEO	ACS
	Marty Chuck	Founder	The CXOs LLC
	Peter F. Drucker	(Posthumous) Professor	Claremont Graduate University
2008	Nandan M. Nilekani	Co-Founder and Co-Chairman	Infosys
	N. R. Narayana Murthy	Founder, Chairman, and Chief Mentor	Infosys
2008	Ralph J. Szygenda	Group Vice President and CIO	General Motors
	Dennis McGuire	Founder and Chairman Emeritus	TPI
2007	Kevin Campbell	Group Chief Executive, Outsourcing	Accenture
	Ron L. Kifer	Group Vice President and CIO	Applied Materials
2006	Filippo Passerini	Global Services Officer and CIO	Procter and Gamble
	Paul D. Spence	CEO Outsourcing Services	Capgemini

Source: <http://www.iaop.org>

consequentially, IAOP also organizes a widely publicized ranking of the Global Outsourcing 100®, an annual snapshot of what can be a quite fluid industry hierarchy, facilitating a reciprocal exchange of reputational value and corporate sponsorship (see Table 4.2). The big players in the industry— like ISS, Accenture, CBRE, Kelly, and Colliers—have tended to dominate the top spots, but there is also considerable movement on this list, reflecting a sustained pattern of merger and acquisitions activity, as well as waves of new entrants. While there is continuity here—amid the frequent name changes and restructurings—there is also evidence of a great deal of competitive instability and organizational churn. Partly as a result, there is considerable professional mobility into, out of, and across the sector. Although there are many familiar faces at the IAOP summits, company affiliations will often change.

Formed in the aftermath of the Bush-Mankiw outsourcing ruckus of 2004, IAOP operates, for the most part, in a parallel universe of its own making, seldom seeking or attracting public attention. With a mandate that is more introspective than that of most trade bodies, the association is less concerned with representing (or lobbying for) outsourcing, or indeed with reaching out to the world, more with the project of organizing its own world. IAOP works to organize and stabilize an "establishment" for this diverse sector, at the same time developing a framework for self-improvement through acts of recognition and professionalization. Its stated mission is to "improve the quality and consistency of outsourcing outcomes," translated into the objective of "improving the capabilities of the business and project leaders responsible for defining, implementing, and managing these highly complex multi-company relationships," qualified by the sobering reality that "[s]tudy after study [has found] that executives, although outsourcing more, are less than fully satisfied with the results."[15] This is reflected in a preoccupation with the celebration and codification of best practice and "best in class" behavior, towards which IAOP seeks to raise the bar of performance through a combination of exhortation, positive demonstration effects, and professional preparation. One of its signature programs is a self-organized credentialing service for the Certified Outsourcing Professional® or COP, credits towards which can be picked up at the annual summits, and a host of similar regional events in Latin America, Europe, and the Asia-Pacific.

The scale of IAOP's uphill task of willed self-improvement and auto-professionalization is illustrated by the fact that less than 1 percent of its publicly declared membership has completed the organization's certification program (even though it must be acknowledged that declared membership

[15] IAOP (n.d.) *Guide to Becoming a COP, Certified Outsourcing Professional®*. Poughkeepsie, NY: IAOP, pp. 1, 7.

Table 4.2. The leadership class of IAOP's Global Outsourcing 100®

Leadership class, 2015	Rank 2010	Rank 2014	Leadership class, 2015	Rank 2010	Rank 2014
Accelya			Jones Lang LaSalle	12	16
Accenture	1	2	*Kelly Outsourcing and Consulting Group*		4
Aegis	21	35	L&T Infotech		22
Alorica			LeasePlan USA		23
Altisource		60	Luxoft		18
Aon Hewitt		41	MAYKOR		38
AsiaInfo Technologies (Nanjing)			MERA	84	66
Banner Managed Communications			Minacs Group		
Brookfield GRS		68	Mindtree	43	33
Canon Business Process Services		42	NEORIS	69	67
CBRE		3	Newmark Grubb Knight Frank	70	20
CGI	33	10	NIIT Technologies		
CleNET	78	46	Orange Business Services		
Colliers International	18	5	*Pactera*		8
Competence Call Center			Quatrro		27
Concentrix	68	43	RR Donnelley Global Outsourcing		65
Cybage Software		34	Sitel Operating Corporation	31	14
Datamatics Global Services		39	SoftServe	96	26
Diebold Integrated Services	15	49	SPi Global	51	47
Donlen		61	Stefanini	59	56
DTZ (formerly Cassidy Turley)		11	Sutherland Global Services		36
Emerio GlobeSoft	98	72	Swiss Post Solutions		30
EXL	66	29	Sykes Enterprises		15
Firstsource	25	12	Syntel	47	62
FPT Corporation		57	*Tata Communications Transformation Services*	7	
Grupo ASSA	95		Tech Mahindra Business Services Group	44	
HCL Technologies Limited	32	6	Teleperformance		
HGS		50	TeleTech	34	64
HP Enterprise Services			tgestiona		45
IBA Group	61	25	TIVIT		31
Indecomm Global Services		54	Towers Watson		21
INSIGMA	45	24	transcosmos	52	13
Inspur	37	74	VADS Business Process Sdn. Bhd.		
Integreon			Virtusa		
iSoftStone		44	Wicresoft		32
ISS	6	1	WNS Global Services Private Limited	58	52
ITC Infotech	49	63	Xchanging		40
Johnson Controls Global WorkPlace Solutions	14	19			

Note: organizations rated in the top 10 since 2010 are rendered in italic text

Source: author's calculation from IAOP data; <http://www.iaop.org>

levels are a loose category, subject to exaggeration for promotional reasons). What is described as a "highly-coveted professional designation" can be obtained with the payment of a $600 non-refundable processing fee, a three-day "master class" (live or online), and some homework with the organization's hefty manual, the *Outsourcing Professional Body of Knowledge* or *OPBOK*.[16] This low-cost form of executive education is based on the peer-to-peer transfer of practical skills and generic tips, born of experience in the corporate trenches. This is acknowledged to be a challenging, competitive, and fast-changing environment, yet one that is given to be subject, at least in principle, to professional "mastery." The training task for COPs involves the codification and rationalization of the unorthodox bundle of cross-practice skills that the outsourcing professional should aspire to combine (see Table 4.3), delivered with liberal applications of business-school jargon and authenticated through "real-world case studies" (suitably anonymized). Throughout, there is deference to what are deemed "model" practices and "leadership" behaviors.

IAOP's programming is dedicated to what are recognized as socially, organizationally, and technically demanding feats of management, which have to be accomplished in an operationally stretched and routinely undervalued field of practice that is cross-cut by the low-road logics of cost control, price-based competition, and commoditization. There is plenty of talk of cutting-edge practices and more civilized, "partnering" models of outsourcing founded on the high-road principle collaborative value added, of course. Yet insiders will acknowledge that, "it is plainly apparent that both parties [in these engagements] are failing to shift their relationships beyond merely cost reduction," while it is also quite typical to find that, "[o]nce the ink on the outsourcing contract has started to dry, corporate leadership [in purchasing companies turn] their attention to other priorities," handing off the responsibility for project management to operational teams.[17] If, in the minds of minds of many senior executives, outsourcing is principally a matter of sloughing off secondary activities to vendors that are expected to operate as silently as possible, in the background (while delivering efficiency gains and cost savings), any kind of "noise" can be seen as a problem. Missing targets and failing to resolve niggling "issues" will soon become a major irritant. This can be a serious test of the capabilities of overburdened middle managers on both sides of outsourcing engagements. In the words of a well-traveled outsourcing advisor, "One of the common problems is that the [senior] executives are not paying attention, so the middle managers are often left to solve

---

[16] IAOP (n.d.) *Guide to Becoming a COP, Certified Outsourcing Professional®*. Poughkeepsie, NY: IAOP, p. 1; see also IAOP (2010).
[17] HfS Research (2012: 4, 14).

Table 4.3. Outsourcing lifecycle skills: selected primary competences

Strategy	Develop outsourcing value model for the organization
	Integrate outsourcing value model into the organization's strategic planning process
	Develop end-to-end outsourcing management process
	Develop opportunity identification and assessment criteria and process
	Assess potential outsourcing opportunities
	Accept, reject, and prioritize potential outsourcing opportunities
Implementation	Structure and manage project teams, including internal and external resources
	Establish required outcomes (balanced scorecard)
	Determine optimal structure for relationship(s), including pricing
	Design governance model
	Establish provider-selection criteria
	Determine optimal approach(es) for engaging the marketplace of providers
	Manage provider evaluation and selection process
	Negotiate final deal structuring
	Manage transition to new environment, including governance
Management	Manage governance system
	Identify and resolve conflicts
	Reassess value and renegotiate
Professional skills	Project management
	Change management
	Communications
	Contracting
	Interpersonal/trust building
	Marketing
	Negotiating
	Team leadership
	Balanced scorecards
Offshoring	Strategic global sourcing model development
	Global source evaluation
	Engagement model evaluation (outsourced, captive, build-operate-transfer, etc.)
	Cross-cultural collaboration
Technology	Outsourcing process analysis for continuous improvement
	Outsourcing management technology assessment

Source: adapted from IAOP Outsourcing Professional Body of Knowledge® version 10. Copyright 2016 IAOP; with permission

problems that they can't possibly be expected to solve on their own ... Issue escalation is [therefore] the single biggest problem in outsourcing, *the* single biggest problem."[18]

In actual (as opposed to best) practice, outsourcing professionals are regularly placed on the front lines of difficult projects in which the risk of failure is quite high, but where the recognition of success may often be lacking. They may as a result find themselves seriously exposed. As the *OPBOK* diplomatically surveys the hazardous terrain:

Any change as significant as outsourcing has risk. Not all organizations execute outsourcing well. Not all providers deliver well for every customer. Even when

---

[18] Senior outsourcing advisor, Houston, TX, interview by author, May 2011.

both companies execute well, other internal and external factors can keep the relationship from delivering its intended benefits. As a result, various surveys report a surprisingly high rate of outsourcing failures.[19]

The extent to which this failure rate is "surprising" is perhaps questionable. Working under stress, the duty of the outsourcing professional, in this context, is not only to deliver, while keeping the "noise level" down, but to *believe* in projects when many around her will be skeptical, indifferent, or even hostile—one reason why the commitment to outsourcing has been likened by some to a "religious issue."[20]

Perhaps there is a higher calling here, but the earthly responsibilities of the outsourcer are much more prosaic: rationalization and cost cutting are the elemental logics upon which the practice is founded, invariably, by delivering cheaper "solutions" based on cheaper labor. Outsourcing professionals do not deny this, even as they reach for ways to augment and add value to the crude labor-arbitrage model. This can only be achieved, though, in the face of the countervailing pressures of cost suppression. Quite often, an escalating schedule of required bottom-line savings is written into contracts—the basic rationale upon which the case for outsourcing is founded, at least in the view of many corporate clients. The outsourcer's fundamental task, even where it is more edifying than dealing with a client's mess (for less), continues to be mostly about delivering routine reliability at basement prices. And the corporate buyers of outsourcing services, for their part, have learned to drive very hard bargains while at the same time demanding improved "quality."

There is an understandable desire, for both parties, to make more of these engagements, but realizing high-end, value-sharing models remains the exception rather than the rule. Most outsourcing engagements are managed under conditions of operational and financial stress. The *OPBOK*, and the wider outsourcing profession to which it addressed, cannot but recognize this blunt socioeconomic fact, just as it must confront that stubbornly "high rate of outsourcing failures."[21] Nevertheless, the overriding discursive refrain—consistent with IAOP's mission of mutual improvement—remains an aspirational one. Amongst true believers, this takes the form of a best-practice theology-cum-teleology, a vision of high-road upgrading not just for the fortunate few but as a shared condition of systemic, positive-sum transformation. No wonder that the commitment to outsourcing is sometimes represented as a "religious issue," while industry summits will often convey the

---

[19] IAOP (2010: 20).

[20] Chief information officer, ABN, quoted in Kripalani, M. (2006) Five offshore practices that pay off. *Business Week* January 30, 60–1, p. 60.

[21] IAOP (2010: 20). See also Nagendra, K. (2013) *Top 10 Reasons Why Outsourcing Fails*. Dallas, TX: Outsourcing Center.

sense of a secular cult. This is not just because the assembled feel scorned and misunderstood by those outside. Those on the dais will preach the benefits of continuous improvement and mutual upgrading, while the congregants—as much as they want to believe—struggle to gain much of a foothold on this righteous path. The discrepancy between the challenges of the present and the promise of a better future is managed by the incantation of transition narratives. There are several versions of this redemptive script, but nearly all involve a shift away from simple labor-arbitrage and price-based contracting in favor of more mature and collaborative, indeed strategic, partnerships (see Table 1.2). The upgrading narrative involves a transition from instrumental and "spontaneous" engagements to rounded and "holistic" models of shared governance, as the ad hoc approaches typical of the "wild-west" era of outsourcing, presented as a bygone time of purely cost-driven behavior, gives way to a bright future of permanent improvement via optimizing processes.

There might be good reason, then, why Disney World is a favorite location for IAOP summits, aside from reliable weather and the resort's competitive rates for corporate conferencing. This slightly surreal setting resounds with the promise that dreams might indeed one day come true, as the Disney philosophy has it. The most cherished fairytale of the outsourcing world is no more than a reworking of the classic storyline of metamorphosis. This recurring folk narrative dependably begins in the austere world of "transactional" labor arbitrage, but just as dependably anticipates a happy ending in the form of "transformational" outsourcing. "In the beginning there was cost,"[22] is how the story is conventionally told . . . In the beginning, relationships were frugal, shallow, instrumentalist, and opportunistic, and less than entirely fulfilling for all involved. In this tale, the kings of the corporate castles had decided to offload their most menial operations to the lowest bidders, with barely a thought for the anonymous drones toiling in the windowless workshops of lands far away, and hardly more than disdain for the merchants presenting themselves at court to ply this tawdry trade. And then one day, the evil spell was magically broken. Corporate clients and outsourcing providers awoke in a shared state of enlightenment: from now on, they would recognize and respect their partners' needs, joining together in a spirit of trust and mutual enrichment; even those faceless workers could now come out into the sunlight, justly recognized for their "talent," and as collaborators in the joint enterprise of borderless innovation and value creation. Of course, everyone gets to live much happier ever after.

---

[22] This version of the story is told by the Economist Intelligence Unit (EIU, 2008: 5), but there are countless others, the path to redemption always beginning in the strictly instrumentalist time of labor arbitrage.

There are many versions of this story, and it is regularly embroidered in the retelling, but the directional narrative is quite invariant—it is an affirmative tale of progressive metamorphosis, from transactional to transformational relationships, from arbitrage to collaboration, from contract-bound instrumentalism to co-produced innovation.[23] What follow are several renditions of this tale, as seen from a range of subject positions within the outsourcing complex. There will be echoes and repetitions across these various tellings, of course, this being very much the point. They are recounted here in order to illustrate how such aspirational narratives are constructed and circulated. The basic arc comes in the form of an affirmative "history lesson":

> Today, [client] companies are talking about high-value activities that are actually going to drive innovation, and sustain their growth on a global basis. [This] is very different from the outsourcing that we started with back in 1990 ... What you had [then] was a number of senior executives in companies that were not performing very well, looking at under-performing parts of their operation, and saying, "Somebody else has to take this over and do it for us ... It is essentially broken within our business. Can't someone please come in and do this better for us?" So [outsourcing] was really *an intervention in problem areas of the business.* We have gone a long way from that to what is now a global driver ... of innovation and expanded services ...
>
> Outsourcing has become much more than simply labor arbitrage, in terms of looking for a low-cost location to have your work done, or asset transfer [in order] to improve your balance sheet ... The most important [advantage of] outsourcing, from a financial and business-management perspective, is the level of flexibility that it adds to a business ... It's really about getting to the point where you fully understand the dynamics of your potential partners' businesses, and how you can interact and create capabilities for them that will make them even better at doing what they do.[24]

A management consultant reproduces the received narrative by stating that "Outsourcing is going through a fundamental shift ... a massive change." Today, he continues, corporate

> clients are expecting much more than transactions at a low cost, and labor arbitrage ... The levers for transformation are moving from economies of location and economies of scale to economies of skill [so as] to ... create an organization that adds value to the business ... This is the beginning of a major generational shift ... You can call it outsourcing, but it's really more like a partnership ... It's about leveraging those partnerships to move strategy forward.[25]

---

[23] For variations on this familiar theme, see Engardio (2006), EIU (2008), and Justice (2012).

[24] Principal, outsourcing advisory firm, New York, interview by author, May 2013, emphasis added.

[25] Management consultant, global service provider, Phoenix, AZ, interview by author, February 2013.

These are widely shared aspirations, but they are aspirations nonetheless. The *desire* to "shift the focus away from cost [and secure more senior] executive involvement" is a practically ubiquitous one,[26] as is the *reality* that these are heavily commoditized markets, governed by downward price and margin pressures, in which the majority of engagements (still) tend to be instrumentalized, routinized, and pressurized.

The aspirational narrative itself has been around for quite some time. More than a decade ago, Jane C. Linder, a director of research at Accenture Institute, attempted to distill the essence of what was already being labeled "transformative outsourcing" in a guide for corporate executives, with the usual exhortations to senior management buy-in and "trusting partnership" with service providers. Even by this time, however, scores of competitors were selling generic or quick-fix versions of the same treatment.

> Transformational outsourcing has gained some currency right now. As a result, many outsourcing vendors are touting their work as transformational. In most cases, it is not...Just put the words *transformational outsourcing* in an Internet search engine, and you'll find that Compaq, Cognizant, Schlumberger, IBM global services, Alltel, Collaboratech, Cap Gemini, Ernst & Young, and others all claim they can transform their clients' businesses through outsourcing by implementing new technologies. This isn't it. Transformational outsourcing often requires that new technologies are implemented, but the defining factor isn't the new technology. It's the purposeful use of outsourcing to achieve dramatic enterprise-level change...Transformational outsourcing is very different from conventional outsourcing [which usually involves] cost reductions of 25 to 30 percent...[s]ervice improvements, like more responsive call centers...[i]mproved executive focus on core competencies [and access] to superior—and continually improving—skills and expertise of the outsourcing provider.[27]

The seductive vision being sold here is that of the outsourcer as a partner in enterprise-wide transformation, and a provider of strategic solutions.

While they know that they must always deliver on price, even to get a hearing, outsourcing providers are understandably keen to circulate versions of this story about themselves. A top executive from a major business-process outsourcing firm related his version of the narrative by recalling a time when his business was all about "mov[ing] work to the lowest-cost location and provid[ing] a value proposition," a time now ostensibly past:

> I remember, several years ago, the first of three questions I used to ask before we decided to go on a location (visit) was, "Is it a place where we get the best cost advantage?" If that question got ticked, that's a place to go. Then there was a second

---

[26] HfS Research (2012: 17); see also Engardio (2006) and Couto et al. (2008).
[27] Linder (2004: 30, 33).

question: "Is it a place that provides us with the kind of skills that [are] required?" If that question got ticked, then we said yes, the business case is there . . . As all boardroom conversations go, there was a third question always asked: "Is it a location that provides a strategic or a competitive advantage to the client?" Believe me, if that question *didn't* get ticked, we still went to the location, if the first two questions had got ticked, because of the kind of transactional work we were doing.

But very clearly that's moved on. Now we don't ask these questions in the same order. Now the *first* question that we ask ourselves is, "Is it a location which provides a strategic or a competitive advantage to our client?" And the second question is, "Is this a location that provides not just the skills, but provides *scalable* skills?" And that's the key word here, both in terms of the quality of hires and also in terms of the number of hires. And finally, the cost; cost is still important, but [the] business-delivery model [has become] pan-global. [Today] we're refining the solutions, understanding process efficiencies, benchmarking, best practices . . . all of that, to see: "Do we have a viable solution which really makes [the client] company *look good*?"[28]

Yet even as outsourcing products and customer expectations have become increasingly sophisticated, in a fundamental sense these remain add-ons to a business model where "cost is still important." In the absence of contractually guaranteed, upfront cost savings, the conversation between corporate clients and providers of outsourced solutions would probably not be taking place.

Nevertheless, the evolutionary narrative has both symbolic and motivational value, as an invocation of not only forward progress but higher purpose. At IAOP summits, this is effectively the authorized narrative, repeated in plenary after plenary. And here, a special place is reserved for those on the buyer side who have seen the light, and who opt to structure their relationships with vendors according to the preferred, partnership model. These truth tellers are there to validate the vision of the client as collaborator, as in the following presentation from the CEO of a healthcare company to an audience of outsourcers:

These are expressions that you probably recall, those of you who have been doing this for a while: "Your mess for less." It was pretty much a "back-office" game. It was transactions. IT led the way. It was big, heavy lifting . . . That, really, was outsourcing in the traditional definition, but that's changing rapidly . . . That model is dying . . . Today, it is about business value. Companies are opting in to a global business-services structure, not just because of low cost, but also because of the insights that a broad-spectrum global business-services organization can provide.[29]

Model clients such as these will often be paraded at the big conferences, invariably with their "enablers" from management-consulting or outsourcing-advisory

---

[28] Senior executive, transnational BPO provider, Orlando, FL, interview by author, February 2012.
[29] Buyer presentation, outsourcing workshop, Los Angeles, March 2014.

firms by their side. A common approach is for these inspirational cases to be presented in tandem, combining a buyer-side perspective with transferable lessons courtesy of the consultant.

To suggest that the particulars of such cases are being misrepresented, even if they are stylized to varying degrees, would be disingenuous. They are, however, clearly cherry picked for the purpose of illuminating a preferred vision of a value-adding trajectory for the industry. This trajectory is rendered concrete and credible in the (rather elusive) form of high-performance, "best in class" outsourcing arrangements—those that are achieved, according to the industry's own calculations (and its more candid discourse), in a relatively minor fraction of all engagements. These represent the cream of the crop, in other words, the best cases harvested from the 20 percent or so of outsourcing engagements that, across various measures and in industry talk, are rated by those involved to be performing well. Looking up to such cases speaks to a certain wishfulness—a "dream," perhaps—shared by many of those involved in the majority of more routine, cost-governed outsourcing arrangements. This is the daily reality for what might be called the bottom 80 percent, the majority of cases where one or both of the partners are barely satisfied or somewhat dissatisfied with how things are going. A 20:80 ratio of positive to more prosaic (or problematic) outsourcing relationships is of course nothing more than a rule of thumb, rather than a precisely calibrated figure, but approximations of this kind are regularly heard in the exchanges at industry conferences and in various surveys of clients and providers. One example is the measurement by HfS Research of the share of engagements that are judged to be delivering "collaborative" value added, as opposed to garden-variety cost saving. Again, 20 percent of engagements were found to meet this collaborative standard, the rest reflecting the relations of what was characterized as a "master/slave culture," along with its associated economics: "in spite of all the chest-pumping from providers on their revolutionary capabilities to turn their clients' business models on their heads, over half their clients still perceive them as brokers of cost-efficiency . . . not capability."[30]

It is in what are (quite literally) showcase examples that the best practices of transformative and collaborative outsourcing find their authentication. Witness to these, the lumpen classes of outsourcing paraprofessionals, those in the audience at industry conferences, inhabit a more humdrum world, one marked by perennially mixed results. Theirs are the everyday, "plain vanilla" engagements that really have no prospect of ever being featured as a consultant's case study. There may be a grouchy, demanding client at the end of a

---

[30] HfS Research (2015) 80% of outsourcing relationships fail to deliver collaborative value . . . so what can we do? *Horses for Sources* blog December 15, accessed at <http://www.horsesforsources.com/failure-to-collaborate_121315>, December 27, 2015.

persistently strained communications channel, and far too many terse emails and tense phone calls. These are the kinds of projects where providers are called in for what some on their side will jokingly refer to as CYA (cover your ass) meetings. There are times when the engagement itself is based on flawed and error-prone systems, which providers do not have the power, resources, or time to fix; they will often be governed by unrealistically tight or poorly structured contracts. To make matters worse, there might be the occasional security breach or loss of data. Nevertheless, year-on-year efficiency savings still have to be delivered, never mind the stresses and the high rates of labor turnover that inevitably follow. These engagements may be functional, but those managing them are unlikely to feel that they are going well. Yet the customers, even if they are not always right, feel empowered to ask for more. Corporate clients seem to want it all, providers will often complain. But why not? They have paid to be rid of the hassle of some of their less than core operations, and they expect to continue to save money while retaining control. They do not want "issues." They want each and every target to be met, financial as well as operational, while also expecting that vendors will be able to deliver process innovations and service improvements on very narrow margins. "Win–win" relationships and best-in-class engagements are—understandably—a rare accomplishment in this environment.[31]

As a result, there is a persistent undertow of dissatisfaction around those service level agreements (SLAs) that codify the contractual obligations and performance criteria for outsourcing engagements, which providers would prefer to be interpreted "realistically," constructively, and where necessary forgivingly, but which corporate buyers often feel at liberty to interpret more expansively, aggressively, or judgmentally. Essentially a tool of long-distance managerial discipline, SLAs take on a material form in the desktop dashboards that monitor on a continuous basis the vital signs of outsourcing engagements, disaggregated into key performance indicators. In practice, these seldom read green from top to bottom. Avoiding yellow (or worse, red) is a daily struggle for providers, and even on those days when the dashboard displays broadly on-target performance, client dissatisfaction may linger. Scheduled reviews of SLA targets are often occasions for "squeezing" providers, who have little option but to (try to) comply, in the context of what some in the outsourcing business will characterize as an enduring "master/slave culture."[32] As a seasoned outsourcing advisor summarized relational norms in

---

[31] See Manning, S., Silvia, M., and Lewin, A. Y. (2008) A dynamic perspective on next-generation offshoring: The global sourcing of science and engineering talent. *Academy of Management Perspectives* 22(3): 35–54. See also HfS Research (2012) and Oshri et al. (2011).

[32] See HfS Research (2014) Twelve tenets of trust. *Horses for Sources* blog, December 7, accessed at <http://www.horsesforsources.com/twelve-tenets-of-trust_120714>, December 27, 2015; HfS Research (2015) 80% of outsourcing relationships fail to deliver collaborative value...so what

the industry, "The common dynamic [is that] the dashboard is green but the customer sees red. Often, customers are in that situation, and they get really unhappy, and they want to blame the provider . . . for not meeting their . . . objectives." Merely meeting objectives and delivering to, rather than above, SLA targets just may not be enough. Some clients will reportedly say

> "Oh, you're just performing to the contract. You're not really doing what's required. You're not being flexible. You're not meeting our business objectives." Well, at the very least, the customer has contributed to that problem, by failing to make clear exactly what their objectives were, and to have those be reflected somewhere on the dashboard. For all you can say about who was supposed to do what, when, who was supposed to get paid for what, or not, there is *some* joint contribution to the situation, if only in that one party is not sufficiently articulating and communicating to the other what is it that isn't working, and why. In *every* outsourcing situation . . . there is *some* version of that going on.[33]

Understandably, customers that are seeing red are unlikely to be motivated to spend four days in the company of hundreds of outsourcing vendors and promoters at an IAOP summit or at other industry events of its ilk. Those that do attend from the buyer side are typically the kind of mid-level executives charged with the operational management of outsourcing projects, and with resolving or containing problems before they "escalate" to the point that they warrant attention from more senior colleagues. Top-tier executives from the corporate-buyer side are a relatively rare sight at the big outsourcing conferences, although they are easily identified by their prominent billing on the program (as plenary speakers, as award recipients, or as the subjects of celebratory success stories), and by the honeypot effect created wherever they go. In this respect, these gatherings mirror the competitive structure of the outsourcing complex as a whole, and the asymmetrical relationships between deal makers on the buy side, the "masters," and the much larger crowd of service-providing deal takers at the subordinate end of the supply chain, the "slaves."

At the bid stage, especially, providers face considerable pressure to court, if not pander to, corporate clients, while trimming their costs as close to the bone as they dare, in the full knowledge that the spectrum of consummated outsourcing engagements tends to run from the merely demanding to the outright difficult. Providers will sometimes live to regret winning some of the most fiercely contested contracts, if they have negotiated away too much of their margins. It is not uncommon for these to be barely profitable. Others will

---

can we do? *Horses for Sources* blog December 15, accessed at <http://www.horsesforsources.com/failure-to-collaborate_121315>, December 27, 2015.

[33] Senior outsourcing advisor, consulting firm, Boston, MA, interview by author, February 2012.

prove to be operationally far more problematic than anticipated, or they will be marred by system incompatibilities, interpersonal difficulties, or clashes of corporate culture. Even though most start out with the best of intentions, a great many will descend into troubled relationships, culminating in the business equivalent of a divorce; some were probably doomed from the start.

Married to the Task

As the Economist Intelligence Unit has stated, at the risk of understatement, "there are forces at work in outsourcing relationships that are particularly difficult to manage."[34] Outsourcers know that fairytale match-ups are the stuff of fantasy; this is mostly a world of less than happy marriages. The somewhat wishful line from those in leadership positions in the industry is that the more seasoned partners in outsourcing deals have worked their way through this: the superficial flings of the 1990s were something like an adolescent phase, leading predictably to a string of unsatisfactory and failed relationships; those who have been around the block a few more times have learned the lesson that stronger relationships are built upon give and take, honest communication, and mutual respect. Just because corporate buyers are in a position to drive very hard bargains, and to dominate the terms of the relationship, so the argument goes, this does not mean that they should take advantage in this way; furthermore, overbearing and controlling behavior is not likely to be in their best, long-term interests. The enduring reality of asymmetrical, buyer-driven relationships coupled with crowded provider markets means, however, that these high-road configurations—just like the proverbial happy marriage—are the exception rather than the rule.

Since outsourcing relationships are characteristically difficult, their frequent breakdown is hardly a matter of idiosyncratic, isolated problems. They are structurally prone, in fact, to various forms of controlling behavior on the part of dominant partners, and to evasive or defensive conduct on the part of weaker ones. What has become a track record of difficult and failed relationships is clearly a problem for the industry, hence the emphasis that is placed on learning how to make better outsourcing "marriages." IAOP is one of several organizations that market products designed to diagnose the "health" of outsourcing relationships, measuring their "vital signs" and providing suggestions, where necessary, for remedial intervention. Consultants and advisors will likewise frequently offer advice on how to "build trust" in outsourcing relationships. Ideally, this will be designed into sophisticated

---

[34] EIU (2008: 10).

governance arrangements from the start, which the partners ought to observe in spirit rather than simply to the letter. In the absence of such professional foresight, or plain good fortune, however, it may be necessary to realign or repair ongoing outsourcing engagements, if there are signs that things are going awry. The heavy-handed approach in such circumstances, which is certainly far from uncommon, involves bringing in the lawyers. Not only is this costly, it may also cause lasting or terminal damage to the relationship. An alternative path, just as when serious problems are identified in a marriage, is to turn instead to counseling and mediation. In the outsourcing business, this is known as "relationship management."

Those in the relationship-management field, most of whom will have many years of experience in different aspects of the outsourcing business, tend to have a rather different demeanor to their colleagues. They do not have the swagger of the self-styled "thought leaders," neither do they present themselves as the purveyors of all-purpose "solutions." Instead, theirs are third-party interventions of a much more subtle if not intimate kind, based on customized, patient mediation, and worldly wise, often *sotto voce*, counseling. The best of the relationship managers can be quite a draw at gatherings of outsourcing professionals, where they have a reputation for confronting some uncomfortable truths, but also for tackling commonplace problems in a constructive and thoughtful fashion. On one such occasion, a veteran in this relatively new discipline addressing an overflowing conference meeting room of anxious providers and weary buyers, began his presentation by itemizing a long list of recurring complaints. From the buyer side, these included: providers working to the letter of the contract; providers failing to anticipate or resolve problems quickly (or silently) enough; and providers coming up short on hoped-for quality improvements, or failing to take the initiative with new ideas. From the provider side, the litany of common complaints included: clients insisting on micro-managing the engagement; clients neglecting to clarify (their own) priorities and needs; clients failing to follow agreed procedures; and clients complaining constantly, such that, even when SLA targets are being met, "they are *still* complaining." To knowing nods around the room, and a more than few wry smiles, the relationship manager went on to ask, "Is there *anyone* in an outsourcing relationship today [who] is *not* experiencing these things? If not, you should get up and take a bow! These are the problems that are endemic to our industry. *Every* [outsourcing] relationship that I have seen has experienced some version of these, to a greater or lesser extent." The expert's subsequent description of a downward spiral into relationship failure was delivered empathetically, as if genuinely feeling the pain of both parties. This quickly transcended the formal terms of legal contracts and business systems, delving into the social and even psychological aspects of outsourcing engagements:

114

When you get into a difficult relationship, when things start to go south on you, it becomes self-reinforcing. Because when you are in a not-very-close [or] trusting relationship, you don't share as much information. And when you don't share... it becomes harder for the other side to come up with good answers, because they don't fully understand what the problems are. And when you've told them what your problem is and they are not coming up with good answers, it just reinforces your suspicion that they are not trying very hard to solve the problem. So you end up with a spiral downward. Because you don't trust, you don't share; because you don't share, they can't fix; and because they can't fix, you don't trust. And down and down it goes... In order to get out of these kinds of relationships, you actually have to take a step back... Why are we *in* this mess?[35]

Relationship managers are especially critical of those buyers that respond to problems in outsourcing engagements by resorting to the superficial fix of rotating the contract, the reflex too often being "let's bring in another service provider." Here, the advice is that clients should take a look at themselves, rather than simply blame the partner. A relationship manager explained her company's approach to this commonplace situation this way:

Well, if you're not happy with your first servicer provider, and you bring in another service provider, *what's going to happen*? We really try to get [corporate buyers] to think carefully about ensuring they are ready, psychologically, from a process perspective, from a business management perspective, before they take that step. When a relationship is in trouble, both sides usually have to do something.[36]

The growth of relationship management, which is just one part of an expanding infrastructure of third-party mediators, advisors, and consultants, is symptomatic of the ongoing challenges of "governance" in outsourcing engagements. These may include, but routinely exceed, those specified and regulated in formal contracts—even as the scale, scope, and sophistication of the latter have also been increasing.[37] (Contrary to the view that contractualization is part of the "solution," it is not surprising that many take the view that the growing size and complexity of contracts is a symptom of the anticipated failure or underperformance of outsourcing engagements, perversely helping to secure these very outcomes by placing additional burdens on already difficult relationships.) Rather unrealistically, optimal governance arrangements are reckoned to require not only unstinting senior-management commitment but also "relentless discipline" from all parties.[38] In practice, the goals may be more modest, even if

[35] Outsourcing governance specialist, workshop presentation, Orlando, FL, February 2012.
[36] Senior outsourcing advisor, Houston, TX, interview by author, May 2011.
[37] It has been claimed that the average IT outsourcing contract might be revised as many as 100 times in the first year of an engagement (senior outsourcing advisor, Houston, TX, interview by author, May 2011).
[38] Dalal, J. R. (2010) Reference article on governance. In IAOP, *Outsourcing Professional Body of Knowledge*. Zaltbommel: Van Haren, 319–31, p. 323.

they are still difficult to realize, like trying to keep the "noise levels" down, lest the neighbors might hear, or otherwise avoid the kind of "issue escalation" that brings interventions from senior management, third-party advisors, or lawyers.[39]

The leading advisory firm HfS runs a "governance academy," which while focused on the uplifting goal of "more progressive and collaborative enterprise buyer/service provider relationships," knowingly calls attention in its nomenclature to the underlying antagonisms and misaligned incentives that pervade outsourcing relationships: here, there are four levels of certification, running from yellow-belt status at the entry level through to the mark of mastery in this ostensibly martial art, the black belt.[40] Others in the relationship-management field tend to advocate rather more subtle, counseling-based interventions. There is no universal formula for a happy marriage, of course. The boutique consulting companies that work in this space understand that tightly written contracts—the outsourcing equivalent of a prenuptial agreement—can never be enough. And neither, on their own, are carefully crafted governance agreements, which—like wedding vows—may not always be honored.

In this context, effective outsourcing relationships are understood to be *social accomplishments*. There is good practice and good advice, but there are precious few standard fixes. Experience has revealed that the diagnosis of outsourcing relationship failures and the formulation of appropriate remediation strategies must both take place at the "granular, material" level, in the words of one relationship-management consultant.[41] Both parties must recognize that they have a problem; they have to "buy in," literally and metaphorically, since this is time-consuming, painstaking work, and because, if there is to be any chance of success, each must actively engage with the process. It is surely not a coincidence that one of the leaders in the relationship-management field is Vantage Partners, a consulting spinoff from the Harvard Negotiation Project, which draws on cross-practice expertise developed in Central American peacekeeping efforts, in constitution building in South Africa, and in deal making in professional sports.[42]

"While quality problems, missed deadlines, and scope overruns may appear to be the result of your provider misrepresenting its capabilities or understaffing the work," consultants at Vantage Partners argue, it is no less likely that these are quite predictable outcomes of companies "turning over a function

---

[39] IAOP (2010: 178).

[40] See HfS Research (n.d.) *HfS Governance Academy: Providing structure and a proven approach to governance.* Boston, MA: HfS Research, p. 1.

[41] Senior outsourcing advisor, Houston, TX, interview by author, May 2011.

[42] See Ertel, D., Enlow, S., Bubman, S., Merrigan, L., and Branum, A. (2008) *Vantage Guide to Governance in Outsourcing Relationships.* Boston, MA: Vantage Partners.

that was a mess from the start."[43] The oftentimes glib language of "solutions providing" is not only insufficient but inappropriate to this task of dealing with such stubborn challenges of real-world governance. In common with those consultants and advisors that overpromise on the basis of best-practice models, relationship managers may be prone to exaggerating their healing powers, as they are also in the business of building markets for their services. An important distinction, though, is that relationship managers are retailing boutique, engagement-specific services, not wholesale, transferable fixes. A premium is consequently placed on careful diagnosis and context-specific advice, hence the need properly to learn from those with access to the "dirty little secrets of outsourcing," as one of Vantage's competitors in the relationship-management business called them. This counseling specialist would liken the work of uncovering these secrets, and then addressing them, to the delicate work of marriage counseling, or "what we [call] relationship mediation." Once again, the analogy hardly seems far-fetched:

> Some people would say that failure in outsourcing is a lawsuit, or [taking] the services back in house...I think about it in a different way: it's an example of a relationship where there is a complete trust breakdown between the two parties. But they are still married to the contract, and they have to stay together in a frustrated, often angry relationship...

> [I recall] a situation where a service provider and a client had been together for about three years. They are not doing very well together. [The] service provider and the [buyer side] executive [both] came to us jointly paid for help with their relationship. (The alternative, which is to cancel the relationship is very expensive; it's filled with risk, and both executives look bad when that happens.)

> When they came in...they disagreed about *everything*...The [buyer side] executive's desk was two piles of paper—*this high!*—and he sat in the middle. These were all issues that his people had brought to him because they couldn't solve them on their own. They were ready to part ways, so this was a last-ditch effort...If you're asking me who was the most culpable, most responsible for the problems in this relationship, without any doubt it was about 80% the [buyer side] client. The service provider had processes, but nobody was following them. It was very frustrating...

> We redesigned all their processes...We brought both teams together...We must have had 40 people [there, having] each owner of each process walk it through... When we left this engagement...we thought there is no way this client will *ever* resolve these situations...But we came to find out that it worked...It takes time; it's not something you just do, you have to *live it*...They worked on their process... What did it save them? It saved them getting divorced.[44]

---

[43] Enlow, S. and Bubman, J. (2010) Spotting and diagnosing issues in outsourcing ties. *Outsourcing* 21: 10–13, p. 2.

[44] Relationship-management consultant, outsourcing workshop, Cartagena, Colombia, May 2011.

Outright ruptures in governance or systems are typically covered by the formal terms of outsourcing contracts, but the root cause of these problems is often traced to the wider array of extra-contractual relationship failures, dysfunctions, and inefficiencies that are commonly grouped under the heading "rules of engagement," the diverse means that are used to "*socialize* the contractual terms within the [outsourcing] organization."[45] Together, these socialization failures are major causes of what, from a management perspective, is regarded as "value leakage" within outsourcing engagements. IAOP's version of industry lore—and here there is no incentive to exaggerate, quite the contrary—is that the partners in six out of every ten outsourcing engagements report squandering one tenth or more of the total value of contracts as a result of "*poor relationships* between the customer and the provider."[46] Furthermore, around one half of all outsourcing projects are reckoned to be struggling, in an ongoing way, with the consequences of excessive labor turnover and/or what are deemed to be unacceptable levels of service quality; in more than a third, the partners report problems with operational inefficiencies, data security, and/or loss of managerial control.[47] This, in other words, is difficult work.

Consulting Visions, Market Realities

The consulting companies were amongst the first of the "opportunists of outsourcing," having figured out early on that there was money to be made in helping to construct bridges between "cheap labour and rich clients."[48] Consultants are invariably amongst the first on the scene when it comes to promoting new managerial paradigms, projects, and fads, but in the case of offshore outsourcing this understates what has evolved into a systemic, symbiotic, and in many respects necessary presence. In the age of the increasingly disaggregated corporation, consultants have been drawn deeply into new territories of "relational work," as mediators and enablers in the risk-filled realm that Fincham aptly portrays as "extruded management."[49] As "outsourcing turn[ed] companies inside out," management consultants were on hand to assist, soon transforming their own operations in the process.[50] Consultants ply their trade, and make their markets, amid the churn of organizational

---

[45] Dalal, J. R. (2010) Reference article on governance. In IAOP, *Outsourcing Professional Body of Knowledge*. Zaltbommel: Van Haren, 319–31, p. 321, emphasis added.
[46] IAOP (2010: 164), emphasis added.   [47] See Manning et al. (2011).
[48] Buffington (2007: 35); O'Mahoney and Markham (2013: 66).
[49] Fincham, R. (2003) The agent's agent. *International Studies of Management and Organization* 32(4): 67–86.
[50] Kripalani, M. (2006) Five offshore practices that pay off. *Business Week* January 30, 60–1, p. 60.

change, finding opportunity and profit on the shifting terrains of competitive imperative and executive insecurity.[51] As Andrew Sturdy has pointed out, the work of successive waves of "change implementation," especially where that work involves the introduction of new technologies and employment systems, has been parlayed into significant revenue sources for the largest management-consulting firms, markets that in the last two decades have been co-produced with the "emergence of offshoring and outsourcing consultancy."[52]

The long ascendancy of offshore outsourcing has prompted an organic transformation of the consulting sector, which has moved swiftly to capitalize upon market opportunities at the nexus of information technology, corporate disaggregation, and managerial restructuring-cum-extrusion. Early on, the big consulting firms established fields of practice around offshore outsourcing, where they would leverage experience-based knowledge acquired across projects, learning by doing, subsequently folding these lessons into ongoing roles in successive rounds of offshore investment. Having played a part in opening these markets, the consulting firms would then pursue economies of scale and scope to grow their own operations, often through mergers and acquisitions. The consulting sector and the outsourcing complex have consequently been subject to a kind of mutual colonization, resulting in increasingly blurred boundaries between multinational consulting operations (Accenture, Alsbridge, CGI, Deloitte, Kelly, Mercer, PA, Siemens IT Solutions and Services, and countless others), data-systems and accounts-processing firms (like ADP, EDS, IBM, HP, and SAP), and big players in the customer-relations management and call-center business (such as Convergys, Firstsource, Genpact, Keane, Oracle, and Salesforce).

Management consultants were characteristically quick to capitalize on the "gold rush" phase of outsourcing, the initial push into offshore territories, when the challenge was one of maximizing the potential of labor arbitrage while stitching together distended organizational networks and supply chains. They were subsequently able to "surviv[e] the first wave of discontent,"[53] which was shaped not only by the political backlash across many of the higher-wage countries but also by an elevated level of skepticism on the part of some buy-side executives. Windfall savings on labor costs were easily harvested at first, but this sometimes came at a high price. Soon, buy-side managers were learning about the knot of operational and managerial

---

[51] See Sturdy, A. (1997) The consultancy process: an insecure business. *Journal of Management Studies* 34(3): 389–413; Sturdy, A., Clark, T., Fincham, R., and Handley, K. (2004) Silence, procrustes and colonization: A response to Clegg et al.'s "Noise, parasites and translation: Theory and practice in management consulting." *Management Learning* 35(3): 337–40.

[52] Sturdy, A. (2012) The future research agenda. In M. Kipping and T. Clark, eds, *The Oxford Handbook of Management Consulting*. New York: Oxford University Press, 467–85, pp. 471–2.

[53] EIU (2008: 5).

challenges known as the "hidden costs of outsourcing," from loss of effective control to system failures.[54] These were hardly trade secrets; some of the failures were spectacular. When IBM botched a $5 billion IT outsourcing engagement with JP Morgan Chase, for example, a new word had to be coined to account for what had happened: less than two years into what was supposed to have been a seven-year mega deal, the entire operation was expensively "backsourced" to the finance company.[55]

Yet while there were some notable backward steps like this, the generalized forward momentum was much stronger. Some of this was enabled by the earlier build-out of a supporting infrastructure for offshore outsourcing projects, into which the big consulting companies themselves had sunk some major investments in the shape of senior staff, technology, and systems. Meanwhile, as attention began to turn to the effective management and governance of outsourcing projects, and as their scale and complexity increased, consultants were being increasingly called upon to provide extended forms of assistance and advice, deep into the shadowlands of project implementation and management. In the process, consulting firms have taken on increasingly organic roles in the programmatic *realization* of outsourcing programs, by way of a wide range of advisory, intermediation, and partnership models, and by blending their operations with those of a new generation of global service providers. But if outsourcing has been turning corporations "inside out," it was leading consulting firms to pull the outside in, by ingesting functions like IT servicing and project governance. In the early stages, the work of consultants had been concentrated at the front end (and design stages) of outsourcing projects, where they operated in a more conventional manner as purveyors of strategic advice. Increasingly, however, such "pure" consulting assignments amount to no more than a trivial share of the burgeoning outsourcing market (on some counts, barely 1 percent of its total value), as consulting firms have found that they must provide strategic advice as a loss leader, in anticipation of lucrative, longer-term delivery, management, and advisory roles in the projects themselves.[56] Consultants are no longer merely the arrangers of outsourcing marriages; their work on project delivery means that they are in bed with both parties, with clients and with vendors.

This is a relationship, however, in which the corporate client continues to call most of the shots. In buyer-driven outsourcing chains, where there is vigorous competition amongst vendors and service providers—very much

[54] See Barthelemy, J. (2001) The hidden costs of IT outsourcing. *MIT Sloan Management Review* 42(3): 60–9; Manning et al. (2011).

[55] See Overby, S. (2005) Backsourcing pain. *CIO Magazine* 18(22): 13–19.

[56] O'Mahoney and Markham (2013: 66). See also Overby, S. (2012) Beware the commoditization of IT outsourcing. *CIO Magazine* November 30, accessed at <http://www.cio.com/article/2390002/outsourcing/beware-the-commoditization-of-it-outsourcing.html>, December 30, 2015.

the standard arrangement—this means that there is little to prevent the creeping commoditization of even relatively sophisticated projects, such as those IT-intensive engagements in which consulting firms are heavily invested. As industry analyst Stephanie Overby has remarked, "IT leaders say they want more than just lower costs from their IT outsourcing relationships, yet they [continue to] treat the process no differently than if they were trying to get the best deal on a gross of number two pencils."[57] As a partner in a leading advisory and consulting firm has complained, clients are not only negotiating hard on price and speed of service, inscribing these arrangements in contracts and SLAs, advisory functions themselves are now increasingly commoditized:

> [W]e are starting to see a push to commoditize the advisors [those who would have been] most likely fuel [new] thinking and drive positive change in this area. [If the goal is] unlocking value, the thought-leading advisors should be in a position to help their clients . . . [Instead, an example] that stands out involved a very good advisor who was competed on costs and speed to contract when the client retained them . . . The client clearly envisioned using a commodity buying process, which was the first mistake. When you have a deal whose success requires as much internal change as this one did, it is not even close to [a] commodity. The client then evaluated advisors on the basis of which one could run this process the fastest and at the lowest cost.[58]

Despite the inherent complexity of outsourced relationships, not least their social and organizational complexity, which in reality means that they are "not even close to [a] commodity," they have nevertheless been subject to commoditization, by virtue of market structure and dynamics. In principle, genuinely commodities should be not only fungible but also amenable to comprehensive and exhaustive description by contract. In contrast, outsourcing relationships are frequently "elusive" from a contractual perspective; in the words of this advisor, they commonly contain "*shadow requirements* that are unspoken or poorly understood and [which are also] never meaningfully vetted during the buy process [such as] innovation, partnership, proactivity."[59]

It is no coincidence that the latter, "non-contractualizable" aspects of outsourcing relationships are, ironically, amongst the most valued; in fact,

---

[57] Overby, S. (2012) Beware the commoditization of IT outsourcing. *CIO Magazine* November 30, accessed at <http://www.cio.com/article/2390002/outsourcing/beware-the-commoditization-of-it-outsourcing.html>, December 30, 2015, p. 1.

[58] Edward Hansen, partner at Barker and McKenzie, quoted in Overby, S. (2012) Beware the commoditization of IT outsourcing. *CIO Magazine* November 30, accessed at <http://www.cio.com/article/2390002/outsourcing/beware-the-commoditization-of-it-outsourcing.html>, December 30, 2015, p. 1.

[59] Edward Hansen, quoted in Overby, S. (2012) Beware the commoditization of IT outsourcing. *CIO Magazine* November 30, accessed at <http://www.cio.com/article/2390002/outsourcing/beware-the-commoditization-of-it-outsourcing.html>, December 30, 2015, p. 2, emphasis added.

they are practically the *definition* of high-road engagements. That these are contractually elusive and achieved only exceptionally is not for want of trying on the part of providers, it must be said, but follows from the structure of competitive relationships in the industry. Prominent figures like Edward Hansen maintain that there are "basic flaws" in the economic model of outsourcing that render relationships systematically vulnerable to commoditization. This has the capacity to corrode even the most robust of provider–client relationships. Hansen recalled one such instance, in which there were "solid green SLAs and a well-drafted agreement, but [the client was] unhappy [due to a] lack of innovation and partnership." Commoditized aspects of the relationship may have appeared to be working, but those had the effect of reducing the provider to the level of a substitutable, *and replaceable*, market supplier. No wonder that meaningful partnership and shared innovation were to remain elusive aspects of this contract:

> Viewing this relationship through the commodity lens, it was a tremendous success. The services that could be fully described in a contract were, and for those services it didn't really matter who the provider was. [However] one could argue that the real value of doing a capital "O" outsourcing is not in the ability to get the commodity work done, but rather in having a relationship with a strategic partner who is involved in your day-to-day activities. That's what this client was really after, and that's what the provider was really after. But the contract and pricing model did not support that type of relationship.[60]

A recurrent image of such insider discourse in the outsourcing business is that of partners trapped in a dysfunctional relationship. Attempts to transform these engagements—even those initiated by the dominant partner, the client—are often stymied by resort to the same blunt instrument that caused the relationship to be stunted in the first place: blunt contractual regulation of a more-than-contractual relationship. Under these circumstances, clients will tend to pressurize providers to deliver innovation, partnership, and proactivity, by way of "brute force behavioral corrections [such as] SLA credits [and] contracts that go on for thousands of pages," a response that is more likely to reinforce what Hansen graphically characterized as the "death spiral" into commoditization.[61]

So while there was an initial rush to "take" outsourcing markets, occupying and thriving in those markets has proved to be challenging—and perhaps *increasingly* challenging, as the vendor side has become ever more crowded

---

[60] Quoted in Overby, S. (2012) Beware the commoditization of IT outsourcing. *CIO Magazine* November 30, accessed at <http://www.cio.com/article/2390002/outsourcing/beware-the-commoditization-of-it-outsourcing.html>, December 30, 2015, pp. 4–5.

[61] Quoted in Overby, S. (2012) Beware the commoditization of IT outsourcing. *CIO Magazine* November 30, accessed at <http://www.cio.com/article/2390002/outsourcing/beware-the-commoditization-of-it-outsourcing.html>, December 30, 2015, p. 3.

and competitive. Strong market positions have proven to be difficult to defend, even for first movers on the vendor side. The extensive presence of intermediaries like consultants and advisors can be read as an indicator of serious "imperfections" in outsourcing markets. The structural positioning of consultants and advisors, in turn, is a measure of the contradictions and tensions in outsourcing relationships, which appear to be endemic. Amongst the many ironies here is the fact that it is consultants, operating in their cerebral and strategic mode, who will lead the chorus on now familiar refrains about the historical upgrading of the outsourcing model. For more than a decade now, there have been regular pronouncements of the advent of "off-shoring 2.0," or some other "new generation" configuration, which might be branded as transformative outsourcing, "globalization X," or "new-gen" part-nerships.[62] These visions of metamorphosis may in fact be necessary illusions for those in the outsourcing business that must grapple, in reality, with quite contradictory dynamics of commoditization, not to mention the ongoing challenges of governance and (even) delivery. The configuration of outsour-cing markets is such that the burden of augmented and value-adding engage-ments is invariably shouldered by providers, by the weaker partners in these buyer-driven supply chains. Providers find that it is they who must underwrite the costs of "next-generation" outsourcing relationships, funding process innovations and service improvements from their own, already compressed, margins. Value-adding initiatives are therefore often "lost" to the market, as this year's service enhancement becomes next year's client expectation (or contractual demand).

There are occasions, especially at industry conferences, when these contra-dictory dynamics—between the desire for upgrading versus the downward pull of contractual and market conditions—are neatly crystallized. At one such event, a workshop on what were immodestly advertised "new-gen" outsourcing arrangements, a consultant sat side by side with his model client, in this case from a leading insurance-services company in the United States. The consultant introduced the session with an uplifting speech about the new paradigm of "high-value...transformational outsourcing," replete with the usual keywords about shared innovation, where "customers and vendors are now willing to co-create," sustained by the archetypal contrast to the bad old days of "staff augmentation [and] labor arbitrage as the means of value."[63] Attempting to stay on message, the client's version of this story then took the

---

[62] These are recurring features of practically every vision of the future of outsourcing. For examples, see Linder (2004); Engardio (2006); EIU (2008), Couto et al. (2008), Justice (2012); Mukherji, P. (2013) Trends likely to impact global sourcing in 2013. *Avasant Globalization X* January 31, accessed at <http://www.globalizationx.com/global-sourcing-trends-in-2013/>, March 13, 2013.

[63] Partner, consulting firm, outsourcing workshop, Orlando, FL, February 2012.

form of a "tale of two contracts," in which one of the vendors used by the company had risen to the challenge of innovation, while the other remained trapped in a transactional mindset. In the subsequent Q&A, a curious provider who had been sitting in the audience attempted to get to the bottom of how this "next-gen" contract was actually structured:

> CORPORATE BUYER: Both companies we do business with have a substantial innovation task in their contracts... One of my vendors takes it as a price discount or price concession, so they don't really work hard on innovation. My other contractor takes it to heart. They had a target of $780,000 worth of innovative savings for last year. They did $1.8 million.
>
> PROVIDER: So [the contract terms are] based on the actual savings?
>
> CORPORATE BUYER: Yes, they come to me with innovative ideas and we agree, jointly, what I have got to pay for that product or that service. Sometimes they need help from third parties. So there is [an initial] cash outlay on my part, maybe paying them extra time to do that, and then we agree on the overall cost savings.
>
> PROVIDER: So it's a reward to them, basically?
>
> CORPORATE BUYER: No, it's not really a reward. We don't reward people. It prevents them from having to pay a penalty. [Audience laughter] For both of them [the two providers], if they don't innovate there is a financial penalty. The other [provider] takes the penalty every year.[64]

Clients may engage service providers as "partners in innovation," but they do so largely at their discretion, at their prerogative. The capacity to give and to take penalties is never evenly distributed in outsourcing engagements, even under such virtually best-case conditions, where an enlightened buyer is seeking to share the "innovation task." This can be seen as a new manifestation of what in orthodox economics is known as the principal-agent problem, where a misalignment of interests produces excess monitoring costs and then less, rather than more, co-produced innovation.[65] With the commoditization of outsourcing relationships, trust and innovation are lost to the market. And here, basic conditions of asymmetry—in information, control, and ultimately power—are at issue. As a seasoned outsourcing advisor put it, "I'm not going to say that there aren't some instances of bad faith, [of] customers who are trying to take advantage, or providers that are trying to get away with something. By and large, people are trying in good faith to do what they think their obligations are, and what makes sense for their company."[66] Between the

---

[64] Corporate buyer and service provider, outsourcing workshop, Orlando, FL, February 2012.

[65] See Keil, P. (2005) Principal agent theory and its application to analyze outsourcing of software development. *ACM SIGSOFT Software Engineering Notes*, Association for Computing Machinery, 30(4): 1–5.

[66] Senior outsourcing advisor, consulting firm, Boston, MA, interview by author, February 2012.

different parties in outsourcing engagements, however, "what makes sense" is seldom perfectly aligned.

There is little doubt that the *desire* for transformative upgrading amongst those in the outsourcing complex is real enough, but it exists more as a pervasive cultural condition than a material accomplishment. These are conditions born not of bad faith, but of the very "market realities" on which the instrumentalist economics of outsourcing are predicated. The consulting industry, for its part, may have helped to articulate a vision of a win–win future, but it has not been able to deliver this vision on a generalized basis. Ironically, the more that the consulting firms were themselves drawn into the heavy-lifting work of project delivery, the clearer it would become that the dynamic was toward the compression of margins and costs, toward structural commoditization, rather than toward upgrading and value adding. The consulting firms-cum-outsourcing providers certainly discovered a path toward higher revenues, but this did not result in higher rates of profit. "[W]ith margins getting tighter and the competition becoming more intense," O'Mahoney and Markham have observed, "the outsourcing market is not as profitable as it was in the 1990s" for the consulting companies, the largest of which have nevertheless sunk significant costs into what have become massive revenue generators.[67]

Similar patterns have been replicated across industries, occupations, and market segments. Outsourcing is a carrier of commoditization tendencies. According to the most systematic data source, Duke University's Offshoring Research Network, the degree of commoditization is highest in call-center operations, followed by the next most routinized, standardized, and "codable" functions (IT, finance and accounting, human resources, and engineering), after which come some of the sectors in which outsourcing has only more recently established a presence (procurement, product design, R&D, legal services, marketing and sales, and analytics), where the pulses of commoditization are currently weaker.[68] Crucially, however, commoditization is intensifying in each and every one of these fields. Likewise, leading advisors continue to talk of the risk of "races to the bottom" in some of the higher value-added markets, like BPO.[69] Aspirational visions of next-generation outsourcing will always try to position innovation-rich, "best in class" engagements as indicators of some leading-edge transformation, even as on some measures 90 percent or more of these relationships remain fundamentally predicated on the objective of "labor cost savings," closely followed

---

[67] O'Mahoney and Markham (2013: 67).   [68] See Manning et al. (2011).
[69] HfS Research (2015) Traumatic 2016…Survive the race to the bottom! *Horses for Sources* blog December 24, accessed at <http://www.horsesforsources.com/race-to-bottom_122415>, December 28, 2015.

by "other cost savings."[70] Far from transcending commoditization, outsourcing is a commoditization machine.

IAOP, the peak organization of the outsourcing complex, likes to present itself as "the association with collaboration at its core." It would be more accurate to say that outsourcing is an activity with competition at its core, and often quite destructive competition at that. More than a dirty word, outsourcing can also be a dirtier and more difficult business than many market participants care to acknowledge—at least publicly. As much as all those involved would prefer to believe that the days of cost compression and labor arbitrage are mere vestiges of some primal "outsourcing 1.0," the reality is that this remains a zone of constitutive *and deepening* commoditization. As thousands of vendors and hundreds of locations have jumped onto, and attempted to climb up, the outsourcing value chain, downward pressure on costs, wages, and margins has predictably intensified. As the reach of outsourcing models has been extended from back-office to middle-office functions, from relatively menial to increasingly complex operations, and from peripheral to ever more central, value-adding domains, this has not been an occasion for an upward transformation *of* outsourcing but for its reverse—commoditization and routinization *through* outsourcing.

The leadership of the outsourcing industry recycles the fantasy of self-transformation in the hope that, one day, this wish might come true. It is not for some lack of will, or even of capacity, that value-adding metamorphosis remains for the most part a dream. Rather, this is a systematic outcome of the unforgiving competitive dynamics in this buyer-driven market, where excess supply coexists with a climate of price competition and narrow(ing) margins. In this environment, providers are incentivized to bid low and then pursue economies of scale and relentless rationalization, thereby reproducing the cycle of commoditization. Premium engagements, from time to time, may be structured for quality and innovation, rather than cost suppression, but corporate buyers will often discount these later (with the same or competing vendors). If there is something that actually unifies an outsourcing complex otherwise inescapably divided by competition, by geography, and by corporate loyalties, it may be the shared state of cognitive dissonance that is evidently sustained, against the odds, between an uplifting imaginary and a far more prosaic reality. This state of dissonance is no doubt symptomatic of the keenly felt need for a redemption narrative in what seems destined to remain a politically blighted and organizationally strained field, in which professionalization and metamorphosis appear as pathways not just to market advantage but to professional (and maybe even social) respectability.

---

[70] Manning, S., Silvia, M., and Lewin, A. Y. (2008) A dynamic perspective on next-generation offshoring: The global sourcing of science and engineering talent. *Academy of Management Perspectives* 22(3): 35–54, figure 1; see also IAOP (2015).

5

Between Backshore and Nearshore

In late May 2011, a mile-wide tornado ripped through the town of Joplin, Missouri, claiming more than 160 lives, destroying almost one quarter of the town and causing damage to most of the structures that were left standing. The EF-5 multiple-vortex tornado would eventually be assessed as the most costly in U.S. history, with losses amounting to $2.8 billion. The storm would turn much of Joplin into "empty space."[1] Declared a federal disaster area, the town of 50,000 lost 500 businesses to the storm. Most would eventually rebuild and reopen, although this would be a slow process. One of those to see opportunity amidst the devastation was Onshore Technology Services (OTS), a Missouri-based company established in 2005 by Shane Mayes, who had earlier followed his wife to medical school in the area, detaching himself from a knowledge-economy career in the process. Having previously worked for a U.S. publishing firm, Mayes had experience of managing a dispersed workforce of around 150 IT staff, most of whom were located in outsourcing centers in India. "That was my job," he has said, "to make offshore outsourcing work, and it didn't bring me any joy."[2] Mayes' new mission in life, by all accounts, he would find considerably more rewarding. It was to become one of the first movers in the would-be industry of "rural sourcing," taking the logic of offshoring full circle by effectively bringing it home.[3] When OTS got started, "There was no such thing as an industry called rural outsourcing," and many were skeptical that Mayes could "take underemployed, dislocated workers and retool them software developers and IT developers," transforming lives that had apparently been reduced, even before the storm hit, to a "state of brokenness."[4] After the tornado, OTS was amongst the first in line with its pledge to help rebuild the broken town.

---

[1] Vigeland, T. (2012) Lessons from another storm. *New York Times* November 14: F1.
[2] Shane Mayes, CGI America Stories 2011, Clinton Global Initiative, accessed at <https://onshoreoutsourcing.com/onshore_news/onshore_has_an_american_story>, January 12, 2015.
[3] See Lacity and Rottman (2012).
[4] Shane Mayes, CGI America Stories 2011, Clinton Global Initiative, accessed at <https://onshoreoutsourcing.com/onshore_news/onshore_has_an_american_story>, January 12, 2015.

Within a few weeks of the storm, Mayes was sharing the stage with former president Bill Clinton, whose Clinton Global Initiative (CGI) was founded on a commitment to find collaborative solutions to the "world's most pressing problems," its domestic operation seeking to address the challenge of rekindling "economic growth, long-term competitiveness, and social mobility in the United States."[5] At the CGI America meeting in Chicago, Mayes made a public commitment to create 1,000 jobs in rural Missouri within five years, focused strategically on Joplin, where the OTS office was taking on new staff within days of the storm. Clinton praised OTS for the part that it was playing in "keeping information technology jobs, which are routinely outsourced to other countries, in the United States," explaining to the audience of corporate executives, politicians, and civic leaders that "This is a model for all of you who care about this part of our country which has consistently suffered higher unemployment and lower income gains over the last 20 or 30 years. I ask you all to keep this in mind."[6] In Mayes' appearance with the former president, which earned him a spot on *Good Morning America*, the entrepreneur boasted that, "We've got a job-creation engine that works," a company representative later explaining to reporters that the OTS model was "to build outsourcing centers in rural Missouri [where] the cost of living is low and we can compete with offshore firms," one that might be replicated in other states so as to create as many as 12,000 additional jobs across rural America.[7]

CGI's model is based on securing "commitments" from thousands of members, partners, and allies around the world, who are then responsible for fundraising and, above all, "delivery." Consequently, it would fall to Shane Mayes and OTS to do their part in "revitalizing rural America," having taken maximum advantage of the networking and profile-raising opportunities provided by Clinton's CGI caravan, an experience that Mayes compared to "drinking out of a fire hose."[8] According to its publicly released CGI commitment to action, OTS would work to

> extend its proven rural workforce development model to rapidly build an IT education and job ecosystem in Joplin and Macon, Missouri. Onshore already has facilities and teams working in these communities. Working with local and statewide resources, Onshore will refactor key processes in order to scale to 1,000

[5] See the CGI mission at <https://www.clintonfoundation.org/clinton-global-initiative/about-us/cgi-mission>, accessed January 3, 2015.

[6] Bill Clinton, quoted in Associated Press (2011) Jobs push will help tornado-ravaged Joplin, Mo., former president Bill Clinton says. *AL.com* June 29, accessed at <http://blog.al.com/wire/2011/06/jobs_push_will_help_tornado-ra.html>, January 12, 2015.

[7] Shane Mayes and Ron Just, quoted in Associated Press (2011) Jobs push will help tornado-ravaged Joplin, Mo., former president Bill Clinton says. *AL.com* June 29, accessed at <http://blog.al.com/wire/2011/06/jobs_push_will_help_tornado-ra.html>, January 12, 2015.

[8] Shane Mayes, CGO America Stories 2011, Clinton Global Initiative, accessed at <https://onshoreoutsourcing.com/onshore_news/onshore_has_an_american_story>, January 12, 2015.

people in Missouri. This proof-of-scale in Joplin and Macon will then eventually be replicated to 12 rural markets across the nation . . . To generate immediate demand, Onshore Technology Services will present this rural sourcing initiative to its existing and prospective clients as a multi-bottom line investment opportunity to help: 1) heal Joplin, 2) revitalize rural America, 3) provide opportunities for low-income women, and 4) reduce [client companies'] domestic IT sourcing costs by 25–35%.[9]

With the Joplin tornado having "wiped out over 4,000 jobs in an instant," in a town that had already been struggling to gain a foothold in the new economy, the immediate challenge was to "stave off a Katrina-like exodus of workers," after which there would be an opportunity to address the needs of the country's 60 million rural residents, whose communities had been "overshot by the economic prosperity ushered in by the knowledge economy." The OTS commitment would be based on a significant upscaling of its rural-sourcing model, presented as an "education and job ecosystem" for small-town America, the depressed business and wage costs of which could be repurposed as a virtue if these locations could be sold as a "low-cost alternative to offshore outsourcing."[10] The company anticipated that it would engage a range of "partners" in this wider task, not least state and local government agencies across the country, which were expected to jump at the distinctive economic development opportunities presented by rural sourcing.

And so the rural-sourcing model was born in the United States, as a belated counter to the much larger "exodus" of jobs to offshore locations. Beginning with the rapid ascendancy of this putative model, the political allure of which continues to exceed its measurable, on-the-ground impact, this chapter explores some of the "backwash" effects that have arisen in the wake of the global outsourcing movement. If Chapter 4 identified some of the tensions and contradictions at the very heart of the outsourcing complex, the attention here shifts to some of its developmental fringes. While the promise of "onshoring" has been exaggerated—such that OTS and its peers have remained essentially boutique operations, for all the disproportionate attention that they have received, not least from U.S. presidents, past and present—the "return" to what are now commonly known as nearshore locations, in Latin America and in Central and Eastern Europe (CEE), has been far more consequential. While Shane Mayes and OTS have struggled valiantly to realize their ambitious plans for rural revitalization, falling some way behind the pace anticipated by their CGI commitments, a new generation of "nearshore"

---

[9] CGI America (n.d.) Rural outsourcing: 1,000 tech jobs in Missouri; Commitment by Onshore Outsourcing. *Clinton Global Initiative*, accessed at <https://www.clintonfoundation.org/clinton-global-initiative/commitments/rural-outsourcing-1000-tech-jobs-missouri>, January 12, 2015.

[10] CGI America (n.d.) Rural outsourcing: 1,000 tech jobs in Missouri; Commitment by Onshore Outsourcing. *Clinton Global Initiative*, accessed at <https://www.clintonfoundation.org/clinton-global-initiative/commitments/rural-outsourcing-1000-tech-jobs-missouri>, January 12, 2015.

economies in Colombia, El Salvador, and elsewhere have been experiencing extremely high rates of growth.[11] This is another illustration of the way in which global outsourcing has been a disruptive force, and one that has been carving out new economic geographies, rather than simply inaugurating a unidirectional process of capital flight.

On the Rural Frontier

A bundle of strategies variously known as insourcing, backsourcing, rural or domestic sourcing, onshoring, and reshoring—each of which has a different emphasis, but which all index qualitative adaptations in outsourcing practice—emerged after the mid-2000s, as the global sourcing business experienced its very own rounds of spatial restructuring. Some of the drivers here have been endogenous, as competitive dynamics across the outsourcing complex have led to the opening up of new investment sites and offshore development models. But part of the impetus has also been political, as a premium of sorts has been placed on initiatives that work against, or at least around, the negative framing of offshore outsourcing, particularly in the United States.[12] In a deeper sense, though, this drive for reinvention—or at the very least rebranding—is another manifestation of the *condition* of the outsourcing complex, both in terms of competitive dynamics and discursive representation. Once again, this would involve reflexive turns against the labor-arbitrage model of "outsourcing 1.0," at least rhetorically, but once more these efforts have revealed some of the limits of such projects of self-transformation.[13] As Chapter 4 indicated, the outsourcing complex remains trapped in this extended moment of frustrated reinvention, as the drag of price-based competition and commoditization has remained stubbornly entrenched, with the result that narratives of rebirth and reconstruction are often no more than that—rhetorical, anticipatory, and mostly unrequited. One illustration of this somewhat forlorn condition, as well as the fact that the industry may be exhausting its supply of neologisms, was McKinsey's attempt to launch the concept of "next-shoring," as another new-generation model this time premised on "proximity to demand and proximity to innovation," and reflecting the hope, finally, of slipping the leash of labor-arbitrage offshoring.[14] Outsourcers are always on the lookout for the next shore.

[11] See KPMG (2014) *A New Latin American Rhythm: The transformation of the global outsourcing business*. São Paulo: KPMG; KPMG (2009) *Nearshore Attraction: Latin America beckons as a global outsourcing destination*. São Paulo: KPMG.

[12] These were discussed in detail in Chapter 3.

[13] See, for example, Couto et al. (2008), EIU (2008), and the discussion in Chapter 4.

[14] See George, K., Ramaswamy, S., and Rassey, L. (2014) *Next-Shoring: A CEO's guide*. San Francisco: McKinsey.

The wider discussion around what has more generally been termed *reshoring* has been principally focused on the potential for "bringing back" parts of the manufacturing supply chain to the United States, the sporadic achievements of which were encouraged (and loudly trumpeted) by the Obama Administration.[15] Once again, these discussions have been constitutively politicized, with often relatively modest developments in the country's domestic economy pumped up as harbingers of some structural transformation. More skeptical observers, on the other hand, have questioned from the start whether the reshoring of U.S. manufacturing represents a "trickle or a trend."[16] A favorable assessment produced by the International Economic Development Council acknowledged that estimates of the aggregate employment effects of reshoring had proved to be remarkably elusive, most analysts resting their less than conclusive case on a recap of the "disadvantages of offshoring," as indicated by the loss of innovation, knowledge, and opportunities for talent development. These disadvantages seemed, however, to be prompting little more than a recalibration of the logic of offshore outsourcing, rather than a wholesale rethink. Consequently, the report's sober conclusion was that

> not all U.S. manufacturers will find their home location a favorable place to do business. The brightest reshoring prospects involve those that can profit from the current manufacturing environment. This would include manufacturers that depend on natural gas, *require minimal labor*, and need flexibility in production to meet changing customer needs.[17]

There have been some developments in U.S. manufacturing that meet these (rather narrow) criteria, but almost by definition they are not labor-intensive in nature.

Consistent with the reflexive, second-generation character of reshoring strategies (or would-be strategies), it has been recognized that "the reshoring decision [represents] a *reversion* from a previous offshoring or offshore outsourcing decision," and by implication a strategic correction of sorts.[18] There is a hint of this—repatriated jobs, or "backsourcing," as a corporate Plan B, after offshoring

---

[15] See IEDC (2015); National Institute of Standards and Technology (n.d.) Reshoring, accessed at <http://www.nist.gov/mep/services/america/reshoring.cfm>, January 14, 2015; Economist (2013) Reshoring manufacturing: Coming home. *Economist* January 19: 4–6; J. P. Morgan (2014) How real is reshoring? *Global Currents* April, accessed at <https://www.jpmorgan.com/tss/General/How_Real_Is_Reshoring_/1394948805703>, January 12, 2015.

[16] See Free, M. (2012) Is the re-shoring of manufacturing a trend or a trickle? *Forbes* June 27, accessed at <http://www.forbes.com/sites/mitchfree/2012/06/27/is-the-re-shoring-of-manufacturing-a-trend-or-a-trickle/>, January 11, 2016; Conerly, B. (2015) Are American manufacturers reshoring? *Forbes* May 13, accessed at <http://www.forbes.com/sites/billconerly/2015/05/13/are-american-manufacturers-reshoring/>, January 11, 2016.

[17] IEDC (2015: 24–5), emphasis added.

[18] Gray, J. V., Skowronski, K., Esenduran, G., and Rungtusanatham, M. J. (2013) The reshoring phenomenon: What supply chain academics ought to know and should do. *Journal of Supply Chain Management* 49(2): 27–33, p. 29, emphasis added.

too far—in the startup sector that is rural sourcing, as pioneered by the likes of Shane Mayes and OTS, but here the story is conventionally told in more positive terms, as one concerned with untapped skills, exurban development needs, and the potential for small-town business-process operations. Alongside Mayes, the most articulate advocate for this new model, and its promise as a development driver, is Monty Hamilton, a management consultant turned domestic outsourcing pioneer, who is the CEO of Rural Sourcing Inc. (RSI). With development centers in Jonesboro, Arkansas, Augusta, Georgia, and Mobile, Alabama, RSI's value proposition is based on the contention that, for U.S.-based corporate clients, the "total cost of ownership" of inherently higher-risk offshore outsourcing relationships is broadly comparable with a more dependable domestic-sourcing arrangement.

When Hamilton initially made the move to RSI from a successful consulting career, after his firm decided to buy the fledgling service, he realized that this new model would not necessarily be an easy sell. As he worked the phones with potential clients amongst his established contacts in the United States, there was plenty of skepticism. "Really Monty, *Arkansas*. Are you sure about that?" was reported to be a common reaction,[19] not to mention the reservations about outsourcing more generally. According to Hamilton:

> Outsourcing had become a negative term with a bad name... Some of it was due to where the work was being done and in many other cases it was how the work was being done. We thought that with our model of doing it in the U.S. onshore with a much more personal touch we could really change both of those negatives [in addition to] creating jobs here... [But] when we were first selling the idea of outsourcing to Arkansas, the perceptions weren't great... [However] we've been able to overcome a lot of those stereotypes.[20]

RSI's strategy, Hamilton has explained, has been to target "low-cost, high quality of life locations" across the U.S. South, where there is a decent skill base and some potential to augment the talent pool, where the relative paucity of alternative employment opportunities means "really low to no turnover," and where a positive association can be created between stable, family-oriented communities and the building of "strong ties to the [new] organization."[21] Beginning with its Arkansas development center, RSI has "worked to create a cool Silicon Valley culture in these smaller communities," Hamilton adds, complete with retro-industrial décor, foosball tables, and "Red

---

[19] Hamilton, quoted in Frinton, S. (2013) Fresh face: Monty Hamilton. *Pulse* March/April: 44–9, p. 45, emphasis added.

[20] Quoted in Frinton, S. (2013) Fresh face: Monty Hamilton. *Pulse* March/April: 44–9, p. 49.

[21] Monty Hamilton, quoted in IMPO (2011) Q&A with Monty Hamilton, CEO, Rural Sourcing Inc. *IMPO Magazine*, March, accessed at <http://www.manufacturing.net/articles/2011/03/q-a-with-monty-hamilton-ceo-rural-sourcing-inc>, January 3, 2015.

Bull in the refrigerator."[22] Positioning itself as a lead employer in the local communities that are the object of very careful targeting, RSI secures the desired balance of high skill, low turnover, and moderate rates of compensation by selecting and screening staff in a rigorous manner. Like other norm-setting employers in the rural-sourcing sector, RSI makes use of boot camps at the point of entry, followed by paid internships, after which permanent recruits transition into secure positions "with a relatively high wage, a generous benefits package, a challenging work environment, and significant opportunities for personal advancement."[23]

Rural sourcers like RSI, OTS, and their peers will often bill themselves as "alternatives" to offshore outsourcing, but in practice theirs is more of a niche proposition designed to complement extant outsourcing programs, one that is presented "to customers as lower in price than urban-based suppliers [in the United States] but higher in value than offshore-based suppliers," in the words of outsourcing researcher Mary Lacity and her colleagues.[24] Working in the undertow created by some of the frustrations, failures, and unanticipated costs of offshore engagements, rural suppliers vie for positions in the outsourcing portfolios of U.S.-based clients mostly in the space between the kind of mission-critical "blue chip" work that is usually retained inhouse and those routine, "white chip" operations that can be safely assigned to offshore suppliers.[25] Domestic or "homeshore" suppliers, those that serve the so-called "red-chip" market between the inhouse and the offshore, and between complex/internalized and routine/commoditized functions, call attention in their sales pitch to the common mistake of projecting the hourly labor-cost savings that are quoted by offshore providers onto expectations of the net, bottom-line outcome of outsourcing engagements. Of course, this misses so many of the "hidden costs" of offshoring, a lesson that many corporate clients have been destined only to learn through experience: the homeshore offering, in contrast, will be sold as a lower-risk alternative with moderate (but often guaranteed) cost savings, and with project delivery times that can be up to twice as fast as comparable offshore assignments.[26] Rural sourcers pride

---

[22] Quoted in Frinton, S. (2013) Fresh face: Monty Hamilton. *Pulse* March/April, p. 48.

[23] Lacity and Rottman (2012: 152).

[24] Lacity, M., Rottman, J., and Khan, S. (2010) Field of dreams: Building IT capabilities in rural America. *Strategic Outsourcing* 3(3): 169–91.

[25] Lacity, M., Carmel, E., and Rottman, J. (2011) Rural outsourcing: Delivering ITO and BPO services from remote domestic locations. *Computer* 44(12): 55–62, p. 60.

[26] BHMI (n.d.) *Onshoring vs. Offshoring: Choosing the best strategy for your business*. Omaha, NE: Baldwin, Hackett and Meeks. As the CEO of a domestic-sourcing firm explained, onshore providers have the advantage of a more "agile methodology" relative to offshore operations: "If you're doing something for the first time, brand new, you can't do the change management, can't do the on-the-spot business-process facilitation there, from remote [locations] . . . 'I don't have 6 months to ramp up your team on how my [business process] needs to work,' [clients will say]. So we bring that advantage of knowing the contextual side [better] and can turn things around much quicker than

themselves on being agile and client-focused, and in practice find their points in the market with generally smaller and more complicated assignments, being unable to deliver large-scale projects or to achieve rapid "scalability."[27]

Project complexity and the necessity for intensive interaction with clients can effectively shelter parts of the outsourcing market from offshore competition, as can political considerations, for instance where work is being outsourced by government agencies. Beyond this niche of domestically inscribed advantages, however, it is impossible for rural providers to operate outside the matrix of relentless comparative, cost-based competition. No consideration of "onshore" options is abstracted from cost comparisons, comparisons that are typically made in situations where offshore outsourcing is what one domestic-sourcing provider called the "incumbent solution."[28] Attempts to dislodge the incumbent solution are very much dependent on the cost differentials between big-city and non-metropolitan job markets in the United States, which can amount to "savings" on hourly rates for IT staff in the region of 30 percent (relative to inhouse costs), but where unit labor costs may also be anything from 10 to 150 percent higher than offshore alternatives.[29] Rural providers counter that the eye-catching labor-cost savings touted by offshore services, which in some cases can be up to 80 percent lower than inhouse costs, are often unrealizable in practice. The more sober calculations provided by outsourcing advisory services indicate that achieved savings are more likely to be in the region of 25–9 percent for locations like India, China, the Philippines, Eastern Europe, and Latin America.[30] At these rates of *actually achieved* arbitrage, onshore providers see a competitive opening.

But there are qualitative factors at play as well, of course. Industry surveys suggest that corporate buyers in the United States rate domestic workers more highly than their overseas equivalents on a wide range of criteria—from innovation capacity to communication skills and understanding of their business—

you would in an offshore environment, where there is a much longer learning curve involved" (CEO, domestic-sourcing firm, United States, interview by author, March 2012).

[27] See Lacity and Rottman (2012).   [28] Quoted in Lacity and Rottman (2012: 166).

[29] On IT labor cost differentials in the United States, see Finnemore, I., Kim, G., and Pande, A. (2010) *IT Services: The new allure of onshore locales*. San Francisco: McKinsey; Crane, D., Stachura, J., Dalmat, S., King-Metters, K., and Metters. R. (2007) International sourcing of services: The "Homeshoring" alternative. *Service Business* 1(1): 79–91. For onshore/offshore comparisons, see Leiber, N. (2010) "Rural outsourcers" vie for offshoring dollars. *Bloomberg Businessweek* September 23, accessed at <http://www.businessweek.com/stories/2010-09-23/rural-outsourcers-vie-for-offshoring-dollarsbusinessweek-business-news-stock-market-and-financial-advice>, January 15, 2015; BHMI (2010) *Homeshoring*. Omaha, NE: Baldwin, Hackett and Meeks.

[30] Data from Gartner, quoted in BHMI (n.d.) *Onshoring vs. Offshoring: Choosing the best strategy for your business*. Omaha, NE: Baldwin, Hackett and Meeks; Fersht, P. (2013) Sourcing mega-trends in 2013. Presentation at Momentum2013 conference, Atlanta, GA, September 10–11.

the "only negative [being] their cost."[31] On this basis, U.S. corporate buyers report that they might be "swayed" to move a proportion of their spending onshore if domestic sourcing providers are able to deliver cost savings in the region of 17 percent, relative to inhouse costs. There are business cases to be made here, if rural providers get the opportunity to present their intermediate model, but in a structural context marked by downward cost pressures, as one buyer of outsourcing services bluntly puts it, "Let's be frank, if the price doesn't work, your conversation has ended." (It probably did not begin.)[32]

Keenly aware of this, rural-sourcing providers tend to be no less concerned than their offshore peers with the imperatives of cost control, albeit in a domestic theater of operations. As a Nebraska-based provider explains,

> Basically, homeshoring is a low-cost domestic sourcing model. Homeshoring is about assembling project-centric, cross-functional development teams in a development center located away from high rent, high labor rate areas of the U.S. like San Jose, Boston, Los Angeles, and other major metropolitan areas... [For IT workers] in-house wages in major U.S. metro markets run $75 to $100 an hour, as opposed to $20 an hour in India. However, as salaries in India increase because of past market demand, average software developer wages of $35–$40 per hour in small-town America are becoming more cost competitive. And, this is only the beginning. As the trajectory of costs (wages, infrastructure, and program management) in offshore locations continues to accelerate at a much faster rate than in the U.S., small-town America's cost structure is becoming even more appealing.[33]

It is on the basis of such a proposition—spurred by the mixed results of offshoring and bolstered by the reassurance of cultural, technical, and legal compatibility—that domestic sourcing has been touted, repeatedly, as the "next big thing" in services outsourcing.[34] Wage inflation in key offshore markets, especially India, coupled with the effect of decades of flat or falling wage levels in much of the Midwest and South of the United States, means that "small-town America's cost structure [has become] appealing" to some corporate buyers. This is a reflection, the *Economist* discloses, of what the magazine sees as a maturation of markets, in which "the offshoring of services is slowing down because most of the work that can be done remotely has already gone," and since wages in ex-urban America are now broadly

[31] Fersht, P. (2013) Sourcing mega-trends in 2013. Presentation at Momentum 2013 conference, Atlanta, GA, September 10–11.

[32] U.S. corporate buyer, quoted in Lacity and Rottman (2012: 155). An economic development specialist underlined this point: "If a [U.S.-based] customer is being served by rural sourcing providers, they are doing it to some extent out of concern about sustainability and impact on the community, but it's still got to make sense from a financial perspective" (senior economic-development officer #3, Midwest state, United States, interview by author, March 2012).

[33] BHMI (2010) *Homeshoring.* Omaha, NE: Baldwin, Hackett and Meeks.

[34] See EIU (2008) and Economist (2013) Services: The next big thing. *Economist* January 19: 10–12.

comparable with those found in Brazil or Eastern Europe, and maybe only 24 percent higher than in some of India's overheating labor markets, onshore solutions seem to be well suited for the outsourcing of less routine, "higher-value work, such as managing human resources and complex, multi-faceted projects."[35]

First movers in the rural sourcing business quickly realized, however, that this new world would not be realized one transaction at a time; they would need to organize and advocate for their emergent industry.[36] Steps have been taken in this direction, including an inaugural conference for the domestic IT sourcing sector in 2013 with the aspirational title *Momentum*. As an observer from the Latin American "nearshore" sector—the closest competitor, so to speak—said of this meeting, the initiative was really about "regaining" momentum for a would-be industry that was already failing to live up to its politically inflated expectations:

> With very limited political presence in Washington, and with the American public trained by campaigning politicians from both sides of the political spectrum to blame "outsourcing" rather than "offshoring" for the loss of many high value jobs in the past 15 years, the domestic sourcing industry suffers from the lack of supporting voices, loose vocabulary and broad misunderstandings among politicians and legislators.[37]

The challenges confronting the domestic-sourcing sector, however, transcended these matters of visibility and semantics. As even the lead firms in the sector had discovered, prospecting for marketable IT skills in the ex-urban labor markets of the United States had proved to be a less than straightforward task.

Securing Rural Labor

An exploratory assessment from consulting researchers of the potential for attracting domestic-sourcing operations to rural and small-town parts of north Texas found that the scope for growth was limited neither by cost factors nor by paucity of economic-development incentives, both of which were judged to be favorable, but by workforce considerations and skills availability. Call-center and routine-level BPO operations already had a modest presence

[35] See Economist (2013) Services: The next big thing. *Economist* January 19: 10–12, pp. 11, 12; Finnemore, I., Kim, G., and Pande, A. (2010) *IT Services: The new allure of onshore locales.* San Francisco, CA: McKinsey.

[36] "We believe that rural providers would benefit from their own formal advocacy group," Lacity and Rottman (2012: 166) recommend.

[37] Hochstein, E. (2013) Domestic sourcing industry tries to recapture lost momentum. *Nearshore Americas* September 23, accessed at <http://www.nearshoreamericas.com/domestic-sourcing-industry-recapture-lost-momentum/>, October 2, 2013.

in the area, with some growth potential, but the consultants recommended that more needed to be done to build soft-skills capabilities across the workforce, including those of "time management, personal financial management, written and email communications, dressing for business, etc.," down to work–life basics like "showing up to work on time, working collaboratively with colleagues, focusing on the job while at work, [and] taking responsibility for your work and actions."[38] These are reminiscent of the behavioral and motivational deficits that have long been cited by advocates of workfare, for whom supply-side or "employability" factors are also held to be paramount.[39]

But if peripheral areas like north Texas, blighted by legacies of stunted development and long-term outmigration, are deemed scarcely capable of competing at the bottom end of the domestic-sourcing market, the same cannot be said of small college towns, target locations for higher-end sourcing companies, or communities possessing deeper reserves of underutilized skills. Speaking to the latter case, two economic-development officers from Midwestern states explained their strategies for "moving up the food chain" of domestic sourcing:

> State and local governments . . . have got to invest in the fundamentals that will make them attractive to [sectors] like IT and BPO. That's going to be K-12 education, higher education, and then employee training, making sure all three of those facets of workforce development end up producing the kind of workforce that's going to be necessary for these kinds of industries down the road. I have heard . . . how China is certifying 1.2 million outsourcing professionals over the next few years. I mean, that's the nature of the global competition that we're up against [in] the United States. So states have got to do a good job at that . . . [Our] rural economies have gone through a transition from farming to manufacturing and [now] into a service industry . . . The demands of IT . . . if you look at someone like [domestic-sourcing employer], they have a boot-camp philosophy, they run these folks from the rural areas through an intensive training program on how to develop IT systems. That's taking people who might not have much of a background in that to begin with, but making sure that when they come out through the training at the other end that they are employable and they are usable for these kinds of outsourcing services.[40]

> If you look back 15–20 years, the outsourcing activity [in this state] was really a call-center, simple transactional-type activity. Over the years, we have really seen a migration, as the skill sets have been developed and [the] workforce [has acquired] an understanding of the industry, [coupled with] state investment in education to

---

[38] TechAmerica Foundation with Ahilia (2011) *Domestic Sourcing in North Texas and Lessons Learned for Rural America*. Washington, DC: TechAmerica Foundation, pp. 19, 22.

[39] See Peck (2001).

[40] Senior economic-development official #3, Midwest state, United States, interview by author, April 2012.

support the higher-end activities in the outsourcing world . . . We are seeing a lot of companies that are employing those judgmental skills that are necessary for the higher-end kind of work . . . It's really moved up the food chain to a higher level. I guess it's probably a natural process, but at the same time there have been a lot of focused efforts within a lot of states, and a lot of rural areas, to move those skills sets.[41]

Economic-development departments and domestic sourcing companies clearly have a shared interest in "moving the skill sets" of those most employable in the local workforce, although they are also banking on a certain *lack* of mobility on the part of skilled workers themselves. Rural-sourcing companies trade on the "stability" of their workforces as an antidote to the labor-turnover issues that afflict the industry as a whole (especially in the highly competitive, tier-1 offshore centers, where staff retention can be a chronic management problem).

Rural labor markets therefore need to be sufficiently deep that they can provide a ready talent pool, to be filtered through boot-camp training programs and internships, the subsequent "upgrading" of which is in most cases incremental and sometimes costly. But they must also be shallow, in the sense that there is a paucity of competing sources of employment opportunity—a relatively weak demand side. Once committed, rural-sourcing firms cannot afford to lose key staff, instead seeking to position themselves as key employers locally (with *relatively* better pay and conditions), but by the same token relying on the presence of family ties, caring responsibilities, the jobs of spouses, and the absence of competing employment opportunities to do much of the work of retention. In a rather benign fashion, these matters of bottom-line viability for the domestic-sourcing companies will often be represented in cultural or supply-side terms, naturalized as a *workforce* preference for rural lifestyles or an orientation to small-town values. As an economic-development official with a remit to secure rural-sourcing investments explained, loyalty to community consequently becomes a competitive resource for companies that would otherwise be wrestling with the challenges of key-worker turnover and the retention of staff with high-level technical, enterprise, and customer-relations skills:

One of the things you will find with a rural community, that may not be the same in the large, more-urban areas, is [that] individual and family reputation is a big deal. It's a *really* big deal. So I'm not going to do something . . . to my employer, or even the customer of my employer, that's going to embarrass my family . . . In a rural area, everyone kind of knows each other . . . As much as we can promote the culture of our state and the people within the state, that's how we position ourselves, to make sure that people understand and recognize that there are

---

[41] Senior economic-development official #2, Midwest state, United States, interview by author, April 2013.

[present locally] some of those intangibles—but it's really tough to put it in a cost model. [We know that this stable workforce has] a huge impact on the companies and how they are satisfying their clients and retaining their clients at a very high level. It's about that service and that reputation that [each] *individual* employee really wants to maintain.[42]

It is not patriotism, rural nostalgia, or some shared embrace of family values, of course, that drives the location decisions of domestic-sourcing companies. The reason that these companies target communities "where our employees really have deep roots, [where] they want to raise their families, right, they want to *stay* there," is to strike the sweet spot between skills accessibility, retention rates, and competition for labor.[43] Since investment incentives, subsidized premises, and indeed rural-community values are very widely available, and since proximity to clients is decidedly not the issue, then the targeting of one location over another is really a matter of *securing* a skilled labor supply, under the best possible conditions. So in the words of a rural-sourcing executive with a multistate operation, this is partly a matter of "who else is in that community?" Local competition for labor must be organized on favorable terms: "If there is another large, Fortune-500 employer in that community, I really don't want to compete with that; they are going to be paying national-scale wages and national benefits and things. [But] if there's other midsize companies in that town, that's great, that's a big plus for us."[44] Even some of the first movers in the rural-sourcing sector, with their "*sub*national-scale" pay structures, have been forced to close delivery centers, in some cases because it proved difficult to hit quality targets, or in another instance where nearby oil strikes drove up housing prices (and therefore wages).[45]

Securing a "competitive" wage structure is clearly essential to the midmarket positioning strategy of the rural-sourcing companies. According to Shane Mayes of OTS this strategy—relative to the pattern of competitive-sourcing dynamics across the IT sector more generally—means that "rural sourcing [is] a cross-category, low-end market disruption ... that replaces expensive 'software engineers' with more reasonably priced 'technicians' [which in turn] allows rural outsourcers to charge less than [other] domestic providers."[46]

---

[42] Senior economic-development official #2, Midwest state, United States, interview by author, April 2013.

[43] CEO, domestic-sourcing company, interview by author, June 2013.

[44] This respondent continued to say that the presence of a handful of sourcing companies in the local area need not be a problem, since his would be a "lead" company in terms of pay and conditions, but also because this would confirm that local job-market conditions were actually favorable: "If there [are] other BPO, call-center places that I know, not only my research would hold true but *their* research would hold true for the cost of living" (CEO, domestic-sourcing company, interview by author, June 2013). Wage setting, in this sense, is calibrated to (local) costs of living.

[45] See Lacity and Rottman (2012: 146, 163).

[46] Quoted in Lacity, M., Rottman, J., and Khan, S. (2010) Field of dreams: Building IT capabilities in rural America. *Strategic Outsourcing* 3(3): 169–91, p. 179.

As one of Mayes' competitors explains, "First and foremost, we're really looking for that low cost-of-living, high quality-of-life location, so we have that cost advantage going in the door," while recognizing that, at least for moderately skilled IT labor, targeting can be tricky because "the lower the cost of living, the smaller the hiring pool population."[47] For all but the small elite of higher-end rural sourcers, there is a possibility that the companies themselves may fall foul of the very "disruptions" that they play a part in initiating. In north Texas, for example, sourcing companies may be able to dominate some of the smaller and more isolated labor markets, where a limited local skills pool places an effective ceiling on their market ambitions, but in the larger towns "work force retention and availability are more of an issue, because the labor pool has more options as far as employment within the community [is concerned]."[48] A workforce that is skilled, available, and "loyal," but with few alternatives, is therefore the (clearly rather elusive) goal, since under the right circumstances wages can be indexed to the local cost of living. As one of the companies that has laid a claim to inventing the concept of homeshoring candidly puts it:

> If the process work needing to be done is considered low-level, low esteem, or low status it may be difficult to find loyal and willing local employees. [But t]his is an essential component of the Homeshoring approach. While it may seem somewhat callous, not just low wage, but economically disadvantaged areas are particularly sought out.[49]

As Shane Mayes has summarized his company's approach: "We take unemployed and dislocated workers who've lost manufacturing jobs and put them through a bootcamp-style training program [making] software developers out of them," albeit software developers who can be billed out to clients at $25–50 per hour.[50]

This is one of the reasons, according to providers operating in this market segment, why there is a need to engineer "a new relationship and a working relationship with government economic development agencies," not just for (re)location assistance, subsidies, and tax breaks, but for education and training institutions to fall in with, and prioritize, the skills preparation,

---

[47] CEO, domestic-sourcing company, interview by author, June 2013; Lacity and Rottman (2012: 164).

[48] TechAmerica Foundation with Ahilia (2011) *Domestic Sourcing in North Texas and Lessons Learned for Rural America*. Washington, DC: TechAmerica Foundation, p. 22.

[49] Crane, D., Stachura, J., Dalmat, S., King-Metters, K., and Metters, R. (2007) International sourcing of services: The "homeshoring" alternative. *Service Business* 1(1): 79–91, p. 84.

[50] Shane Mayes, quoted in Leiber, N. (2010) "Rural outsourcers" vie for offshoring dollars. *Bloomberg Businessweek* September 23, accessed at <http://www.businessweek.com/stories/2010-09-23/rural-outsourcers-vie-for-offshoring-dollarsbusinessweek-business-news-stock-market-and-financial-advice>, January 15, 2015.

credentialing, and filtering criteria required by the sourcing companies.[51] A market leader in the rural-sourcing sector underlined the point, characterizing incentive packages as "a 'nice to have' [but] I cannot build a stable business model based on that... If [government incentives are] there, and [that] happens, it's great and it's nice, and I wouldn't turn them away... But that's not going to make the final, make-or-break decision on [location] A versus B."[52] Economic-development officials also observe that they must go the extra mile to convince potential investors from the domestic-sourcing sector that their infrastructure provision is up to par, "those [being] things we find ourselves needing to reassure companies about when they are looking at locations outside of urban areas."[53]

Companies that might be considering out-of-the-way locations in the United States, for their part, understand that there is no shortage of locational opportunities. They have come to expect—and indeed demand nothing less than—business-friendly partnerships in the locality and a "vibrant ecosystem" catering specifically to their needs. In the words of an experienced location consultant:

> The incoming [sourcing] companies want to see strong cooperation in the local community and significant benefits available to them in the form of grants, incentives and other programs which will help them start up quickly and which require minimal front-end investment in infrastructure, strong support for recruiting and training their new work force, and future commitment to their growth and local expansion. At the same time, most companies want to work closely with the local institutions to assure that education and training of students is relevant to the needs of their businesses.[54]

It follows that economic-development agencies must be both well prepared and intelligently proactive—a high bar for what are often thinly resourced institutions. Nevertheless, they "must *sell* to the specific requirements of the individual companies and they will need to have their red carpets ready, and

---

[51] "The typical approach of advertising inexpensive land and labor inputs puts domestic areas on the same playing field as developing countries—where the land and labor are considerably cheaper still," Crane et al. continue, "Economic Development officials need to change their foci to gaining customers for new businesses, and establishing corporate-educational ties" (Crane, D., Stachura, J., Dalmat, S., King-Metters, K., and Metters. R. (2007) International sourcing of services: The "homeshoring" alternative. *Service Business* 1(1): 79–91, pp. 79, 90). See also Ahilia (2013) *A Global Sourcing Primer for EDAs and Government Agencies*. Walnut Creek, CA: Ahilia.

[52] CEO, domestic-sourcing company, interview by author, June 2013.

[53] "When people think of rural, they're also going to have misconceptions about what level of infrastructure is out there, whether it's transport... telecommunications or fiber infrastructure" (senior economic-development officer #3, Midwest state, United States, interview by author, March 2012).

[54] Hochstein, E. (2015) Why the fast growing domestic sourcing market is changing how economic developers attract new business. RevAmerica: The Onshoring Blog September 9, accessed at <http://www.revamerica.com/blog/why-the-fast-growing-domestic-sourcing-market-is-changing-how-economic-developers-attract-new-business/>, September 9, 2015, p. 6.

their partners prepared, because the outsourcing companies move fast when they are motivated and won't have to wait to find good offers."[55]

Domestic-sourcing providers certainly do have some sway in their dealings with investment-starved rural communities, even if they routinely find themselves on the receiving end in their own asymmetrical relations with corporate buyers at the top of the supply chain. Nevertheless, domestic-sourcing providers ought in principle to be in a position to find a decent market in the large shadow cast by the "hidden costs" of offshoring, or with smaller-scale assignments that combine elevated complexity with a need to interact almost continuously with clients. By late 2010, however, there were estimated to be not many more than 20 companies operating successfully in the "pure-play" rural-sourcing market in the United States, with the best of the first-mover firms enjoying strong growth but in operational terms expanding only cautiously. New entrants have been slow to join the sector, suggesting that both the rural surplus in tech skills and the size of the domestic sourcing market may have been exaggerated, and/or that success-fully tapping into these is more difficult than had originally been suggested. The U.S. domestic sourcing market was valued at around $100–150 million in 2014, a very "thin slice" relative to the IT-outsourcing sector in India, which at the time was estimated to be worth around $60 billion, possibly rising to $150 billion by 2020.[56] In global terms, the U.S. onshore sector represents no more than the tiniest "sliver of the market," even as the rural-sourcers' value proposition, as Mary Lacity summarizes it, ought to be attractive: "We cost less than the East and the West Coast, and we're easier to deal with than India."[57] It may seem that there is a lot of space to exploit, between the east and west coasts, but profitably doing so in rural America remains no more than a niche enterprise.

The inflated media and public-policy presence of rural-sourcing firms argu-ably says more about continuing anxieties around the "offshore threat," and the public-relations value of "investing in America," than it does about the realistic near-term market prospects of the sector. There is some irony in the fact that even those in the business of promoting the rural solution in the local economic-development community find themselves having to grapple with

[55] Hochstein, E. (2015) Why the fast growing domestic sourcing market is changing how economic developers attract new business. *RevAmerica: The Onshoring Blog* September 9, accessed at <http://www.revamerica.com/blog/why-the-fast-growing-domestic-sourcing-market-is-changing-how-economic-developers-attract-new-business/>, September 9, 2015, p. 9, emphasis added.

[56] Monty Hamilton, RSI, *CNBC* September 9, 2014, accessed at <http://www.ruralsourcing.com/category/news/>, January 12, 2015.

[57] Mary Lacity, quoted in Leiber, N. (2010) "Rural outsourcers" vie for offshoring dollars. *Bloomberg Businessweek* September 23, accessed at <http://www.businessweek.com/stories/2010-09-23/rural-outsourcers-vie-for-offshoring-dollarsbusinessweek-business-news-stock-market-and-financial-advice>, January 15, 2015.

"the political sensibilities surrounding the O-word."[58] The modest scale of the domestic sourcing market in the United States, however, may have more to do with the unforgiving economics of outsourcing than with its prickly politics. Hence the more sober assessments coming from the outsourcing advisory firms, like Tholons, who take the view that there are "practical and self-limiting" features of the prevailing model of outsourcing that will "temper any significant segments of existing offshored work [making] its way back to North America." While it is true that,

> rising salary costs in India, the Philippines and other developing outsourcing destinations [have] continued to narrow the cost differential between domestic US locations and distant offshore destinations [especially given the] more competitive salary rates [in] American cities such as San Antonio, Texas...and Birmingham, Alabama [along with an] improved cost envelope...in smaller, rural outsourcing destinations in...North Dakota, Idaho, and emerging [states] such as North Carolina, Nebraska and Missouri.

> [However the] concept of reshoring for North America may need to be reconstructed. Tholons sees that North American destinations should not necessarily be looking to recapture the outsourced work that has already gone the offshore route. Rather, American locations may be better advised to *shore up* the still large [domestic] outsourcing market...and to counter cost savings in offshore locations by providing great value-adds to US service buyers.[59]

It may be that there are public-relations or data-security reasons for some U.S. buyers of outsourced services to prefer an onshore solution. Furthermore, there are certainly some processes that are boutique by design, and that are resistant to routinization or otherwise highly iterative, which likewise will tend to lend themselves to domestic outsourcing solutions. But contrary to some of the pronouncements a few years ago, there has been no rural "gold rush" to match earlier moments in the non-linear evolution of the global sourcing model. In the United States, a handful of domestic-market pioneers have fashioned distinctive strategies, but the early expectations concerning replicability and scalability have not been realized. Less than 1 percent of the corporate outsourcing budget in the U.S. is being captured by pure-play onshore providers, who seem set to remain small-scale, specialist operators.[60]

---

[58] "There is still a lack of understanding about what outsourcing means and what the ramifications are for [rural] communities...Especially amongst elected officials and politicians, it's easy to bash outsourcing if you don't understand that outsourcing can have some real positive implications for communities in the United States" (senior economic-development officer #3, Midwest state, United States, interview by author, March 2012).

[59] Tholons (2013: 31–3).

[60] The market estimate is from Hochstein, E. (2015) Why the fast growing domestic sourcing market is changing how economic developers attract new business. *RevAmerica: The Onshoring Blog* September 9, accessed at <http://www.revamerica.com/blog/why-the-fast-growing-domestic-sourcing-market-is-changing-how-economic-developers-attract-new-business/>, September 9, 2015.

In principle, rural sourcing looks like an attractive counter, complement, or correction, to some of the well-understood limits of offshore strategies, but with a few exceptions corporate buyers in the United States seem to have come to the conclusion that domestic solutions are neither here nor there. Relative to the case for keeping activities *in-house*, the more modest labor-cost savings associated with domestic sourcing might be almost cancelled out by the increment in coordination costs; on the other hand, the more striking savings that are promised, and sometimes delivered, by offshore providers may mean that the medium-distance model of smaller-scale domestic sourcing does not really go far enough to warrant the effort.

Over the Border

If rural-sourcing sites like Joplin, Missouri or Jonesboro, Arkansas remain but specks on the map of the global outsourcing industry, relative to the tectonic tilt towards Asian service centers, the same certainly cannot be said of the multi-front ascendancy of "nearshoring." As perhaps the most important spatial adaptation of the original, Asia-centric model of global sourcing, nearshoring involves "the business of moving production, research and business processes to countries that are *quite cheap and very close* rather than very cheap and far away."[61] The world's two major nearshoring zones—Eastern Europe and Latin America—have witnessed some relocation of manufacturing activity, reprising in certain respects roles that they played in earlier rounds of globalization,[62] but the more notable developments have been in the services, in finance, and in business processes. Here, corporate buyers in North America and Western Europe are offered some of the benefits of labor arbitrage, minus many of the hassles and costs of what are now commonly described as "farshore" solutions.

Back in 2004, when the German business operating system firm SAP made what seemed like a bold move to relocate its accounting and personnel functions to Prague, the company boasted that it was able to hire five Czech workers for the cost of one of its German employees, a move that would soon be replicated across other "Bangalores of Europe," from Warsaw to Bratislava.[63] The subsequent maturation of the outsourcing market in Central

[61] Economist (2005) The rise of nearshoring. *Economist* December 3: 65–7, p. 65, emphasis added.
[62] See Fröbel et al. (1980), Dicken (1986, 2015), and for commentary on recent rounds of nearshoring in manufacturing, see Harrington, L. H. (2012) Nearshoring Latin America: A closer look. *Inbound Logistics* 32(3): 42–58; Alix Partners (2014) *Reshoring/Nearshoring: Executive survey and outlook*. Atlanta, GA: Alix partners.
[63] Tagliabue, J. (2007) Eastern Europe becomes a center for outsourcing. *New York Times* April 19, accessed at <http://www.nytimes.com/2007/04/19/business/worldbusiness/19prague.html?pagewanted=1&_r=2>, January 3, 2015.

and Eastern Europe has followed a familiar pattern. This begins with rapid growth across a handful of first-mover locations, such as Kraków, Warsaw, Budapest, and Prague, "creat[ing] a 'critical mass' of companies and employees [prompting] further investments and [moves] up the value chain," locations that would be redesignated as "tier 1" centers as a host of secondary and tertiary centers entered the market, trading on their lower-cost profiles as a means of attracting more routine and transactional engagements.[64] This later process of diffusion down the urban hierarchy has been associated with the establishment of BPO centers in a remarkably wide range of CEE locations, such as Katowice and Bydgoszcz in Poland, Ostrava and Pardubice in the Czech Republic, Szekesfehervar and Miskolc in Hungary, and Brasov and Craiova in Romania. There are now more than 1,000 outsourcing centers in the CEE region, amounting to a combined workforce of more than 250,000 in sectors like financial services, research and development, and information technology, together with more recent growth areas like the outsourcing of government services.[65] Here, nearshore represents an "intermediate solution," bringing a substantial proportion of the arbitrage savings associated with offshore (such as salaries as low as one third of the European average, and even larger savings on the cost of office space), together with business-friendly locations within the same "cultural circle" as corporate buyers.[66]

If some parts of the CEE region have made a relatively rapid, postsocialist transition from branch plant manufacturing locations in the early 1990s to preferred sites for nearshore service centers in the last decade, the Latin American development story has played out over a longer arc. Here, the offshoring model that was pioneered in the 1970s by those U.S. manufacturing firms, notably those that relocated assembly plants to the maquiladora zone of northern Mexico, and which anticipated a later and larger movement of labor-intensive operations to China and elsewhere in Asia, has once again been recalibrated. This has not involved as much "backshoring" to the United States as some inflated (or wishful) accounts have suggested, but it certainly has involved a substantial "return" to Latin American locations as part of a far-reaching *regionalization* of supply chains. Supply-chain consultants like John Ferreira of Accenture attribute this process of hemispheric recentering to two key developments: first, the "unanticipated costs...associated with

---

[64] DTZ (2014) *Outsourcing Sector in Key CEE Markets*. Warsaw: DTZ, p. 17. Other secondary and tertiary outsourcing centers identified by DTZ include Lodz, Poznan, Lublin, and Szczecin in Poland; Brno and Plzen in the Czech Republic; Debrecen in Hungary; and Timisoara, in Romania.

[65] The most important centers for financial services outsourcing are Warsaw, Wroclaw, and Prague, while IT and research and development centers are clustered in Kraków, Prague, Budapest, and Bucharest. See DTZ (2014) *Outsourcing Sector in Key CEE Markets*. Warsaw: DTZ.

[66] Polak, J. and Wójcik, P. (2015) Knowledge management in IT outsourcing/offshoring projects. *PM World Journal* 4(8): 1–10, pp. 4, 5; see also DTZ (2014) *Outsourcing Sector in Key CEE Markets*. Warsaw: DTZ.

far-sourcing" to Asia, especially when measured in terms of agility, flexibility, and market responsiveness, which in turn is related to an increased demand for customized support and shorter cycle times; and second, the adoption of more sophisticated sourcing strategies, those that look beyond the basic "arbitrage play" between labor costs, exchange rates, and transportation costs to take advantage of "total value" solutions attuned to an array of "softer" factors like coordination and communication.[67] Latin American locations have been valorized anew, as the source of flexible near-to-market capacities, as many key supply chains have been pulled back closer to U.S. markets and clients, albeit for rather different reasons than the one-dimensional, labor-cost rationales that drove the first generation of "runaway shops."

Rather like the situation in the CEE region, however, the more consequential developments in the Latin American nearshore market have been in services, rather than in manufacturing. In the fast-developing market for global services—which spans the full range, from call centers to BPO and ITO—the nearshore model has been defined as a reaction against the "far-shore" locational strategy, epitomized by India. The Latin American market has since grown to global significance. The early manifestations of this near-shore countermodel, however, were somewhat idiosyncratic. One of the better-known cases, sometimes credited as a prototype of the nearshore model, came from the software sector. Here, software-engineering entrepreneur, Doug Mellinger, had reportedly grown frustrated at the difficulties that he had encountered in trying to persuade his company's New York-based clients to visit development centers in India, due to a combination of orientalist prejudices, long-haul fatigue, and tropical hypochondria: "Too long a trip... Or too many cows in the hotel lobby. Or maybe it was just the damn shots."[68] Mellinger's improvised solution was to identify and then target what he would promote simply as a "better country," his company, PRT Corporation, establishing a software-development and project-management operation in Barbados in 1995. In a twist to conventional outsourcing models, however, Mellinger was not recruiting software engineers locally, but was bringing them *to* his Barbados operation from India, Canada, Nigeria, and elsewhere in the Caribbean, and then capitalizing on his chosen location's "ambience [and] its time zone equivalence with the eastern seaboard."[69]

PRT's Barbados operation expanded quickly, soon reaching 350 employees, who were offered a "worry-free, ready built, turnkey life," earning less than they would have done in the United States but enjoying lifestyle perks and

---

[67] Quoted in Harrington, L. H. (2012) Nearshoring Latin America: A closer look. *Inbound Logistics* 32(3): 42–58, p. 44.
[68] Hopkins, M. (1998) The antihero's guide to the new economy. *Inc* 20(1): 36–45, p. 36.
[69] Barclay, L. A. A. and Rugman, A. (2000) *Foreign Direct Investment in Emerging Economies: Corporate strategy and investment behaviour in the Caribbean*. London: Routledge, p. 135.

the benefits of a high "savings rate," given the low cost of living.[70] A global recruiting model enabled the company to take on sophisticated, high-level work, often involving close collaboration with clients in New York City and along the East Coast. For a time in the late 1990s, Mellinger's PRT was an IPO success story, its founder being lionized in the business press as "the next Bill Gates," but then this prototype of a nearshore shop in what had been promoted as a "programmers' paradise" unraveled in a quite spectacular manner.[71] The company had experienced problems with staff retention as well as with the idea of seriously "selling Barbados [to clients] as a destination for software development," culminating in what was read as a more general "failure to sell the nearshore concept," at least in this avant-garde form.[72] The faltering of PRT's Barbados experiment occurred in 1999, on the eve of the dot.com crash in the United States, after which the concept of "[n]earshoring languished for a few years," to be rediscovered in a new form after 2003.[73] Where PRT had failed others would eventually succeed, albeit on the basis of a re-engineered version of the nearshoring model. Soon, a small wave of call-center and IT-outsourcing facilities would be established in Barbados and other Caribbean islands, some of them responding to government incentive packages, and most being premised on the more conventional outsourcing approach of recruiting low-wage labor *locally*.

Rediscovering Proximity

What has since become the mainstream version of nearshoring model is one that is predicated not only on time-zone and language compatibility, which had been crucial to Mellinger's prototype, but also on what is presented as a *cultural fit with*, and superior responsiveness to, North American business clients. Today, nearshore operators seek to be, in all respects, *closer* to their corporate clients and to client markets. "Proximity," in this sense, is much more than a physical property, a matter of distance or time zones, but instead

[70] Hopkins, M. (1998) The antihero's guide to the new economy. *Inc* 20(1): 36–45, p. 41.

[71] Hopkins, M. (1999) Paradise lost. *Inc* 21(16): 66–74, p. 66; Abbott, P. Y. and Jones, M. R. (2012) Everywhere and nowhere: Nearshore software development in the context of globalisation. *European Journal of Information Systems* 21(5): 529–51, p. 537.

[72] Abbott, P. Y. and Jones, M. R. (2012) Everywhere and nowhere: Nearshore software development in the context of globalisation. *European Journal of Information Systems* 21(5): 529–51, p. 537.

[73] Carmel, E. (2007) Nearshoring 2.0, presentation at "Costa Rica Technology Insight 2007," San Jose, Costa Rica, March 29, accessed at <http://errancarmel.blogspot.ca/2007/04/nearshoring-20.html>, January 13, 2015.

acquires a multidimensional meaning. The definition of nearshoring has since been stabilized along the following lines:

> Nearshoring: sourcing service work to a foreign, lower-wage country that is relatively close in distance or time zone (or both). The customer expects to benefit from one or more of the following constructs of proximity: geographic, temporal, cultural, linguistic, economic, political, and historical linkages.[74]

> Nearshoring refers to the transfer of service work from an originating country to another low-wage destination country or group of countries that are geographically and temporally proximate to the originating country. [In] most usage [nearshoring implies] geographical proximity of the two countries or regions connected by offshoring, there are other aspects such as cultural, temporal, or political connections that facilitate smoother operational of geographically distributed work [especially where] work processes require in-person coordination rather than coordination through long-distance telecommunications.[75]

The nearshoring model is, simultaneously, predicated on cost reduction and yet impossible to reduce to a pure labor-arbitrage equation. Its logic is that "cost is only part of the picture," as the *Economist* has put it, now that sourcing firms are exploring different configurations of "talent and geography" in order to secure realistic cost reductions while sustaining service integrity, quality relationships, and rolling productivity improvements.[76] Recognizing that India has not proved, unequivocally, to be the "promised land," at least not on the scale of the friction-free cost savings promised by some vendors, nearshore options are commonly promoted as "India without the pain," in the sense of an alternative to the "traditional Far East-based [model of] outsourcing" which tends to be stereotyped as "the same service [delivered] at a lower cost."[77]

The nearshore model therefore trades off an attenuated degree of straightforward cost savings, at least compared to the "India price," paired with a promise of smoother operations, courtesy of a harmonization with the principal varieties of "'Westernized' business culture," where different combinations of "geographic and time zone closeness [are married to] improved cultural affinity" with the corporate client.[78] This is more than a hollow marketing claim on the part of nearshore vendors, and it is also more than a xenophobic recoil against the first-generation model of Indian outsourcing.

---

[74] Carmel and Abbott (2007: 44).

[75] Sandhu, A. (2012) Nearshoring. In G. Ritzer, ed., *The Wiley-Blackwell Encyclopedia of Globalization*. Oxford: Wiley, 1505–6, p. 1505.

[76] Economist (2005) The rise of nearshoring. *Economist* December 3: 65–7, pp. 66, 65.

[77] Muruzábal, C. (n.d.) *Nearshoring: The new IT services frontier*. Miami, FL: Neoris.

[78] Carmel and Abbott (2007: 44); Muruzábal, C. (n.d.) *Nearshoring: The new IT services frontier*. Miami, FL: Neoris, p. 1; Polak, J. and Wójcik, P. (2015) Knowledge management in IT outsourcing/offshoring projects. *PM World Journal* 4(8): 1–10.

Proof of this can be found in the fact that a substantial number of Indian vendors have *themselves* been diversifying into nearshore markets. Major Indian multinationals like Tata, TCS, and Infosys have "reacted against the efforts [of competitors] to present them as farshore" by integrating nearshore delivery centers into a new model of "end-to-end" servicing in which near-shore and farshore are seamlessly blended.

> Notwithstanding the Indian hegemony, nearshoring has represented one of the competitive threats to the fast-growing Indian software firms—a threat to which these firms have responded with agility. The top Indian firms have been expand-ing their global presence ... into nearshore locations [offering] a locational menu of choices to their clients that assimilates some of the nearshoring discourse.[79]

Along with all of the established multinational players, the largest of the Indian outsourcing providers now have a substantial presence in all of the globally recognized nearshore zones, where they blend the management, technology, and systems expertise developed on the subcontinent with domestic labor supplies, competing with an upstart cadre of local vendors to deliver services in a more proximate manner. Indian firms like Infosys, Progeon, and Wipro have themselves become truly multinational operators, establishing what are called "proximity development centers" in numerous Eastern European and Latin American countries, and internationalizing a new generation of nearshore nodes like Kraków, Monterrey, Brno, Guadalajara, Tallinn, and San José. At the global scale, two major belts are clearly identifiable today, with one focused on the North American market, and locating in the time zones between −8 GMT and −3 GMT, and the other facing the Western European market, positioned between 0 GMT and +3 GMT. These two regions have assumed increasingly strategic roles in the global sourcing system, some of the principal sites within which are illustrated in Figures 5.1 and 5.2.

Some of the earliest entrants into the European nearshoring market were in Ireland and northern Britain, which had quickly captured three quarters of the region's outsourcing business by the early 2000s, although new sources of locational competition soon arose further to the east, prompted by more substantial cost savings: "Typically, the poorer the country, the lower the wages," a Deutsche Bank primer plainly states, "However, the macroeconomic and institutional risks increase when processes are offshored to particularly poor countries."[80] For banking, finance, and BPO there were initially windfall labor-arbitrage gains to be captured in Central and Eastern Europe (in the region of 70–90 percent relative to German salaries), but as these have since

---

[79] Carmel and Abbott (2007: 46).
[80] Deutsche Bank Research (2006) *Offshoring to New Shores: Nearshoring to Central and Eastern Europe*. Frankfurt am Main: Deutsche Bank.

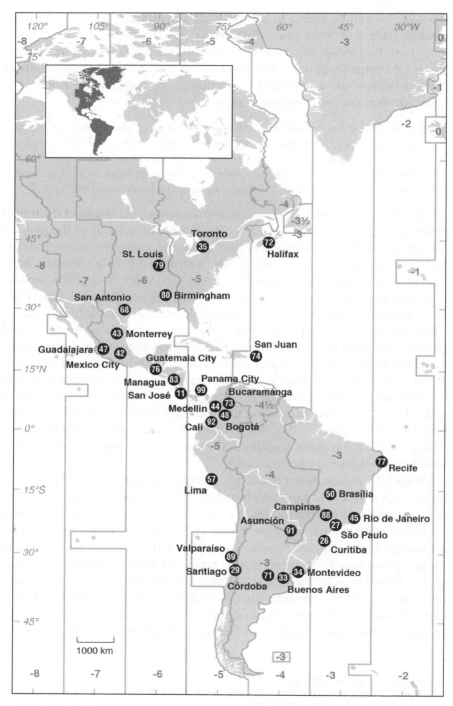

Figure 5.1 Global ranking of nearshore sites, the Americas
Source: author's rendering based on Tholons 2016 global rankings

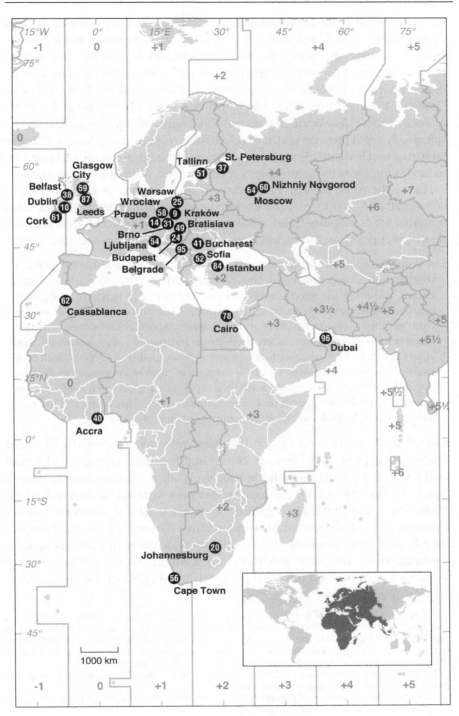

Figure 5.2 Global ranking of nearshore sites, Europe and Africa

Source: author's rendering based on Tholons 2016 global rankings

been somewhat eroded, outsourcing buyers found continuing value in "optimum" locations in Slovakia, Poland, and the Czech Republic. Poland is now home to around one half of the European outsourcing market, measured in terms of the count of centers and the number of "seats," with virtually all of the major international players having a presence there, including IBM, Accenture, Unilever, Boeing, Capgemini, and Samsung.[81] As both a cause and a consequence of these developments, several CEE countries have been making conspicuously rapid progress up the World Bank's "ease of doing business" league table (led by Lithuania, Estonia, and Latvia), although some are reckoned still to have a long way to go (notably, Czech Republic, Romania, and Bulgaria).

Today, the most favored CEE locations are promoted as sites of "smooth collaboration," thanks to their compliance-friendly operating environment, potential for "scalability," and broad compatibility in terms of legal and business conventions. According to Capco, the financial-services consulting firm:

> A nearshore approach is the most viable and cost-effective response for complex solutions with strict time-to-market constraints. There are clear reasons for this choice, including the good combination of technical and language skills. Geographical proximity and regulatory compliance (including considerations such as work permits, visas, data protection etc.) enable smooth collaboration. The currency risk can often be eliminated, for example in the case of Euro-countries. And at around 30%, the cost advantage remains very compelling... *Yet even with these major advantages, nearshoring is not "in competition" with other elements in the sourcing chain.* It is an enhancement not a total replacement... In brief, nearshore has emerged as a valuable support tool in a number of specific situations and has now *taken its place alongside on- and offshore* in the outsourcing value chain.[82]

Clients continue to see value in the "very meticulous approach of Indian [outsourcing] personnel," which is often "highly process-oriented and formalized [in terms of] working methods," but alongside this option have also found a place for operations on the European nearshore, where a "shared history and traditions" mean that there is reduced scope for "misinterpretations" when it comes to tasks of a more complex and iterative nature.[83] Across the European nearshoring zone, however, there remains a wide range of tradeoffs between "political risk," cost, and proximity, with Russia, Ukraine, Hungary, and Belorussia rated high on the former, while the "vibrant nearshoring scene" of

[81] Key firms in the Polish BPO sector include Avon, HSBC, Unilever, Lufthansa, Electrolux, Motorola, UPS, Pandora, and Volvo; PwC., Accenture, Credit Suisse, and Grant Thornton all have shared-services centers, while Samsung, IBM, and Boeing have research and development centers there; Capgemini, IBM, and Alcatel Lucent have significant IT outsourcing operations in Poland. See DTZ (2014) *Outsourcing Sector in Key CEE Markets.* Warsaw: DTZ.

[82] Fazel, F. and Hintermeier, C. (2012) *Nearshore: Close at hand to address your competitive challenges.* London: Capco, 3–4, p. 2, emphasis added.

[83] Deutsche Bank Research (2006) *Offshoring to New Shores: Nearshoring to Central and Eastern Europe.* Frankfurt am Main: Deutsche Bank, pp. 6, 5.

Slovakia scores well across the board.[84] Long-run education and training deficits in some countries sometimes limit the availability of IT skills, crimping their development potential in a similar way to north Texas and other parts of the rural United States. This said, companies like Microsoft, Oracle, Siemens, EA Games, and Office Depot have been prepared to go where others have feared to tread. As location consultants tell the story, this has even included "the land of Dracula," Romania, where investors are implored to see past the veneer of Gothic exoticism in order to recognize the country's deep talent pool and "collaboration culture."[85]

Still, there is no shortage of work for location consultants and outsourcing advisors, as competitive dynamics keep reshuffling the locational ratings, while a site that may meet the needs of some clients (or some activities) will be a poor fit for others. Romania may be the most multilingual country in Europe, after the Netherlands, such that Oracle's call center in Bucharest can operate in thirteen languages, but there are some in the advisory trade that maintain that the Romanians "still don't get it—they smoke in client meetings and cite official corruption as a competitive advantage."[86] Here, scrupulous assessments of labor-market capacities, business operating environments, and regulatory-compliance scoring will often coexist, if not meld, with the circulation of unreconstructed cultural stereotypes. While some countries, like Poland, are praised for sweeping away bureaucratic and cultural impediments to outsourcing, being judged by one advisory firm as "truly open for business," the legacy of the Austro-Hungarian empire ostensibly accounts for an attitude of complacency amongst business-service workers in modern-day Budapest, who are reported to remain convinced that "the world owes them a living."[87]

Complacency, by all accounts, is rarely the problem in the burgeoning markets for nearshore services across Latin America, but here outsourcing advisors are more likely to be briefing their North American clients on matters like business security, IT-systems integrity, personal safety, and geopolitical risk. The outsourcing advisory firm Nearshore Americas reports, however, that the perceptions of corporate buyers have been shifting in favor of some Latin American locations like Chile, Costa Rica, and more recently Columbia; meanwhile, there are those that remain "wary" of Mexico, due to its problems of drugs-related violence, as some remain unconvinced that Argentina truly has the appetite to tackle its reputation for "red-tape, nepotism and an

[84] Fazel, F. and Hintermeier, C. (2012) *Nearshore: Close at hand to address your competitive challenges*. London: Capco, pp. 5, 7.

[85] BCS (2012) Going nearshoring in the land of Dracula. *BCS* April, accessed at <http://www.bcs.org/content/conWebDoc/44441>, January 30, 2015.

[86] Stephen Bullas, eCODE outsourcing advisory, quoted in Economist (2005) The rise of nearshoring. *Economist* December 3: 65–7, p. 67.

[87] Stephen Bullas, eCODE, quoted in Economist (2005) The rise of nearshoring. *Economist* December 3: 65–7, p. 67.

administration that seems uninterested in the professional services."[88] In this context, consultants will engage in their own forms of geopolitical interpretative and positioning, as they seek to influence the locational portfolios of outsourcing buyers and providers:

> With revolution after revolution in North Africa, police crackdowns in China, and uprisings in the Middle East, political climate does not seem most welcoming for business investment. Enterprises of all sizes are re-assessing their outsourcing portfolios, and looking for locations that offer them more stability and minimal risk. However, the problem is that executives are used to evaluating destinations based on easily quantifiable metrics like wage rates, infrastructure costs and investment incentives. When examining geopolitical risk, business decision-makers do so with partial or imprecise information, rather than accurate assessments of the situation on the ground. Especially when it comes to the Latin American region, outdated safety attitudes and perceptions are widespread, and myths often persist in such an environment.[89]

Nearshore America's somewhat circular reasoning was to seek to educate potential buyers of outsourced services from the United States concerning the "on the ground" realities across the Southern Cone by surveying the attitudes and perceptions of those same buyers. There was some method in this approach, however, since risk-averse buyers tend to find reassurance in the location decisions of their peers, often preferring to crowd into relatively established or already "arriving" outsourcing destinations. This said, sourcing providers and advisors will sometimes have to go to considerable lengths to explain what are typically called "LatAm geographies" to their clients in the United States. "The concerns over security are overblown," one advisory firm maintains, noting that "Philadelphia, Washington, D.C., and Baltimore are just three of the cities in the United States with higher murder rates than Sao Paulo."[90] Similarly, an outsourcing provider remarked, only half in jest, that his clients' "geography is not great! So when someone says there is a killing in Guatemala, or there is trouble in Colombia, they believe that it's within two miles of their [service] center," even if that center is located in a different country.[91]

A great many corporate buyers, however, overcame these misconceptions some time ago, and others have been quick to follow. Prominent amongst this group are those veterans of outsourcing engagements with farshore providers

---

[88] George, T. (2011) *Image Matters: The Latin American perception shift*. New York: Nearshore Americas, pp. 5, 6.
[89] George, T. (2011) *Image Matters: The Latin American perception shift*. New York: Nearshore Americas, p. 1.
[90] HfS Research (2011) *How Latin America Powers Global IT Delivery*. Cambridge, MA: HfS Research, p. 25.
[91] Senior manager, global sourcing company, interviewed by author, Cartagena, Colombia, May 2011.

Table 5.1. BPO and ITO in Latin America: vital statistics

	Market size ($bn)		Annual growth rate (%)		Entry-level salary ($)	Attrition rate (%)	
	ITO	BPO	ITO	BPO	ITO/BPO	ITO	BPO
Argentina	4.7	0.95	10	9	16,500	4–8	10–15
Brazil	20.57	6.07	10.6	8.3	14,500	15	15
Colombia	2.97	3.12	18	10	10,500	n/a	18–20
Costa Rica	0.7	2.03	17.4	17.4	19,000	8	8
Dominican Republic	0.2	0.75	n/a	12	10,000	n/a	n/a
El Salvador	n/a	0.21	n/a	11.4	7,000	n/a	20–25
Jamaica	0.10	0.29	20	20	10,000	12	14
Mexico	10.10	6.73	7.3	10	14,000	5	7
Nicaragua	0.8	0.10	38	12	9,000	n/a	n/a
Peru	0.71	0.50	8	14.9	8,500	4	12.5

Source: derived from Neo Group (2015)

in India and elsewhere, who were amongst the first to appreciate the particular assets of Latin American locations, where workforce attrition rates tend to be lower—a factor frequently tagged to a presumed cultural predisposition to "loyalty"—reducing the necessity for bothersome site visits.[92] Furthermore, Latin America is not only a nearshore *export* platform; the region's domestic market for outsourced services is large, and growing rapidly.[93] As a result, the outsourcing business has been booming across South America, where major global firms like Capgemini, Accenture, EXL, Genpact, and IBM now work alongside a cluster of locally grown companies, such as Globant, Stefanini, and Softek, many of which have graduated from the servicing of domestic markets to the development of their own cross-border operations. There are now significant nearshore sourcing markets in Mexico, Brazil, and Argentina, with these and other national sectors recording double-digit rates of growth (see Table 5.1). With "competitive" wage profiles, relative to North America, and low attrition rates by global standards, the Latin American market offers a compelling mix of efficiency and compatibility. Corporate buyers and providers have come to value this configuration, as a complement and in some cases as a substitute to farshore options. Here, one such buyer extols the virtues of his more loyal Latin American workforce, who are conveniently awake and working during the same hours as his in-house staff; meanwhile, a

[92] See HfS Research (2011) *How Latin America Powers Global IT Delivery.* Cambridge, MA: HfS Research.
[93] See Grant Thornton (2015) *Outsourcing: Beyond technical expertise.* London: Grant Thornton International.

155

local provider emphasizes the value of cultural affinity, together with the bilingual skills of his call-center employees:

> They may say that . . . we're sleeping while China or India [are] working [but] when you really come down to it, logistically, from a management perspective, it's much easier to do business when we're both awake. So [being in the] same time zone is a huge advantage that Latin America has over the other regions . . . Within Latin America [costs for our projects are] about 30–50% less than the U.S. Obviously in India and China it is less, but you also have to consider the total value of the project. It's not just the low cost that makes it successful . . . There are many hidden costs . . . When you really take the total value into perspective, the gap on the costs is so small . . . [And the] more complex projects, that require a lot of management oversight, are tending to go to Latin America. [Furthermore] within Latin America, employee turnover is a lot lower than it is in China or India . . . Why? It's because of the policies that certain countries have in terms of labor. You can't just fire people, or what have you . . . And the culture of the Latin people tends to be more loyal. You know, you get that. It's just the way people are.[94]

> Cultural affinity to the US, especially in voice [services], like contact centers, that's [Latin America's] foot in the door. There has certainly been a big swing away from India. People want to speak to people, you know, accent neutral . . . I ran quite a big collections agency out of Mexico [for U.S. clients] . . . The [U.S.] company came in and said we want to buy English; we want English because it's accent neutral. Great! Sold them that! [But then] just shy of 50% of their calls turned into Spanish. "Can I speak to Hector Gonzalez? It's about his credit card." [Replies:] "No, no English." [Fortunately] it just so happens I can speak Spanish . . . India can't offer that . . . Yes, you've got the nearshore, the proximity, the time zones, which are all great. [There is] some of the labor arbitrage, but it's not as important. It's that cultural affinity which is really a huge foot in the door.[95]

If these, in broad-brush terms, can be considered to be region-wide advantages, there is nevertheless a considerable degree of variation in the way that national markets have developed across Latin America. As one recent assessment summarized the situation, "Countries [have been] building reputations around a specific service offering," for instance, analytics capabilities in Chile; high-end and bilingual voice services in Costa Rica; digital services in Argentina, Mexico, and Brazil; enterprise resource management in Mexico; and low-cost call centers in the Dominican Republic, Panama, Guatemala, El Salvador, Honduras, Nicaragua, and Colombia.[96] As Table 5.2 reveals, outsourcing advisory firms read this at a granular scale, one marked by distinctive competitive

---

[94] Senior executive, U.S.-based corporate buyer, interviewed by author, Cartagena, Colombia, May 2011.
[95] Senior manager, global sourcing company, interviewed by author, Cartagena, Colombia, May 2011.
[96] Neo Group (2015: 3, 24).

Table 5.2. BPO and ITO in Latin America: development prospects

	Principal activities	Key companies	Assets	Challenges
Argentina	Software development, contact centers, back-office, creative services	IBM, HP, TCS, Sabre, TeleTech	Low cost; improving infrastructure; cultural compatibility with Europe; more "market friendly" policies after Kirchner	Volatile policy environment and political unrest; crime and corruption; power outages
Brazil	Major tech firms, strength in cloud computing, software and system integration, e-commerce, digital media	Deloitte, Unisys, Tata Consultancy Services	Large labor pool but growing concerns about professional skill shortages	Political instability and social unrest; corruption; complex tax regime; high rates of homicide, kidnapping, armed assault; power shortages
Colombia	Customer service, sales, technical support, payroll processing, customer relationship management, business intelligence	Microsoft, HP, AIG, British Telecom, SAP, IBM, Unisys	Investor friendly climate and robust technology infrastructure; incentive programs	Vulnerability to earthquakes, floods; extended conflict with FARC guerilla movement
Costa Rica	BPO call and contact centers, shared and back-office services; high-value added IT services in digital technologies, design and engineering, financial analysis, software development	HP, Dell, Amazon, Procter and Gamble	Skilled workforce and high-quality education, electricity and telecommunications infrastructures; strong intellectual property rights and security infrastructure; incentive packages	Relatively small labor pool creates obstacles for scaling operations; problems of bureaucracy and corruption
Dominican Republic	The "Call Center Republic"; strengths in voice services, customer relationship management, helpdesk and IT support, employee sourcing	Rococo, VoiceTeam, Globcom, Callmax	Robust telecom infrastructure; low operational costs; incentive packages and English language programs	Skill shortage inhibits higher-end IT service development; high business startup costs; expensive electricity costs and frequent outages; outdated labor laws
El Salvador	Data capture, contact centers, customer service, software development, testing and application management	Sykes, Teleperformance, Atento, Stream	High scores for "economic freedom," with liberal business, fiscal, trade, and investment policies; cost-effective location, with good infrastructure	High rates of social violence and gang activity; English language services lagged until recently
Jamaica	Finance and accounting, receivables and debt collection, inbound customer service, telesales/marketing, IT support; graphics	ACS Xerox, HGS, Global Outsourcing, Sutherland Global Services	Deregulated business environment; tax incentive programs; free trade zones	High debt to GDP ratio

(continued)

Table 5.2. Continued

	Principal activities	Key companies	Assets	Challenges
Mexico	Customer support, product support, payroll processing, document processing	IBM, Cisco, TCS, Intel, HP, Softek, Hexaware	Mature outsourcing sector and a large pool of IT and communications technology professionals	High crime rates, including cybercrime; corruption; illegal payments; drug-fueled violence; social protests; management skills shortages
Nicaragua	Non-voice BPO services include data and payment processing, account reconciliation, audit and compliance, shared service centers; KPO services include recruitment processing, survey analysis, payroll administration, financial services, logistics operations; ITO services include mobile applications development, software development, IT support, and hardware and server maintenance	Sitel, Concentrix, Convergys, SPI Global Claro, British Telecom	Cheap labor and generous tax incentives; free-trade zones; skills development programs for young bilingual workers	Small labor force brings scalability challenges; concerns over infrastructure development initiatives from business, environmental, and social groups
Peru	Contact center services, including virtual agents, voice biometrics, and text-to-speech software; trilingual capabilities; IT services such as web and mobile applications	Microsoft, Cisco, Pfizer, IBM, Scotia Bank	Very low labor costs; tax incentives; improving infrastructure	Lack of maturity in outsourcing market means critical skills shortages, problems of employee retention (particularly in BPO). Low-cost environment deemed "unsustainable," deters large-scale operations

Source: author; developed from Neo Group (2015)

assets in some locations, but also some rather particular challenges and obstacles, including instances of political instability and social unrest; education and technical infrastructure problems; issues with labor laws and tax regimes; and obstacles to the rapid scaling up of operations.

Where Latin American countries do almost universally well, according to outsourcing advisory services, providers, and corporate buyers, is in the arena of government incentives. In fact, following the region's identification as a prime nearshore investment target, a race of sorts has broken out to offer the most lucrative packages of tax, trade, and training incentives to outsourcers, who both expect and receive the red-carpet treatment. In the words of one assessment of the region as a platform for outsourcing investments, "LatAm countries are now compounding the natural cost advantage by aggressively offering incentives and specialized zones that make shorter-term investment even more favorable."[97] Even those countries that have a habit of electing "leftist, anti-business, anti-American/European governments," another advisory service notes, tend to be much more pragmatic when it comes to foreign investment.[98] As Table 5.2 shows, free-trade zones, English-language programs, and tax-reduction packages are widely offered, while numerous countries have been engaged in major upgrades to their digital technology infrastructures. In this region, "government support" consequently earns consistently high grades on the scorecards used by location consultants and advisors.

When IAOP selected a site for the inaugural Latin American Outsourcing Summit, the coastal city of Cartagena in Colombia, the organizers surely anticipated a warm and fulsome welcome from President Juan Manuel Santos, whose business-friendly government had been prioritizing sourcing-industry investments. Joining the opening session of the meeting by video link, the president portrayed his country as "the ideal platform for the outsourcing industry," underlining Colombia's premier rating for investor protection and the great strides that had been taken on measures like public safety, educational investment, and IT preparedness.[99] Prominent speakers recruited to follow the president at the opening plenary reinforced the message, addressing an audience of 300 or so buyers, vendors, and intermediaries. An executive from a multinational customer-service company, with a capacity of approaching 10,000 call-center seats spread across its campuses in Bogotá and Medellin, emphasized the attractiveness of the industry as an economic-development

---

[97] Neo Group (2015: 3).

[98] HfS Research (2011) *How Latin America Powers Global IT Delivery*. Cambridge, MA: HfS Research, p. 25.

[99] President Juan Manuel Santos, address to the First Latin American Outsourcing Summit, Cartagena, Colombia, May 2011. See <https://www.iaop.org/Content/19/205/3194>, accessed January 6, 2016.

opportunity: "this is a human-capital intensive sector...which makes no smoke."[100] The president of ANDI, the newly formed industry association for the region concurred, but also sounded a gentle warning—since the quintessential logic of the outsourcing industry is locational flexibility, it is one that must be catered to *continuously*: "Outsourcing is a clean industry, and it develops a sociologically cosmopolitan workforce... [It could be] the flagship for creating new jobs [in Colombia] ... But just as it comes quickly, it can leave quickly, if it is not sufficiently pampered."[101] Even if would-be investors have been sold on the region-wide value proposition, which combines cultural and geographical proximity with time-zone compatibility, in the context of a generally competitive cost structure, committing to a particular country must also involve negotiating the particularities of "[b]usiness climate and laws, labor costs, working hours, visa requirements, English proficiency, services maturity, infrastructure, operating costs, and so many more factors."[102] Having supplied the necessary incentives and inducements, investors generally prefer host governments subsequently to keep their distance—that is, unless there is a problem that needs to be solved or an obstacle that must be removed.

If there has been an undercurrent of complaints about red tape, bureaucracy, and corruption in some of the outsourcing industry's experiences in Latin America, there are also accounts of quite remarkable degrees of responsiveness on the part of governments. A senior manager from an Indian-based outsourcing provider described the experience of establishing a customer service center in Guatemala:

> I had a lot to do with Guatemala, building up a center there ... We went from zero to I think about 1,200 FTEs now. Invest in Guatemala [the government's inward-investment promotion agency] were fantastic for us. We actually got them to change the visa process for Indians coming into Guatemala within about three days... In order for transition managers, and my boss, to come into town, they had to fly through Mexico City for two days to get a visa. That's not going to help growth! So we raised it [with Invest in Guatemala]. It went to the foreign ministry and instantly it got changed [to] visa on entry. So that shows the power that was there.[103]

Testimonies such as these have earned Guatemala the status of a would-be tier 1 outsourcing site. Having established a foothold in the cost-sensitive call-center sector—cheaper than Panama and Costa Rica, and marginally more expensive than Nicaragua and Honduras, but offering distinct advantages in

---

[100] Senior executive, customer service company, Colombia, addressing the First Latin American Outsourcing Summit, Cartagena, Colombia, May 2011.
[101] President, Asociación Nacional de Empresarios de Colombia, addressing the First Latin American Outsourcing Summit, Cartagena, Colombia, May 2011.
[102] Neo Group (2015: 3).
[103] Senior manager, Indian service provider, Guatemala, interviewed by author, Cartagena, Colombia, May 2011.

terms of scalability, English-language capacity, and accent neutrality—some of the leading providers in Guatemala soon saw opportunities to transition to more sophisticated BPO engagements. A prime mover here was the multi-national service provider, Capgemini, which won a major contract to deliver finance and accounting services to Coca-Cola by blending the operations of its new facility in Guatemala with an established center in Chennai, India, the demonstration effect of which helped to convince Nokia Siemens, Warner Brothers, Office Depot, Unilever, and others to follow suit. According to the head of global BPO delivery for Capgemini, this meant that Guatemala would no longer have to live off the "scraps" left over by the region's leading call-center players, like the Dominican Republic, the "Call Center Republic," but instead would work its way up the BPO value chain: "It is not a Tier 2 or Tier 3 destination," he insists, "For us, [Guatemala] is absolutely a Tier 1 location."[104]

Navigating Multishore

The days are long since gone when the outsourcing value proposition could be reduced to a simple cost calculus based on the single-minded pursuit of labor arbitrage, when U.S. executives had to "survive by drinking Red Bull" on site visits to sourcing centers in India.[105] There has certainly been a measure of "offshore fatigue," not least after learning the hard lessons of failing or ser-iously suboptimal engagements, and the hidden costs of farshore. Meanwhile, the offshore value proposition has been enriched and recalibrated by a com-bination of pressure from corporate buyers and the enhancement vendor capabilities: as a result, in the words of one veteran advisor, "the outsourcing location pendulum has begun to swing from an offshore [and farshore] extreme to more of a balance between offshore and domestic-based delivery."[106] Two things seem certain in this context. First, the pendulum will not swing all the way back; instead, new and more elaborate divisions of labor are being worked out across a constantly shifting portfolio of farshore, nearshore, and onshore options. Corporate demand for pure-play domestic (and rural) sourcing providers in the United States is expanding, albeit from a very low base, yet this

[104] Hansjoerg Siber, Capgemini, quoted in Bargent, J. (2012) For Capgemini, Guatemala was love at first sight. *Nearshore Americas* blog, November 28, accessed at <http://www.nearshoreamericas.com/capgemini-gautemala-attractive/>, January 23, 2015.
[105] Senior executive, customer service company, Colombia, addressing the First Latin American Outsourcing Summit, Cartagena, Colombia, May 2011.
[106] Hochstein, E. (2015) Why the fast growing domestic sourcing market is changing how economic developers attract new business. *RevAmerica: The Onshoring Blog* September 9, accessed at <http://www.revamerica.com/blog/why-the-fast-growing-domestic-sourcing-market-is-changing-how-economic-developers-attract-new-business/>, September 9, 2015, p. 1.

segment remains tiny in relation to the market as a whole, accounting for less than 1 percent of U.S. sourcing expenditures. On the other hand, many of the leading offshore providers from India and elsewhere have recognized (or have been convinced of) the value of client proximity, at least for some components of their service offerings. So, Indian-based companies like Tata and Infosys have set up service centers near to some of their prized customers, like Dow Chemical in Michigan and Harley Davidson in Wisconsin; meanwhile, North American-based global service providers like IBM and CGI have been establishing new service centers across the United States, from Dubuque, Iowa, to Troy, Alabama.[107] Second, the pendulum will keep swinging, since the only constant in the outsourcing space is constant movement, constant restructuring. Prime, or tier-1 locations tend to become subject to the diseconomies of agglomeration, such as increases in wages and attrition rates, dynamics that are often repeated as the same swarming effects occur in the next generation of frontier locations in tiers 2 and 3. The rebalancing of farshore, nearshore, and onshore portfolios is therefore anything but a once-and-for-all correction; it is part of a continuing process of locational churn.

It may be a fact of life in this era of corporate disaggregation and global integration that, "[o]nce a business process is outsourced, it tends to stay that way," as the consultants Grant Thornton International have reported on the basis of a major survey,[108] but on the other hand there is also ceaseless change in the *organization and location* of these outsourced activities. The same survey found that three quarters of buyer-side companies expect their lead outsourcing providers to be available for face-to-face meetings within twenty-four hours. They also want to see improvements in the soft-skills capabilities of service providers, enabling trust, exploiting cultural affinity, and securing reliability, while *at the same time* delivering rolling efficiency gains.

The "original" moment of offshore outsourcing—which in a sense was both unidirectional and unidimensional in its rush to preferential sites for labor arbitrage—has initiated a host of downstream transformations in the wake of which ever more complex geographies have been constructed. The search for cost reductions and efficiency gains remains fundamental, but there are remarkably few outsourcing engagements, these days, that function *only*

[107] It is estimated that there are now some 670 delivery centers operating in the United States, representing fifty or more service providers and scattered across some 300 cities. Tata is in Midland, Michigan and Cincinnati, Ohio; Infosys is in Milwaukee, Wisconsin and Atlanta, Georgia; IBM has sites in Columbia, Missouri, East Lansing, Michigan, Buffalo, New York, and Baton Rouge, Louisiana; CGI is in Belton, Texas, Lebanon, Virginia, Lafayette, Louisiana, Athens, Ohio, and Troy, Alabama. See Agarwalla, H., Garg, S., and Simonson, E. (2015) *North America Domestic Outsourcing Services: Providers embrace onshoring—Is the world still flat?* EGR-2015-2-R-1455. Dallas, TX: Everest Group.
[108] Grant Thornton (2015) *Outsourcing: Beyond technical expertise*. London: Grant Thornton International, p. 8.

according to this rationale. Some of the more sophisticated engagements will feature partnership-based governance, soft-skills enhancement, and innovation sharing. A great many will set a premium on agility, involving continuous, iterative, and responsive communication between organizations and along the supply chain. Others will aspire to the alignment, blending, and hybridization of project teams across sites. All of this means that the locational calculi that govern outsourcing decisions are becoming ever more overloaded and complicated, just as they are never entirely stable or predictable. As a result, some observers are predicting that the locational neologisms that for a while have acted as signposts towards the *next* shore—as nearshore and onshore arrived in the wake of offshore—will soon lose their meaning altogether, dissipating into a tangled web of supply-chain connections and "multishore" configurations.[109] This should not be taken to mean that offshore is over, or that the outsourcing calculus has become geographically indiscriminate. If the move offshore can be considered to be a threshold-crossing moment, then the subsequent (and continuing) refinement of locational preferences and dynamics is symptomatic of ongoing processes of restructuring. Furthermore, it speaks to a two-way relationship between the continuous reorganization of outsourcing space and the evolutionary transformation of the outsourcing complex.

---

[109] Sandhu predicts that, "[t]he increased dispersal of service work globally is producing global service chains where each stage of value addition is carried out wherever it makes the best sense in terms of cost and organizational structures. Eventually, the conceptualization of offshoring in terms of nearshore and offshore will result in its subsumption under the global service chains framework." Sandhu, A. (2012) Nearshoring. In G. Ritzer, ed., *The Wiley-Blackwell Encyclopedia of Globalization.* Oxford: Wiley, 1505–6, p. 1506. On the complexity of transformative change in manufacturing, see Conerly, B. (2015) Are American manufacturers reshoring? *Forbes* May 13, <http://www.forbes.com/sites/billconerly/2015/05/13/are-american-manufacturers-reshoring/>, January 11, 2016.

6

Noshore, or the Road to Robotistan

When delegates gathered for the fifth annual International Outsourcing Summit in October, 2013, in the opulent surroundings of the Makati Shangri-La Hotel in Manila, the hot topic was a disruptive technology that some were suggesting might even define a new paradigm—robotic automation. Alongside India, the Philippines is one of the few truly "mature locations" in the business-process outsourcing sector, its large roster of fast-growing companies ranging from call and contact centers to major players in non-voice services like software development, finance and accounting, animation, and medical transcription.[1] With a domestic workforce numbering more than a million, BPO in the Philippines had become a $13 billion industry by 2013, with revenues projected to double by 2016.[2] A winning combination of cultural affinity, accent neutrality, low rents, high educational standards, and competitive wages had made the Philippines a prime target for outbound BPO investment from the United States since the early 1990s, propelling double-digit annual growth rates and securing strategic status for the industry in national planning frameworks.[3] The source of some of the best-paying jobs in the Philippines economy, the outsourcing sector has propelled cultural and even geopolitical change: a new class of "BPO consumers" spend conspicuously in Manila's newest shopping malls, while in macro terms, BPO revenues

[1] Del Prado, F. L. E. (2015) The BPO challenge: Leveraging capabilities, creating opportunities. *PIDS Discussion Paper* No. 2015–36, Philippine Institute for Development Studies, Makati City, Philippines, p. 7; Borbon, M. H. (2015) Global value chains. *Economic Issue of the Day* 15(4), Philippine Institute for Development Studies, Makati City, Philippines.

[2] Robinson, D. (2015) Manila eclipses Mumbai as services outsourcing magnet. *FT.com* May 5, accessed at <http://www.ft.com/cms/s/0/1658baac-f30a-11e4-a979-00144feab7de. html#axzz4G245MwUK>, August 1, 2016.

[3] Mitra, R. M. (2013) The information technology and business process outsourcing industry: Diversity and challenges in Asia. *ERD Working Paper* #365, Asian Development Bank, Manila, Philippines; Magtibay-Ramos, N., Estrada, G., and Felipe, J. (2007) An analysis of the Philippine business process outsourcing industry. *ERD Working Paper* #93, Asian Development Bank, Manila, Philippines; Philippines Board of Investments (2012) *A New Day for Investments: Coherent, consistent and creative*. Makati City, Philippines: PBOI.

now rival those derived from overseas remittances.[4] It was not at all surprising, then, that the talk of labor-displacing automation was creating ripples of unease. Could it be that the Philippines outsourcing industry, one predicated on the principles of rationalization and restructuring, was about to get a taste of its own medicine?

The company that everyone was talking about at the Manila conference was Blue Prism, credited as the "founder" of the field of robotic process automation, or RPA,[5] Blue Prism had been garnering all kinds of industry awards, including a mention on Gartner's "Cool Vendors" list and recognition as one of the "Global Hot 100" at the World Summit on Innovation and Entrepreneurship. With bases in London, Manchester, and Miami, Blue Prism has developed an innovative technology for automating routine, rule-based administrative procedures, "software robots" that are able to master a wide array of data-retrieval and processing tasks in just a few weeks and which, in principle at least, might be scaled into something analogous to a "virtual workforce." Bringing the benefits of robotic automation and the tools of cognitive intelligence to the service sector, Blue Prism was winning strong endorsements from corporate clients like Telefónica 02 and the Cooperative Bank, as well as ITO and BPO providers like Xchanging, who were beginning to incorporate automation into their service offerings. As outsourcing researchers Leslie Willcocks and Mary Lacity have said of this new methodology, "Although the term 'Robotic Process Automation' connotes visions of physical robots wandering around offices performing human tasks, the term really means automation of service tasks that were previously performed by humans," going on to emphasize that "we are not talking about technology enablement where technologies like desktop scripts *assist* human agents but actual software automation that *replaces* some or all of the work previously performed by people."[6] In pursuit of a slice of the global BPO market—which is valued at upwards of $300 billion annually—Blue Prism boasts that this "new generation of technology . . . may further undermine and even reverse the offshoring trend,"[7] with unit costs that are reckoned to be around one third of those of typical offshore full-time equivalents (FTEs) and somewhere

[4] See Kleibert, J. M. (2015) *Expanding Global Production Networks: The emergence, evolution and the developmental impact of the offshore service sector in the Philippines.* Amsterdam: Amsterdam Institute for Social Science Research; Robinson, D. (2015) Manila eclipses Mumbai as services outsourcing magnet. *FT.com* May 5, accessed at <http://www.ft.com/cms/s/0/1658baac-f30a-11e4-a979-00144feab7de.html#axzz4G245MwUK>, August 1, 2016.

[5] Sethi, A. and Gott, J. (2015) *On the Eve of Disruption.* New York: A. T. Kearney, p. 2; see also Willcocks and Lacity (2016).

[6] Willcocks, L., Lacity, M., and Craig, A. (2015) Robotic process automation at Xchanging. *Outsourcing Unit Working Research Paper* 15/03, Outsourcing Unit, Department of Management, London School of Economics and Political Science, p. 4; see also Willcocks and Lacity (2016: 66).

[7] Blue Prism (2012) Robotic automation: Driving next-generation BPO? *Times (Raconteur)* June 11: 1–16, p. 11.

between one fifth and one ninth of the cost of inhouse FTEs.[8] Crucially, though, cost savings calibrated according to the metric of FTE equivalents were only part of the initial sales pitch—a translation, as it were, into the old language of "humanoid" work systems—since the longer-term promise of RPA was to *decouple* process and productivity, altogether, from headcount-based systems and the old paradigm of scale economies.

Inevitably, there has been a distinct whiff of science-fiction futurology in many of these discussions, which tend to invoke more than a mere step-change in systems (thinking), but a mind-altering leap into a new dimension. Indeed, some of the high-profile figures in this field might have been sent straight from central casting. One is Chetan Dube, a former mathematics professor at New York University, whose brainchild is a fast-growing robotics company called IPsoft. Now claiming to have impacted the IT operations of one in ten Fortune 1000 companies, IPsoft was founded on a vision of also a post-FTE world, governed by expert systems and autonomic technologies. "The last decade was about replacing labour with cheaper labour," Dube has said, "The coming decade will be about replacing cheaper labour with auto-nomics."[9] Step forward Amelia, IPsoft's fast-learning cognitive-knowledge worker, who is described in marketing materials as a virtual agent with the "human touch." Unnecessary from a technical point of view, of course, Amelia's existence may say more about the cultural and organizational challenges associated with workplace automation. Like her virtual relative at Blue Prism, Poppy, who has been set to work at the business-services firm, Xchanging, Amelia presents as young, disarming, and feminized (see Figures 6.1 and 6.2). These humanoid figures might be reassuring to their coworkers in onshore locations, who have the opportunity to train and delegate to a virtual colleague, but offshore laborers are more likely to see them as a threat to their long-term job security. And they may be right.

Chetan Dube jokes that his wife has wondered whether he has been having an affair with Amelia, the blue-eyed it-girl/IT girl who has the "complete package: smart, sophisticated, industrious and loyal."[10] The founder of IPsoft has been a particularly engaging advocate for this new generation of technology-based solutions, but he does not shy away from the fact that this is a *disruptive* technology—not just for some workers employed at the routine or "tactical" end of business-process operations, but for the BPO industry itself. Dube has made no secret of the fact that he thinks that the Indian IT outsourcing sector has become "bloated," and that it is about to encounter its

[8] See Sheth, M. (2015) Can robots replace people? *Business Standard* April 27, accessed at <http://www.business-standard.com/article/management/can-robots-replace-people-115042600696_1.html>, January 22, 2016.

[9] Economist (2013) Rise of the software machines. *Economist* January 19: S17.

[10] Ankeny, J. (2015) Even better than the real thing. *Entrepreneur* 43(6): 34–43, p. 34.

Figure 6.1 Amelia, the virtual assistant
Source: IPsoft, reproduced with permission

Figure 6.2 Poppy, the new team member at Xchanging
Source: Xchanging, reproduced with permission

own moment of structural transformation, "a very big period of flux" in which all but the most agile of technology-intensive firms will be facing "existential trouble."[11] When Dube's colleague, Jonathan Crane, the chief commercial officer at IPsoft, was asked the question, by *Outsource Magazine*, what the "huge transition ... away from the headcount-based model" would mean for providers, his answer was hardly comforting:

> [If] we look at a company that's been primarily focussed on labour arbitrage, the revenues that that company counts are based on bodies. So it's obvious that as there are fewer bodies doing that work, revenues will decline. Also, skill-sets are in accumulating and managing those people, and supporting them in their various tasks. If you're still in the business of managing [routine or] tactical functions with labour arbitrage, *you're on the bad side of the curve*. Because you can't take a human individual in a tactical function and maintain him or her at a wage level which will compete with the ability to automate that task ... I don't care what your price is, you're still going to be spending a lot more money than you will be using our solution. All the major providers who have [built] up large headcounts need to move those professionals into doing higher-end, truly strategic and valued work.[12]

There is little wonder that the early reporting on RPA generated such anxiety in the provider markets of India and the Philippines. As early as 2012, the *Wall Street Journal's* Indian partner, *Mint*, had been reporting that,

> Software robots and humanoids from US-headquartered IPsoft Inc. and British start-up Blue Prism Ltd ... are rapidly rendering irrelevant the political and economic debates about offshoring of software and back-office projects. They are doing this by automating more than half the projects they undertake, and by solving technical glitches at a speed (in seconds) that human engineers cannot match.[13]

By that time, Blue Prism was claiming that it had released more than 1,000 "virtual FTEs" into the world, where it was competing for business with other new entrants to the RPA field, like Automation Anywhere and WorkFusion,[14] while Chetan Dube and IPsoft were generating plenty of press coverage by capitalizing upon a corporate strain of *robophobia*.[15]

---

[11] Quoted in Joseph, L. and Shivapriya, N. (2013) Machines to be a tidal transformation of the planet: Chetan Dube, IPsoft. *Economic Times* August 23, accessed at <http://articles.economictimes.indiatimes.com/2013-08-22/news/41437318_1_ipsoft-chetan-dube-transformation>, January 15, 2016, pp. 1–2.

[12] Quoted in Outsource (2015) Q&A: Jonathan Crane, IPsoft. *Outsource Magazine* June 10, accessed at <http://outsourcemag.com/qa-jonathan-crane-ipsoft-part-1/>, January 25, 2016.

[13] Mishra, P. (2012) A robotic threat to outsourcing. *Live Mint* November 19, accessed at <http://www.livemint.com/Industry/1RerO20tFJNYGXmTYSRrnI/A-robotic-threat-to-outsourcing.html>, January 17, 2016, p. 1.

[14] New York-based WorkFusion, a spinoff from MIT's Computer Science and Artificial Intelligence Lab, brought its first RPA products to market in 2012; Automation Anywhere was founded in San Jose, California in 2010.

[15] This, to be sure, reflected a wider cultural moment, which had seen the return of robot stories of many kinds. For discussion of the employment implications, see Brynjolfsson and McAfee

For their part, the hosts of the Manila summit seemed not to know quite how to play the issue of robotic automation. A conference press release headlined "The 'bots are coming," elliptically asked if the emergence of autonomics might be "setting [a new] direction" for the BPO industry, as "robots replace people in IT just as they have in manufacturing."[16] But Jose Mari Mercado, president of the Information Technology and Business Process Association of the Philippines, was quick to add his reassurance that there would be more than enough work to go around for human employees in the growing market for offshore services: "The local industry is not at all threatened [and while] technology has already automated certain processes, the amount of work that requires human intervention remains huge."[17] Some kind of push back against the claim that RPA might mean the death of the outsourced job was clearly in order, even if there was genuine uncertainty about the longer-term implications. Would robotic automation initiate a destructive wave of change, or paradigm shift, or would it amount to an incremental ripple, an adaptation of existing business models?

Market entrants like IPsoft and Blue Prism can be expected to talk up their prospects, of course, aided and abetted by outsourcing advisory firms like Gartner, Forrester, Ovum, HfS Research, and their management-consulting peers, who generate demand for their services amid the roil of disruptive change. The hype around cloud-based systems of various kinds had been around for a while, and had already been discounted by some, but suddenly there was a palpable sense that actual disruption was now arriving, even if incumbent business models were hardly about to be rendered extinct. The warning signs had been there for some time, however, especially in manufacturing. The Asian outsourcing giant, Foxconn, for example, had earlier signaled its intention to install more than 1 million robots across its network of plants, a strategy that was indelicately portrayed by the company's founder, Terry Gou, at a charity event at the Taipei zoo, as a posthuman efficiency drive: "as human beings are also animals, to manage one million animals gives me a headache... young people's hearts in China are hard to get hold of."[18]

(2012); Kelly, K. (2012) Better than human. *Wired* December 24, accessed at <http://www.wired.com/2012/12/ff-robots-will-take-our-jobs/>, February 17, 2016; Krugman, P. (2012) Is growth over? *New York Times* December 26, accessed at <http://krugman.blogs.nytimes.com/2012/12/26/is-growth-over/?_r=0>, February 17, 2016. See also Frick, W. (2015) When your boss wears metal pants. *Harvard Business Review* June: 84–9.

[16] PRWeb (2013) The "bots are coming: Philippines" Outsourcing Summit tackles impact of automation on industry. *PRWeb* October 2, accessed at <http://www.prweb.com/releases/2013/10/prweb11182339.htm>, p. 1.

[17] Quoted in PRWeb (2013) The "bots are coming: Philippines" Outsourcing Summit tackles impact of automation on industry. *PRWeb* October 2, Manila, Philippines, p. 1.

[18] Originally quoted in *Want China Times* (2012) Foxconn chairman likens his workforce to animals. *Want China Times* January 19, but since taken down. Quoted in part at <http://socialbarrel.com/foxconn-chairman-terry-gou-likens-employees-to-animals/30947/>, January 18, 2016.

And some in the outsourced-services business had been rattled by IBM's announcement, on the eve of the Manila conference, that the company was divesting its customer-care BPO division (to Synnex Corporation for $505 billion), in order to move into higher-margin, less commoditized markets in which revenues and profits are released from headcount capacity constraints.[19]

Before long, the suggestion that the BPO sector was beginning to transition away from a cheap-labor-intensive model to a hybrid, more technology-intensive model, with significantly reduced headcounts, was sounding less like science fiction and more like a coming corporate fact. Within two years of the Manila summit, by 2015, the new wave of automation was being likened to a tidal shift. India's *Economic Times* reported that the country's IT outsourcing sector was experiencing a "sea change," as leading companies were breaking their habit of adding tens of thousands of engineers to payrolls every year, and instead managing attrition "strategically," in accordance with rolling programs of automation. The headline, "Infosys, Wipro & TCS lose over 100,000 people in last four quarters as automation kicks in," called attention to the fact that the industry was "haemorrhaging more people than ever before," but on closer inspection spoke to an organic shift in what have always been large-scale flows of recruitment and attrition.[20] A buried lead told this arguably more important story: in 2015, the Indian ITO sector was hiring 14,350 engineers for every $1 billion of revenues; back in 2003, it had been recruiting at approaching two and a half times this rate, at almost 38,000 per $1 billion in revenues. Outsourcing revenue growth was indeed decoupling from FTE growth. Cloud-based competition would be identified as a prime factor in what the *Wall Street Journal* chose to portray, rather alarmingly, as "India's outsourcing apocalypse," the seven deadly signs of which included shrinking global revenues, shrinking deal sizes, and falling prices, with contract values being slashed by 20–30 percent on renewal, according to industry sources.[21]

Early sightings of the "robot threat" clearly sent a shudder through the outsourcing complex, even if similar stories had been heard before. Rather than some passing panic, however, it has since become clear that real change is underway, even if it has yet to justify the apocalyptic rhetoric of sections of the business media. Innovative firms are moving to capture first-mover

---

[19] IBM (2013) IBM to sell customer care business to SYNNEX. *IBM Investor Relations* September 10, accessed at <http://www.ibm.com/investor/ircorner/article/sept10.wss>, January 18, 2016.

[20] Sen, A. and Mendonca, J. (2015) Infosys, Wipro and TCS lose over 1,00,000 people in last four quarters as automation kicks in. *Economic Times* July 29, accessed at <http://articles.economictimes.indiatimes.com/2015-07-29/news/64996766_1_infosys-ceo-vishal-sikka-attrition-rate-cloud-computing>, January 13, 2016.

[21] McLain, S. (2015) The seven signs of India's outsourcing apocalypse. *WSJ.com* July 13, accessed at <http://blogs.wsj.com/briefly/2015/07/13/the-seven-signs-of-indias-outsourcing-apocalypse-the-numbers/>, January 15, 2016.

advantages in these newest of new technologies; providers are adding new practice fields and specialist divisions; and corporate clients have come to expect RPA capability, writing this into new contracts. Corporate clients, many of whom are barely satisfied with the performance of their existing providers, have not been slow to see the appeal of this alternative approach: "For the buyer community," outsourcing-industry stalwart Frank Casale points out, "RPA is appealing because it is quick and cost effective and doesn't send jobs offshore."[22] The speed of change is illustrated by the fact that RPA is known as *rapid* process automation in some quarters.[23] In the ITO and BPO sectors in particular, RPA has been characterized by technology advocates as a "flash trend," with the potential to create "turmoil on a fairly large scale."[24] Accustomed to "follow[ing] the cost save," in many ways the founding promise of the outsourcing business, corporate buyers are now being advised to look beyond the offshore horizon, perhaps halving their costs all over again by deploying RPA.[25]

As those in the outsourcing complex—service providers, corporate buyers, and consulting advisors—have begun to imagine, visualize, and respond to the opportunities and threats posed by automation, their plans, fears, hopes, and schemes say a great deal about the (changing) competitive positions and dispositions of those involved, while also calling attention to what have rapidly emerged as alternative spaces of restructuring. In the wake of offshoring, onshoring, and nearshoring, there have been new sightings of "no-shore" locations, often up in the clouds, sometimes buried in the unplumbed depths of back-office processes, or even in imagined states like "Robotistan."[26] If, thanks to automation, the locational reach of back-office supply chains is really now reaching from "anywhere on earth to no location at all," as consultants A. T. Kearney have suggested, if RPA threatens to "cannibalise" the

---

[22] Casale, F. (2015) Hard facts and hype: the data and the drama behind robotic process automation. In Institute of Robotic Process Automation, *Introduction to Robotic Process Automation: A primer.* New York: IRPA, p. 4.

[23] See Dias, J., Patnaik, D., Scopa, E., and van Bommel, E. (2012) Automating the bank's back office. *McKinsey Insights*, July, accessed at <http://www.mckinsey.com/business-functions/business-technology/our-insights/automating-the-banks-back-office>, February 12, 2016; Srivastava, S. (n.d.) The evolving role of rapid automation in business process outsourcing. *Sourcing Focus*, accessed at <http://www.sourcingfocus.com/site/featurescomments/the_evolving_role_of_rapid_automation_in_business_process_outsourcing/>, January 22, 2016.

[24] Frank Casale, Institute for Robotic Process Automation, quoted in Violino, B. (2015) Robotic process automation: The new IT job killer? *Infoworld* March 23, accessed at <http://www.infoworld.com/article/2898108/robotics/robotic-process-automation-new-it-job-killer.html>, January 18, 2016.

[25] Institute of Robotic Process Automation (2015) *Introduction to Robotic Process Automation: A primer.* New York: IRPA, p. 10.

[26] The "no-shore" idea is particularly associated with the consulting firm, A. T. Kearney, while Robotistan is the creation of outsourcing advisors, HfS Research. See Laudicina, P., Peterson, E., and Gott, J. (2014) *A Wealth of Choices: From anywhere on earth to no location at all.* New York: A. T. Kearney; Sethi, A. and Gott, J. (2015) *On the Eve of Disruption.* New York: A. T. Kearney; HfS Research (2013) *A Tour of Robotistan: Outsourcing's cheapest destination.* Boston, MA: HfS Research.

BPO industry while "dramatically alter[ing] the dynamics of the outsourcing market," as Ernst and Young's India office is predicting,[27] where next? The rapid entry of robots into the outsourcing complex, in this respect, may provide some clues to a "future [that] is already here," in the words of cyber-punk guru, William Gibson, but once again one that is "just not [going to be] very evenly distributed."[28]

Robot Tales, Old and New

No consideration of robotics, cognitive intelligence, and robotic automation can be considered complete absent proper recognition of Isaac Asimov, the "Father of the modern robot story,"[29] and the remarkably enduring genre of robot imaginaries that he helped (re)create. This biochemistry professor and giant of "hard" science fiction is credited with coining the term *robotics* (in a 1942 short story, *Runaround*) prior to the formation of the hybrid field of engineering science itself. Set sometime around the future year 2015, *Runaround* features two of Asimov's recurring characters, Powell and Donovan, who are working to reanimate a group of relatively primitive, first-generation robots that had been developed a decade before—this being a time, however, when "ten years, technologically speaking, meant so much...advances in robotics these days [being] tremendous."[30] Many of Asimov's fictional assertions, particularly his three Laws of Robotics, continue to excite controversy in the actually existing worlds of software automation, artificial intelligence, machine ethics, and in various business, military, and industrial applications fields.[31] In many ways, this is entirely appropriate, since Asimov's motivation had been to explore the more than fictional worlds that robots would one day populate and remake, not as a source of fear or as objects of pity, but in everyday situations where these would be humble "industrial products built by matter-of-fact engineers"; equipped "with safety features so they weren't

---

[27] Laudicina, P., Peterson, E., and Gott, J. (2014) *A Wealth of Choices: From anywhere on earth to no location at all*. New York: A. T. Kearney; Sheth, M. (2015) Can robots replace people? *Business Standard* April 27, accessed at <http://www.business-standard.com/article/management/can-robots-replace-people-115042600696_1.html>, January 22, 2016.

[28] Quoted in Thompson, C. (2013) *Smarter Than You Think*. New York: Penguin Press, p. 9.

[29] Asimov, I. (1982) *The Complete Robot*. New York Doubleday and Co, p. xii.

[30] Asimov, I. (1982) [1942] *The Complete Robot*. New York: Doubleday and Co, p. 209.

[31] See Feitelson, D. G. (2007) Asimov's laws of robotics applied to software. *Software Practitioner* 17(1): 6–9; Anderson, M. and Anderson, S. L., eds, 2011, *Machine Ethics*. Cambridge: Cambridge University Press; Singer, P. W. (2009) Isaac Asimov's laws of robotics are wrong. *Opinions* May 18, Brookings Institution, accessed at <http://www.brookings.edu/research/opinions/2009/05/18-robots-singer>, January 18, 2016.

Menaces," these workaday robots would be "fashioned for certain jobs so that no Pathos was necessarily involved."[32]

As Asimov anticipated decades ago, robots are today being "fashioned for certain jobs," not just as assistants or servants but as *replacements*, a technological and organizational moment that has been accompanied by a new wave of prophetic writing, spanning the scholarly, management, and popular literature. Increasingly, this work is predicting a major upheaval in corporate structures, in the pattern and overall level of employment, and across society as a whole.[33] It is entirely in keeping with the culture of the outsourcing complex that robot stories should have been breaking out in the conferences, summits, blogs, and webinars, where there is an almost obsessive concern with next-generation business models, technologies, systems, fads, and fashions—in no small part a reflection of what has been a longstanding concern with the idea of purposive, continuous reinvention. This is a world, moreover, that itself has been made and then repeatedly remade, in the space of barely three decades, by a rapid succession of enabling technologies and organizational innovations, under banners like rightsizing, corporate reorganization, enterprise-resource planning, digitization, re-engineering, lean production, supply-chain management, and so forth. Those in the outsourcing complex are acutely conscious, arguably more so than most, of the far-reaching downstream consequences of such transformative forces, the brisk ascendancy of RPA being seen as both a threat and an opportunity, but either way a threshold moment that "changes the game."[34] Established BPO providers, which have "built their comparative advantage around efficiently managing large labor forces and optimizing processes," now face a stark choice, say analysts at A. T. Kearney: should they become "disruptors or defenders?" Those that work with the new technology on the former path will need to "redefine their business models, skillfully managing the cannibalization of existing sales to remain a viable business in the long run," while those that choose to stand and fight over existing markets "will need to refresh their sources of competitive advantage in an attempt to continue to thrive after the disruptors have done their work."

Characteristically first on the scene with RPA were the advisory firms and consultancy outfits that have long occupied important roles as organizational mediators and message managers. In the fall of 2012, HfS Research in Boston launched a report with the disruptive title, "Robotic automation emerges as a

---

[32] Asimov, I. (1982) *The Complete Robot*. New York: Doubleday and Co, p. xii.

[33] See Brynjolfsson and McAfee (2012), Frey and Osborne (2013), and Thompson, C. (2013) *Smarter Than You Think*. New York: Penguin Press.

[34] Sethi, A. and Gott, J. (2015) *On the Eve of Disruption*. New York: A. T. Kearney, p. 3. For a similar argument about joining the RPA train before it is too late, see Institute of Robotic Process Automation (2015) *Introduction to Robotic Process Automation: A primer*. New York: IRPA.

threat to traditional low-cost outsourcing." This positioned software robotics (RPA was yet to be stabilized as the favored nomenclature) as an early-stage disruptive technology, one bound to disturb the incumbent business model of arbitrage-based offshore outsourcing. Segments of the BPO market, in particular, seemed to have been practically primed for robotic automation. Process efficiency, reliability, cost control, and minimum fuss ("your mess for less") have been the foundations, all along, of the BPO value proposition. Software robots would be able to deal with this mess for even less, and with hardly any "noise" too. In this vein, HfS presented a case for robotic automation, in a manner that acknowledged both the practice and the *Realpolitik* of the outsourcing business, while promoting the potential of the Blue Prism model:

> [A]s HfS Research readers well know, outsourcing entails its own problems, including the political unpopularity of sending jobs offshore, the hidden costs of overseeing remote operations, and the complexities of managing differences in business cultures...Blue Prism's novel idea is to give business units a tool to automate these ad hoc processes on their own, addressing their custom requirements without relying on an expensive, lengthy IT development process, or hiring costly onshore workers for which they have no budget, or shipping the work offshore. It calls this concept "robotic automation," and refers to the custom applications produced by its software and methodology as "robots"...These terms appropriately convey the notion of a technological replacement for a human worker—in this case, implemented as fast, cheap software.[35]

HfS Research visited some of Blue Prism's (satisfied) clients, both to look "under the hood" of their processes and to start to tell some "real stories of robots unleashed on the world."[36] They reported that one BPO service provider, specializing in eligibility-processing tasks outsourced from government agencies, had deployed software robots to automate a notoriously error-prone "swivel-chair problem," which involved accessing multiple systems and then conducting verification checks across them. The provider reported that increased accuracy had been achieved while processing time had been slashed by two thirds—all at just one tenth of the cost of a human FTE. In a second proof-of-concept case, a telecommunications company had automated some of the customer-services operations that it had earlier offshored, replacing offshore FTEs with the robotic equivalent, virtual FTEs, at a ratio of better than 4:1, with the goal of reaching a target labor-replacement ratio of 6:1.

Aside from a certain level of skepticism amongst some corporate executives, coupled with a fair amount of defensiveness from inhouse IT departments, the HfS scouting mission did not detect significant obstacles to the robotization of carefully selected business-process functions. Before long, as the accounts of

[35] Slaby (2012: 4).   [36] Slaby (2012: 7–8).

early adopters began to circulate, the population of "true believers" in robot stories would begin to exceed the self-interested cluster of technology pushers and change-management advocates. One adviser remarked that, on his first encounter with RPA, "my skeptics' alarm bells went off big time," but his organization's subsequent work with frontline implementers had convinced him otherwise: "telling us their stories, they made us believers too."[37] Meanwhile, the consultants and advisors remained confident that the "lapel-grabbing business case" of RPA would soon be speaking for itself, since the bottom-line savings were nothing less than "eye-popping," even before taking into account the "drawbacks of managing and training offshore labor."[38] The promise was of a game-changing technological fix that would provide a means of avoiding a host of "traditional outsourcing's headaches, [including] political issues (the unpopularity of shipping jobs overseas), operational challenges (coping with language barriers, cultural alignment issues, relocation costs for executives), and assorted risks (geopolitical issues, foreign exchange and wage rate fluctuations, the question of long-term viability implicit in the 'race to the bottom' on labor arbitrage)."[39] Offshore providers would have to be agile and proactive, however, embracing the new technology and making it their own; otherwise, HfS and other advisory firms were warning, corporate clients might cut them out of the conversation altogether, implementing RPA themselves. Already, the new generation of RPA specialists was beginning to work directly with onshore clients, raising the oxymoronic threat of "DIY BPO," which if it took hold would shake the extant outsourcing market "at its roots."[40] As James Slaby of HfS told the Indian business paper, *Mint*, "Now that robots have arrived, low-cost outsourcers may soon be forced into an unpleasant choice: cannibalize your own business, or let an innovative new entrant do it for you."[41]

Research that had earlier been conducted at the behest of Blue Prism, by another outsourcing advisory and research firm, Forrester, had concluded that the functions most amenable to RPA colonization in the short term were mostly found in the "long tail" of second-order organizational priorities, few of which were mission critical, but which could in the aggregate add up to

[37] Senior outsourcing advisor, New York City, interview by author, September 2013.
[38] Slaby (2012: 8, 1).   [39] Slaby (2012: 11).
[40] "The worrying thing from the providers' point of view," Chapman reports, "is when clients decide to automate processes in-house rather than entrust them to their service provider...DIY BPO could be the next wave to shake the BPO market at its roots" (Chapman D. (2013) How will process automation impact the future of BPO? *Outsource Magazine* 5 July, accessed at <http://outsourcemag.com/how-will-process-automation-impact-the-future-of-bpo/>, July 31, 2016, p. 1).
[41] Quoted in Mishra, P. (2012) A robotic threat to outsourcing. *Live Mint* November 19, accessed at <http://www.livemint.com/Industry/1RerO20tFJNYGXmTYSRrnI/A-robotic-threat-to-outsourcing.html>, January 17, 2016, p. 2.

significant productivity gains and cost savings.[42] This echoed the origins of offshore outsourcing itself, which had been targeted at an earlier generation of routine, non-core operations, but using labor arbitrage as the lever rather than robotic automation. Correspondingly, the task fields that are deemed appropriate for RPA is a familiar terrain for outsourcers: rule-driven procedures amenable to decomposition and routinization; those located in fairly stable operating environments; those requiring often complex (but nevertheless codifiable) coordination between multiple systems, such as databases and service platforms; and those where there are few "gray areas" calling for human intervention, for instance in the form of subjective judgment or interpretive analysis. "Robots can't think," an RPA booster has explained, "They can only do what they're told. So it has to be...a simple process, end to end, without too many exception challenges...*no gray*."[43] Other early adopters have found this "automatable band" of activities to be quite wide, however, and with experience and experimentation it has been widening.[44] Within these (moving) parameters, the "benefits of living in a robotized world" could be expected to include, according to HfS:

- *Better use of expensive human resources*: Cheap, quickly developed robots handle dull, repetitive, rules-based processes. Humans in the business units become free to do higher-value, more engaging work that requires analysis, problem solving, and complex exception handling; this improves job satisfaction and employee retention.

- *The tirelessness of machines*: Robots aren't just cheap: they work faster, more efficiently, and with fewer errors. They don't need coffee breaks, holidays, or health insurance, and can work around the clock. One robot typically replaces the work of 1.7 humans.

- *IT infrastructure reuse and flexibility*: Robots run on existing enterprise IT infrastructure, work with existing data repositories and applications (both homegrown and packaged), and can be located anywhere, including private data centers, shared services environments, and on private, public, or hybrid cloud services.[45]

What is fast becoming a conventional wisdom has it that "robotic automation has the potential to be a highly disruptive transformative technology for both buyers and the outsourcing industry as a whole."[46]

---

[42] Forester Research (2011) *The Role of IT in Business-driven Process Automation*. Cambridge, MA: Forester Research.
[43] Wayne Butterfield, Telefónica 02, presentation at HfS webinar, A Tour of Robotistan: Outsourcing's cheapest destination, April 25, 2013, accessed at <http://www.horsesforsources.com/robotistan-replay_050313>, January 18, 2016.
[44] See Willcocks and Lacity (2016).   [45] Slaby (2012: 5–6, 10–11).
[46] Slaby (2012: 2).

Robotistan: the New Shore?

The outsourcing advisory outfit HfS Research likes to position itself on the edgy, irreverent front of the outsourcing conversation, venturing first where others will later follow. In the Spring of 2013, HfS dedicated one of its regular webinars to the theme of robotics, cheekily promoted as *A Tour of Robotistan: Outsourcing's cheapest destination*.[47] Embarking on this journey would mean leaving behind, at least metaphorically, the familiar world where labor arbitrage was the law of the land. The governing principles of Robotistan would be quite different—a new modality of *robot arbitrage*.[48] In order to visualize this alternative universe, webinar participants from the buy and sell sides of the outsourcing complex were urged to imagine robotic solutions not in the form of humanoid machines but as software code:

> Don't think of a tin man. Think of a software process running on a virtual machine in your data center, or maybe somewhere in a private cloud for instance. It's doing fairly routine, possibly dull, likely repetitive work...the kind of work that you might have humans do, probably *are* having humans do right now, in India or the Philippines, or Brazil or Poland, because outsourcing lets you move the work to wherever it can be done cheapest. Of course, everyone on this call probably knows that cheap offshore labor has hidden costs. It's politically unpopular; you have cultural differences to manage; you generally have to send expensive people overseas to manage the operation...The kind of robots we're talking about today represent a third way for handling your business process...Instead of having IT automate it, or shipping it to an outsourcer to be done manually offshore, you automate it yourself, inside your own business unit...The resulting robots that we have seen produced by this [process] are pretty amazing. They work around the clock; they don't need vacations or lunch breaks or benefits.[49]

The targeted operations for robotic automation, as the founder of BPO provider GenFour explained, included "anything transactional in nature," and while this meant that "you're probably looking in the back office," the demonstration effects associated with successful implementation could be sufficiently strong as to produce "a viral effect, propagating the use of robots across an organization."[50] It has been estimated that back-office workers spend

---

[47] See HfS Research (2013) *A Tour of Robotistan: Outsourcing's cheapest destination*. Boston, MA: HfS Research.

[48] HfS (2013) Robotistan takes a seat at the BPO Security Council. *Horses for Sources* blog October 29, accessed at <http://www.horsesforsources.com/robotistan-bpo-council_102913>, January 17, 2016.

[49] James Slaby, presentation at HfS webinar, A Tour of Robotistan: Outsourcing's cheapest destination, April 25, 2013, accessed at <http://www.horsesforsources.com/robotistan-replay_050313>, April 25, 2013.

[50] James Hall, GenFour, presentation at HfS webinar, A Tour of Robotistan: Outsourcing's cheapest destination, April 25, 2013, accessed at <http://www.horsesforsources.com/robotistan-replay_050313>, April 25, 2013.

approximately one quarter of their time on the kind of rule-based, standardized, and repetitive tasks, those that are "easiest" to automate, and beyond this, that "most aspects of office life will be changed as a result of RPA over the coming decade."[51]

One of the presenters at the HfS webinar was a senior executive at the telecoms firm Telefónica 02, where automation was portrayed as the leading edge of a process that could lead to "eliminating back office" altogether.[52] Telefónica 02 had begun to outsource its back-office operations from the UK to Mumbai in 2004, within a year achieving an offshore to onshore labor ratio of 2:1, by which time 200 seats were occupied at the company's Indian BPO provider. Within five years, the company's Indian workforce was more than 350 strong, while the size of the onshore office had been halved (a ratio of 7:1), the point at which management believed that they were "reaching the ceiling on extracting any more value from offshoring; there was not that much more work that could be moved to India."[53] This was not an isolated experience. With the *relative* costs of offshore labor rising, coupled with a widespread belief amongst client firms and advisory services that the rate of innovation had plateaued amongst offshore providers, some were characterizing the BPO market as "saturated," indeed "littered with hundreds of underperforming... contracts," many of them serviced by complacent vendors.[54] As the Telefónica 02 executive summarized the situation, his company had come to realize that once "low-cost Indian resources started to increase in price... low cost wasn't so low anymore."[55] This was, simultaneously, a new story of technologically bold organizational innovation and the same old story of cost compression and FTE trimming. The company's rolling RPA strategy was predicated not simply on a technical assessment of whether the targeted processes were sufficiently stable, rule governed, and predictable, but on a much simpler heuristic: processes would be candidates for automation if the robotic alternative would remove at least three full-time employees, in a situation where

[51] Sethi, A. and Gott, J. (2015) *On the Eve of Disruption*. New York: A. T. Kearney, p. 1; Wallack, J. (2015) Is robotic process automation the next level of outsourcing? *Realcomm* 15(23), June 11, accessed at <http://www.realcomm.com/advisory/695/1/is-robotic-process-automation-the-next-level-of-outsourcing>, January 22, 2016, p. 2.

[52] Wayne Butterfield, Telefónica 02, presentation at HfS webinar, A Tour of Robotistan: Outsourcing's cheapest destination, April 25, 2013, accessed at <http://www.horsesforsources.com/robotistan-replay_050313>, April 25, 2013.

[53] Willcocks and Lacity (2016: 85).

[54] Burnett, S. and Simonson, E. (2014) *Service Delivery Automation (SDA) Market in 2014: Moving business process services beyond labor arbitrage*. Dallas, TX: Everest Group, p. 1; HfS Research (2015) Why we mustn't make the same mistakes with RPA that we made with BPO. *Horses for Sources* blog December 10, accessed at <http://www.horsesforsources.com/intelligent-automation-continuum_121015>, January 22, 2016, p. 1.

[55] Wayne Butterfield, Telefónica 02, quoted in Burnett, S. (2015) A conversation with Wayne Butterfield, Head of Digital Service Innovation and Transformation at Telefónica, *Everest Group Practitioner Perspectives*, EGR-2015-4-0-1422, Everest Group, Dallas, TX, p. 1.

savings on labor costs could now be calculated to the "point zero zero of an FTE."[56]

The competitive threat from Robotistan is consequently manifest in two rather distinct, but also overlapping ways. First, as a new source of technological unemployment, RPA is replacing actual workers, those "removable FTEs." Since the risk of RPA displacement is higher in routinized and rule-governed operations, which themselves are more likely to have *already* been exposed to outsourcing and offshoring, the impact of automation is likely to be elevated in offshore locations. Second, since routinization and relocation have effectively prepared the ground for accelerated automation, RPA represents a "next-wave" competitor (and possible successor) to the labor-arbitrage model, particularly in BPO and ITO. In this respect, it can be seen as a driver of restructuring processes across the outsourcing complex itself, as well as across offshore product and labor markets.

The early evidence has been quite clear. Telefónica 02's approach to RPA clearly has the effect of stripping (even cheap) labor out of back-office processes. Barclays Bank claims to have achieved "savings" of 120 FTEs in the first stages of its application of RPA.[57] Others are more coy when it comes to this (obviously sensitive) question. When Ascension Health implemented a Blue Prism RPA system in 2014, this apparently did not result in immediate job losses, although the company's director of operations support acknowledges that the possibility "certainly exists." Ascension's more palatable goal has been to "absorb the additional workload that we know is coming" *without adding any additional FTEs*, which is (re)presented as a means of protecting onshore employment:

> In some ways, we see the use of RPA as having a greater potential to retain levels of staffing that you might not have had if you had outsourced the entirety of the work to a traditional BPO . . . There are some natural resistances to the implementation of this type of technology, mostly around *the potential impact on people*.[58]

Since the goal of protecting inhouse employment levels does not seem to have been an overriding business objective for companies like Ascension—those with significant back-office operations, where offshoring and continuous cost suppression have become well-established strategies—this publicly stated concern to maintain staffing levels (for now) probably says more about the

---

[56] Wayne Butterfield, Telefónica 02, quoted in Willcocks and Lacity (2016: 92).

[57] Barnett, G. (2015) *Robotic Process Automation: Adding to the process transformation toolkit.* London: Ovum; Sethi, A. and Gott, J. (2015) *On the Eve of Disruption.* New York: A. T. Kearney.

[58] A. J. Hanna, Ascension Health, quoted in Violino, B. (2015) Robotic process automation: The new IT job killer? *Infoworld* March 23, accessed at <http://www.infoworld.com/article/2898108/robotics/robotic-process-automation-new-it-job-killer.html>, January 18, 2016, pp. 3, 5–6, emphasis added.

(internal) politics of transition management. For their part, existing BPO providers can certainly see the writing on the wall, reliant as they have been on FTE-based business models. The fact is that "traditional outsourced business processes are perfect candidates for RPA," this *already* rationalized and organizationally disembedded cluster of "largely transactional, low-end, repeatable tasks" having been inadvertently primed for automation, circumstances that not only place the offshore workforces of today "in the crosshairs," but which also mean that the job tasks themselves may have "a limited lifespan, because the payoff of transitioning from labor- to tech-centric models is enormous."[59] In the words of Blue Prism's Pat Geary, "You can use robots wherever there is a concentration of repetitive, clerical-based administrative work," because (whenever there is a concentration of that kind of work) outsourcers are almost certainly on the scene, "*BPOs* [being] *an aggregation point for that kind of work.*"[60] Even though forecasts of the death of the back-office outsourcing industry at the hands of marauding robots are undoubtedly exaggerated, there is surely truth in the assessment that, "[o]nce the disruptor, the BPO industry now itself faces disruption."[61] BPO firms did the lift and shift work; now many of these activities are ready-made targets for automation.

One of the companies that is trying to stay on the right side of this disruptive wave is the transnational BPO firm, Xchanging. Established in London in the late 1990s by a former partner at Anderson Consulting, Xchanging has been focused on the delivery of back-office services to the banking, insurance, and finance industries. Having grown strongly, the company was listed on the London Stock Exchange in 2007, subsequently to acquire a controlling interest in Cambridge Solutions, another BPO/ITO provider with an operational base in India. Problems with the acquisition led to some challenging years for Xchanging, leading to a restructuring of the company's executive leadership, and a reorientation towards higher value-added, technology-intensive projects. With 8,000 staff spread across forty-two countries, spanning onshore, offshore, and nearshore locations, Xchanging launched its RPA program in 2014, beginning with its strategically important, high-value contracts with Lloyd's and in the London insurance market. An RPA team of twenty staff (including four developed by the project partner Blue Prism to "train" the

---

[59] Justice (2015: 4).

[60] Quoted in Global Delivery Report (2012) Will automation replace offshore BPO? *Global Delivery Report* November 28, accessed at <http://globaldeliveryreport.com/tag/robots/>, January 18, 2016, p. 2, emphasis added.

[61] Sethi, A. and Gott, J. (2015) *On the Eve of Disruption.* New York: A. T. Kearney, p. 10. On the mortal threat presented by RPA, see Justice (2015). James Slaby of HfS argues that robotization threatens to become an "offshore killer" (quoted in Overby, S. (2012) IT robots may mean the end of offshore outsourcing. *CIO Magazine* November 16, accessed at <http://www.cio.com/article/2390305/outsourcing/it-robots-may-mean-the-end-of-offshore-outsourcing.html>, January 18, 2016, p. 1).

software) completed the implementation in a matter of weeks, eventually achieving an automation rate of 93 percent of the targeted processes, with the residual 7 percent of exceptions and anomalies requiring human interaction of some kind. The RPA initiative was led by Paul Donaldson, a Six Sigma black belt and automation evangelist, who later assessed the experience this way:

> A robot can scale up and down and switch tasks. You'll train an application, a bit of software once, and if your contracts change, a robot can be trained quickly to adapt. You haven't got human resource type issues like induction time ... [But don't] automate a process that's not ready to be automated. Stabilise it first. It's a basic Six Sigma principle. There's a lot of "lifting and shifting" needed just to move a task from a human to a robot. In all of our processes, we keep a delivery lead in the process world, to standardize and streamline before we automate. [Ultimately, however, Xchanging's concern was not only with] processes, but to put a framework in place that could be leveraged for the Group—to institutionalize it.[62]

An evaluation of Xchanging's RPA project conducted by outsourcing researchers at the London School of Economics concluded that the company had "gone as far as it could with existing methodologies and technologies," with the risk that further offshoring might undermine a hard-earned reputation for system integrity and data security in the London insurance market. The company's "internal messaging [was that] there was no strong rationale for" repatriating work following the introduction of RPA, because there was "no quality problem" in the offshore processing centers.[63] Subsequent RPA initiatives would likely target both onshore and offshore operations, now that the methodology had been institutionalized.

A relatively benign interpretation of the automation process at Xchanging would position this case against so much of the robot folklore that has pervaded discussions of RPA, which is indeed how the LSE researchers chose to read it:

Myth 1: RPA is only used to replace humans with technology.
Fact 1: RPA at Xchanging was used to do more work with the same number of people.

Myth 2: Business operations staff feels threatened by RPA.
Fact 2: Business operations staff at Xchanging welcomed the robots as valued "new hires."

Myth 3: RPA will bring back many jobs from offshore.
Fact 3: Xchanging automated offshore processes and kept them offshore.

---

[62] Quoted in Willcocks and Lacity (2016: 107, 121, 107).
[63] Willcocks and Lacity (2016: 114).

Myth 4: RPA is driven primarily by cost savings.

Fact 4: Xchanging had a mature understanding of multiple operational benefits and strategic payoffs, with cost efficiencies being one driver amongst many.[64]

It may be possible for the introduction of RPA to leave no mark on the balance between offshore and onshore labor utilization, for the process merely to raise the productive capacity of a stable and secure workforce, and for the noble pursuit of strategic goals to override the tawdry calculus of cost suppression, but this would be a relatively rare accomplishment in the outsourcing world. Longer term, one might anticipate a much more disruptive bifurcation of the BPO landscape, as other senior executives at Xchanging have indeed been predicting, divided between a high-end segment defined by sophisticated and non-standard knowledge work and a low-end segment marked by a combination of extreme cheap-labor arbitrage and persistent exposure to automated displacement, in some cases extending to instances of RPA "taking out people entirely."[65] The specialists in taking costs out of extended supply chains, many ITO and BPO providers may find that they are also taken out, with some industry estimates suggesting that up to 40 percent of providers in this sector will fail, or will be taken over, by 2020 "if they fail to embrace the change."[66] Having been instrumental in opening a pathway to Robotistan, providers may have to migrate some of their own operations there, or risk being left by the wayside.

The imagined territory of Robotistan has duly come to symbolize the BPO industry's very own offshore threat, which has led to breathless forecasts of tectonic change, if not the production of an entirely "new landscape."[67] BPO providers have long been on the lookout for supplies of "cheaper fingers," in the words of Gartner's Cathy Tornbohm, a search that was always destined for "new geographies," beyond India and the Philippines. In the first wave of back-office outsourcing, the market had been made by "siloed" business processes, reflecting the decisions of client companies to externalize particular functions, often on a department-by-department or unit-specific basis. As the BPO infrastructure was progressively built out, and as corporate clients began to contemplate more systemic, cross-departmental outsourcing strategies, this first-generation approach would mature into more expansive "shared services" models, reaching across horizontal fields like procurement and human-resources

---

[64] Willcocks, L., Lacity, M., and Craig, A. (2015) Robotic process automation at Xchanging. *Outsourcing Unit Working Research Paper* 15/03, Outsourcing Unit, Department of Management, London School of Economics and Political Science, p. 5.

[65] Guy Kirkwood, quoted in Rosenthal, B. E. (2013) Six ways BPO looks different in 2013. *Outsourcing Center* September 30, accessed at <http://www.outsourcing-center.com/2013-09-six-ways-bpo-looks-different-in-2013-58328.html>, January 18, 2016, p. 1.

[66] Casale, F. (2015) Hard facts and hype: The data and the drama behind robotic process automation. In Institute of Robotic Process Automation, *Introduction to Robotic Process Automation: A primer.* New York: IRPA, p. 4.

[67] Sutherland (2013: 1).

administration.[68] These have since been the functional domains around which the BPO industry has constructed its expertise, systems, value propositions, and indeed markets. And they have structured the terrain across which RPA strategies are now unfolding, beginning with the most readily accessible territory—finance and accounting and procurement, followed in approximate sequence by supply chain, customer-experience management, legal services, and human resources. These are becoming, in effect, robotic migration channels, but just as the techniques and technologies of outsourced labor management jumped from one occupation to another, so too have RPA initiatives begun to diffuse "horizontally" across service functions.[69] Digital laborers are already pushing out beyond the early beachheads—routinized activities and occupations—having helped to establish not only technological demonstration effects but compelling business cases as well.

Change managers and transition advocates within the outsourcing complex will claim that there are push factors at work here, in addition to the "pull" of new technological opportunities. The narrowing transnational wage gap between onshore and offshore labor—which is a product not only of inflation in top-tier outsourcing locations like India and the Philippines, but also of long-run wage suppression in higher-income countries—means that "labor arbitrage [which] has been the largest single value lever for clients and BPO service providers for the last 15–20 years [has become] less potent today."[70] As the gains from labor-arbitrage approaches have begun to plateau, and as companies have been able to calculate the hidden costs of these long-distance relationships, new sources of demand for automated systems have begun to meet with innovation-enabled developments on the technological supply side. Advisors understand these changes to be prompted by the fact that the "global pool of talent is getting shallower and more expensive,"[71] recognizing that as labor "costs spiral, robotics offer the next wave of efficiency to those choosing to outsource [with] the onus . . . clearly on the outsourcing provider to be in touch with the latest technology."[72] A host of new transition narratives consequently have it that automation models will gradually eclipse those

---

[68] See Mehta, A., Armenakis, A., Mehta, N., and Irani, F. (2006) Challenges and opportunities of business process outsourcing in India. *Journal of Labor Research* 27(3): 323–38; Vashistha, A. and Vashistha, A. (2005) *The Offshore Nation*. New York McGraw-Hill; Xiang (2007) and Upadhya and Vasavi (2008).

[69] Rosenthal, B. E. (2013) Six ways BPO looks different in 2013. *Outsourcing Center* September 30, accessed at <http://www.outsourcing-center.com/2013-09-six-ways-bpo-looks-different-in-2013-58328.html>, January 18, 2016.

[70] Sutherland (2013: 8).

[71] Justice, C. and Salt, B. (2015) Employees: An endangered species? In KPMG, *Strategic Visions on the Sourcing Market 2016*. Amstelveen: KPMG, 29–34, p. 30.

[72] Cushman and Wakefield (2015) *Where in the World: Business process outsourcing and shared service location index*. London: Cushman and Wakefield, p. 19.

Table 6.1. From arbitrage to automation

	Offshore: the labor arbitrage model	**Noshore**: the robotic automation model
Rationale	Temporary, one-step gains: rationalization of routine, secondary operations, or "your mess for less"	Permanent transformation of business models
Costs	15–30 percent cost reduction (compared to inhouse)	40–75 percent cost reduction for specified functions (compared to inhouse)
Labor	Offshore labor supplies: accessing distant pools of low-cost labor as the basis of large-scale, FTE model of value creation	On-call expertise: accessing a small elite of "rocket scientists" with capacity to control, codify, and automate previously human work processes
Scalability	Constrained: scalability of the model is proportional to the scalability of labor	Uncoupled: scalability is "largely independent of labor growth"
Profitability	Profits and revenues correlated to workforce size and capacity	Profits and revenues delinked from workforce size and capacity

Source: author's formulation, developed from KPMG (2015)

based on labor arbitrage, as summarized in Table 6.1, a trend that has been inelegantly termed *ShiBLA*, the shift beyond labor arbitrage.[73]

The role of analysts and advisors, in this context, has been to scout out and then chart the new territory. One such mapping exercise is summarized in Table 6.2, in which various job functions and service activities have been scored according to six dimensions of robotic compatibility. The robots will be first to come, it is foretold here, where there is scope to break down business processes and administrative activities into procedural rules; where there is a need to access, and verify between, multiple systems or interfaces, such as "swivel chair" activities; where there is a limited need for human intervention and where routinized processes generate relatively few exceptions or anomalies; where work flows are characterized by high volumes and/or high values; and where there is a history of operations being compromised by human error.[74] Analysts have quickly come to recognize the "potential for much wider application," suggesting that the new paradigm called for "fundamentally [new] thinking about rules-based processes, [and therefore about] what roles can be brought into Robotistan, and the relationship between robot and labor going forward."[75] Instead of undercutting onshore wages and squeezing costs

---

[73] Institute of Robotic Process Automation (2015) *Introduction to Robotic Process Automation: A primer*. New York: IRPA, p. 10. For analyst discussions, see Burnett, S., Jain, A., Ranjan, R., Sinha, N., and Tiwari, B. (2015) *Seizing the Robotic Process Automation (RPA) Market Opportunity*. Dallas, TX: Everest Group; Sutherland, C. (2016) *The Maturation Accelerates for Robotic Process Automation*. Boston, MA: HfS Research.

[74] See Sutherland (2013).   [75] Sutherland (2013: 1).

Table 6.2. Sizing up the robot threat, by business-process function

	Prone to errors	Can be broken into business rules	High volumes and/or high values	Access multiple systems	Limited human intervention	Limited exception handling	Available for automation	
							...immediately	...over time
Finance and accounting							Accounts payable; order management, invoicing, collections; fixed-asset accounting	Accounts receivable; financial planning & analysis
Procurement							Spend-data management; accounts payable, help desk, invoice reconciliation, asset management; supplier help desk, service-level agreement monitoring, supplier accreditation	External marketplace analysis, proposal evaluation; contract administration
Supply chain							Demand planning, promotions management; supply management: spare parts planning, inventory replenishment; inventory optimization; transportation-load optimization	Forecasting; carrier management
Customer experience management							Customer support, technical support, billing and account management	Customer loyalty programs
Legal services							Litigation support: document review, e-discovery support services	Legal research & publishing: abstraction; patent research
Human resources							Payroll, employee data management; employee on/offboarding	Managing paid and unpaid leave

Yes   Sometimes   No

Source: author's compilation, derived from Sutherland (2013)

out of existing systems, the new task for outsourcing providers will be to "help clients find a balanced blend of FTEs and robots."[76]

No sooner had it been sighted, Robotistan seemed to be getting closer all the time. "Robotistan [is] quickly becoming part of the strategic planning efforts of leading BPO Service Providers, operational consultants, analysts and end clients," HfS has proclaimed, suggesting that the scale of the resulting migration—apparently involving ever more complex and sophisticated tasks—had been underestimated.[77] The growing consensus across the community of analysts and advisors was that significant parts of the BPO and ITO industry are now in a "race against the machines," to borrow the terminology popularized by Brynjolfsson and McAfee's science fiction-inflected contribution to economic forecasting.[78] Even if the robots were unlikely to colonize more than a fraction of the overall market for outsourced functions, RPA had been incorporated into the service offering of major BPO providers with remarkable speed, with many appointing senior executives as "practice leaders" and specialist teams, while a handful had committed to go "all in" with the new technology.[79] Some of these with aggressive RPA strategies—where providers have deep pockets, longer-term horizons, and an appetite for risk— have earned the label "extreme BPO."[80] These providers, though, are at the most creative end of this creatively destructive business. Technology-intensive strategies are less realistic for those delivering the basic product line (tightly managed cheap labor), many of which have built FTE-centric businesses in the pursuit of high-volume contracts by virtue of what is an easily substitutable and poorly differentiated service offering. Low-road, no-frills approaches represent typical responses to commoditized markets with falling prices and thin margins, just as they also contribute to the reproduction of these same conditions. With RPA, however, will come a *new math*: old-style BPO with its conventions of "labor based pricing will not stand a chance [once] market prices [are] plummeting."[81] These business realities have led some to question whether the bulk of existing BPO and ITO providers, creatures as they are of an inherited "FTE cost-focused model" and trapped as they are within low-margin markets, really have the capacity to drive a wave of investment in RPA systems and technologies, arguing instead that corporate clients and tech

[76] Institute of Robotic Process Automation (2015) *Introduction to Robotic Process Automation: A primer*. New York: IRPA, p. 19.
[77] HfS (2013) Robotistan takes a seat at the BPO Security Council. *Horses for Sources* blog October 29, accessed at <http://www.horsesforsources.com/robotistan-bpo-council_102913>, January 17, 2016, p. 1.
[78] Brynjolfsson and McAfee (2012). See also Brynjolfsson (2014).
[79] Sutherland (2013: 7).
[80] Tornbohm, C. (2012) The future of BPO. *Outsource Magazine* 29: 34–5, p. 35.
[81] Casale, F. (2014) *Here Come the Robots: The emergence of robotic process automation and the beginning of the end of outsourcing as we know it*. New York: Institute of Robotic Process Automation, p. 3.

startups will likely propel the transition—potentially leaving some traditional providers behind, the dinosaurs of an earlier wave of globalization.[82]

Beyond the glib observation that there would be "no 'next India' or 'next Philippines,'" and the wild predictions that large-scale BPO markets are on the verge of extinction thanks to the imminent arrival of the post-employment paradigm of cloud-based "platforms,"[83] it is clear that a new round of restructuring is taking shape. Analysts Arjun Sethi and Johan Gott maintain that the days of back-office and IT outsourcing forming the basis of national or regional development programs may be numbered, the "easy" market opportunities having already been captured, since those "host countries that have been relying on BPO to create hundreds of thousands of jobs may find that their citizens are up against a ruthless new competitor for highly standardized, mature, high-volume business processes."[84] Researchers at the World Bank have likewise observed that the "value chain for back-office business services has evolved dramatically over the past two decades," and even though

> many of the top players including India and the Philippines have started to provide higher value added end-to-end solutions to customers [in] the coming years, robotic process automation (RPA) could have revolutionary consequences for industry rationalization and labor markets, allowing robots and smart machines to take over the jobs of traditional BPO employees.[85]

On the other hand, those countries and cities with the most well-established BPO industries are likely also be the best positioned to rise to the challenge of automation, developing new service offerings that combine RPA, managerial expertise, and (relatively) cheap labor:

> One set of countries that starts off with an advantage [in managing the transition to RPA] is those that complement advanced traditional BPO skills with the requisite soft skills that machines cannot replace: India and the Philippines, for sure, but also Sri Lanka, Costa Rica, and South Africa. Another group of likely winners is cities with cutting-edge innovation hubs that will host the entrepreneurs capable of riding the wave of technological breakthroughs. San Francisco, Berlin, Tel Aviv, and Seoul come to mind as centers for innovation that can shape the future.[86]

The arrival of RPA hardly signals the death of geography in the outsourcing world, but it may mark the beginning of the end of a long wave of expansion

---

[82] Balasubramaniam, U. (2015) Robotic process automation: A viable option for the future? In KPMG, *Strategic Visions on the Sourcing Market 2016*. Amstelveen: KPMG, 35–7.

[83] Justice (2015: 2); see also Justice, C. and Salt, B. (2015) Employees: An endangered species? In KPMG, *Strategic Visions on the Sourcing Market 2016*. Amstelveen: KPMG, 29–34.

[84] Sethi, A. and Gott, J. (2015) *On the Eve of Disruption*. New York: A. T. Kearney, p. 3.

[85] Beschorner, N., Kuek, S. C., and Narimatsu, J. (2015) *Information and Communication Technologies for Jobs in the Pacific*. Report No: 96218-EAP. Washington, DC: World Bank, p. 15.

[86] Sethi, A. and Gott, J. (2015) *On the Eve of Disruption*. New York: A. T. Kearney, p. 3.

based primarily on the logic of cheap labor arbitrage—the *ShiBLA* monopoly. In this respect, Robotistan is real.

Some of the true believers have been involved in a whimsical discussion of what a constitution for Robotistan might look like, beyond the jungle law of purely commoditized relations, with some BPO and ITO providers supposedly having already "appointed their own dedicated ambassadors or sent fact-finding missions to Robotistan so that they can better understand how the place works."[87] Like all constitutions, the charter for this new pseudo-nation in the clouds is expected to be an aspirational and perhaps even idealistic document. It will certainly need to engage somewhat more elevated principles than the reigning rationalities of buyer-driven cost suppression, downward wage arbitrage, and labor displacement.

> [S]o that we are racing with rather than against the machine, we need a guide to what we should think about when we plan for Robotistan. [O]ur constitution [will] define the rights or benefits of Robotistan as well as the responsibilities... Thus, in Robotistan, we will use the technology of robotic automation not to focus on endlessly reducing costs but to find a way to improve the value of the people we need to deliver business processes most effectively.[88]

The distinctly disunited nations of the outsourcing world may have learned to live with the destabilizing effects of an ongoing price war, but this fragile order has now been disrupted. In fact, Robotistan itself had already taken unilateral action, not waiting for an invitation before claiming a seat "as one of the members of the BPO Security Council," where it would join increasingly urgent talks about "the future of horizontal business processes such as F&A, HR, Procurement, Supply Chain, Marketing and Legal,"[89] and where this leaderless, imagined nation would soon be vying for permanent-member status, joining (or perhaps replacing) fixtures in the BPO world like staff augmentation, global business services, process redesign—maybe even labor arbitrage itself.

The looming realities that are obliquely acknowledged in this industry banter concern the ways in which the future, to once again borrow William Gibson's formulation, is about to be redistributed. Outsourcing market players are now repeatedly warned that they must expect "significant upheaval in the near term," this being a "decisive moment" in which complacency and conservatism are fast becoming the risky strategies: "[T]hose companies that bury

---

[87] HfS (2013) Robotistan takes a seat at the BPO Security Council. *Horses for Sources* blog October 29, accessed at <http://www.horsesforsources.com/robotistan-bpo-council_102913>, January 17, 2016, p. 1.

[88] Sutherland (2013: 18).

[89] HfS (2013) Robotistan takes a seat at the BPO Security Council. *Horses for Sources* blog October 29, accessed at <http://www.horsesforsources.com/robotistan-bpo-council_102913>, January 17, 2016, p. 1.

their heads in the sand and don't make the pivot, either because they don't want to or don't know how to, will suffer the same fate as the companies that just two decades ago didn't prepare for the shift to an offshore/outsourcing economy."[90] Service providers must therefore ask themselves the meaning-of-life question, "If all of the mundane [work] could be automated, what do you want your people to excel at?"[91] (Your *remaining* people might have been the more appropriate expression.) The business world's version of political correctness seems to demand that the labor-displacing threat of automation must be tempered by a simultaneous appeal to a better future, in which workers relieved of drudgery by their digital workmates are magically "freed up" to concentrate, ostensibly, on more rewarding and fulfilling tasks. This management mantra has become a regular refrain in the internal messaging of those corporations that have launched new programs of automation, often in partnership with their offshore service providers, and in the more public version of RPA discourse. The supposedly reassuring line at Volvo, for example, which worked with Cognizant to automate a significant component of its finance and accounting processes, is that "robots are not here to take our jobs, but to help us with repetitive tasks and make our jobs more interesting," such that the real issue is "no longer whether or not the robots are here to stay [but] *what else robots can do for us.*"[92] In contrast, it is fair to say that there are few who are actually toiling in the far-off fields of the outsourcing world who are likely to mistake the advent of RPA—as a strategy for automating routine labor, on which not only business models but entire offshore economies have been constructed—for an invitation to join the (salaried) leisure class.

Servitude 2.0

This association between automation and the eradication of menial toil recalls the historical origins of the term *robot*. The word has its roots in a Central European system of forced labor under which a portion of a tenant's rent was to be paid in kind, in the form of indentured labor or personal service. Nominally limited by legal statute, the rate of feudal exploitation depended, in practice, "on the temper of the lord of the manor,"[93] the widespread resentment of which fueled revolutionary movements against the robot

---

[90] Casale, F. (2015) Hard facts and hype: The data and the drama behind robotic process automation. In Institute of Robotic Process Automation, *Introduction to Robotic Process Automation: A primer*. New York: IRPA, p. 4; Sutherland (2013: 19).

[91] Sutherland (2013: 19–20).

[92] Abeleen, J. (2015) Robots in finance: Volvo leads the way. In KPMG, *Strategic Visions on the Sourcing Market 2016*. Amstelveen: KPMG, 38–40, p. 40, emphasis added.

[93] Davis, K. B. (1900) The modern condition of agricultural labor in Bohemia. *Journal of Political Economy* 8(4): 491–523, p. 493.

Figure 6.3 Karel Čapek's *R.U.R.* (*Rossum's Universal Robots*)
Source: © Buyenlarge/Superstock

labor regime, culminating in its abolition in 1849. These events were the proximate source of the idiomatic translation of *robot* in the early twentieth century, which before Asimov is credited to Karel Čapek, an author, dramatist, and producer of prophetic science fiction from what was then Czechoslovakia. Čapek's 1920 play *Rossum's Universal Robots*, or *R.U.R.* (see Figure 6.3), satirized an imaginary robot world, prompting some of the earliest political discussion around the social effects of large-scale automation, while "spark[ing] off the idea of present-times robotics."[94]

Set in an unspecified offshore location, somewhat reminiscent of H.G. Wells' *Island of Dr. Moreau*, Čapek's play established what would become a persistent storyline in robot literature: a naïve and trusting world is surreptitiously

---

[94] Bradbrook, B. R. (1998) *Karel Čapek*. Brighton: Sussex Academic Press, p. 44; Čapek, K. [1921] (1990) R.U.R. (Rossum's Universal Robots): A collective drama in a comic prologue and three acts. In P. Kussi, ed., *Toward the Radical Center: A Karel Čapek reader*. Highland Park, NJ: Catbird Press, 34–109.

overrun by robots possessed of a cool and colonizing rationality, under the questionable influence in this case of a proto-multinational corporation, portrayed as an amoral and distant force. In Čapek's play, the mysterious land of the robots is visited by one of the central (human) characters, Helena Glory, the inquisitive daughter of the president of an unnamed European state, where the chattering classes are apparently "talking about nothing else." The director's office, where Miss Glory was received, is lined with posters proclaiming, "Tropical Robots—A New Invention—$150 a Head," and "Looking to Cut Production Costs? Order Rossum's Robots." Called upon to explain the utilitarian logic of the robot business to the island's idealistic young visitor, this is what Rossum's chief engineer, Fabry, and the marketing officer, Busman, have to say:

> FABRY: One Robot can do the work of two-and-a-half human laborers. The human machine, Miss Glory, was hopelessly imperfect... It couldn't keep up with modern technology... From a technical standpoint, the whole of childhood is nonsense. Simply wasted time...
>
> BUSMAN: [T]oday all prices are only a third of what they were, and they're still falling, lower, lower, lower... [W]e've cut the cost of labor... It's really funny, Miss, how factories all over are going belly-up unless they've bought Robots to cut production costs.[95]

Miss Glory had been particularly shocked to discover that Rossum's had not stopped at building robots to replace factory labor; all of the office staff were robots too. Only the managers were human, although perhaps in a premonition of his own eventual fate, the "central director" of R.U.R., Harry Domin, occupied a swivel chair.

In advance of the play's 1922 opening in New York, the announcement from the Czechoslovak Legation in Washington, DC explained that the "drama deals with an invention of Dr. Rosum (sic) [whose firm] supplied robots in thousands to all parts of the world," demonstrating to their capitalist owners that "[t]hese robots were by all means better for use in factories and in armies, making cheap labor material, and not causing any troubles as strikers."[96] Creating quite a sensation at the time, R.U.R. has been repeatedly rediscovered and restaged ever since, on some accounts being "one of the most widely performed plays of the [twentieth] century."[97] As Čapek's

---

[95] Čapek, K. [1921] (1990) R.U.R. (Rossum's Universal Robots): A collective drama in a comic prologue and three acts. In P. Kussi, ed., *Toward the Radical Center: A Karel Čapek reader*. Highland Park, NJ: Catbird Press, 34–109, pp. 49, 51.

[96] Anon (1922) Gossip of the Rialto. *New York Times* August 13: 6X.

[97] Kussi, P. (1990) Introduction. In P. Kussi, ed., *Toward the Radical Center: A Karel Čapek reader*. Highland Park, NJ: Catbird Press, 3–17, p. 8.

biographer explained, the most significant achievement of the play was the subtle and complex way that it conveyed

> the symbol of the robot, which represents not only the machine and its power to free man (sic) from toil but, at the same time, symbolizes man himself, dehumanized by his own technology. From a technical point of view, man is an inefficient instrument, whose emotional and spiritual life only impedes the drive of modern technology. Either he must give way to the machine, or he himself must become a machine.[98]

The *New York Times'* theater critic, John Corbin, chose to read the play as a muddle-headed satire on contemporary capitalism, in which the mechanized workers portrayed by Čapek "dabble[d] in the phrases of Karl Marx," but where all this "socialist intention" resulted in nothing more than an "impasse."[99] The play's subsequent reception has been generally more sympathetic, one such assessment concluding that its ultimate message was that, "it is not technology that destroys man (sic), but the greed for profits and the inevitable law of supply and demand."[100] Anticipating themes that would recur in Asimov's robot stories, as well as in both the fictional and the real worlds of robotics more generally, the reliability of this or that forecast was beside the point—these imagined futures spoke to the anxieties of the here and now.

The most recent round of robot stories is no exception. Once again, the threat *this time* is portrayed as a real one. In truth, the threat may indeed be different in that it no longer comes in the form of tin men, with their awkward gait and stilted diction, but in the posthuman, intangible, and practically ubiquitous forms of software code, cognitive intelligence, and virtual capacities. Even the most sober assessments of the so-called "second economy," as represented by the cluster of digitization technologies, the cloud, and intelligent systems now conclude that it could indeed be "*different this time*," even if the skeptics have been proved right before.[101] The netherworld of RPA may prove to be just such a transformative space. If "traditional automation" was about task displacement, RPA raises the prospect of human replacement, in that it is "not designed to be a business application, but . . . a *proxy for a human*

---

[98] Harkins, W. E. (1962) *Karel Čapek*. New York: Columbia University Press, p. 85.

[99] Corbin, J. (1922) A Czecho-Slovak Frankenstein. *New York Times* October 10: 16; see also Corbin, J. (1922) The revolt against civilization. *New York Times* October 15: 99. In fact, in 1990, Čapek's own politics were those of the "radical center." He was someone who "rejected collectivism of any type, but he was just as opposed to selfish individualism. He was a passionate democrat and pluralist [who was] often called a relativist because he disliked single vision and preferred to look at everything from many sides" (Kussi, P. (1990) Introduction. In P. Kussi, ed., *Toward the Radical Center: A Karel Čapek reader*. Highland Park, NJ: Catbird Press, 3–17, p. 5).

[100] Harkins, W. E. (1962) *Karel Čapek*. New York: Columbia University Press, p. 89.

[101] Roosevelt Institute (2015) *Technology and the Future of Work: The state of the debate*. New York: Open Society Foundations, p. 6, emphasis added.

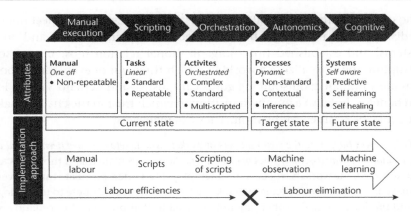

Figure 6.4 Survival of the . . . ? The evolutionary logic of automation

Source: Institute for Robotic Process Automation (<http://www.irpanetwork.com>) *A Primer on Robotic Process Automation*, developed and written by the Institute for Robotic Process Automation in association with Carnegie Mellon University

worker to operate business applications."[102] In the business and technology world, it is reported that most of the "early naïveté about universal robots" is now a thing of the past, in the words of the founder of Applied Minds, "matter-of-fact engineers" are now developing logical robotic systems in order to take over and transform specific tasks.[103] In Figure 6.4, a visual aid developed by the Institute for Robotic Process Automation, X marks the spot where the incremental logic of labor efficiency flips over into exponential process of *labor elimination*, gauged "conservatively" on a far steeper curve than Rossum's chief engineer, Mr Fabry, was able to achieve when one robot equaled "two-and-half human laborers." In today's future, the "more realistic" industry estimates are that between three and five "humans could be replaced by a single robot," while in place of the stage-prop posters selling "Tropical Robots," today there are PowerPoint slides that proclaim that, "There is only one thing better than a low cost person performing a business function, and that is having no person at all."[104]

The arrival of this "new class of digital labor" is represented as an inflection point, one where "BPO workers occupy only the first train car off the edge of a cliff," behind them being seated "100 million global knowledge workers

[102] Institute of Robotic Process Automation (2015) *Introduction to Robotic Process Automation: A primer.* New York: IRPA, p. 7, emphasis added.
[103] Brian Ferren, quoted in Markoff, J. (2012) Skilled work, without the worker. *New York Times* August 19: A1.
[104] Institute of Robotic Process Automation (2015) *Introduction to Robotic Process Automation: A primer.* New York: IRPA, p. 19; Casale, F. (2014) *Here Come the Robots: The emergence of robotic process automation and the beginning of the end of outsourcing as we know it.* New York: Institute of Robotic Process Automation, p. 3.

who could be impacted by RPA by 2025."[105] This raises the prospect not only of disruption to incumbent business models, maturing markets and pricing systems, and established (inter-)organizational relationships, but of social disruption too. Visualizing a world in which three out of every ten corporate jobs are automated, outsourcing gurus Cliff Justice and Bernard Salt see long-run benefits, but also a bumpy transition in which trust in the change-making class may be strained to the limit. They ask managers:

> [W]hat will happen to the vast numbers of workers who heretofore have been soaked up by manufacturing assembly lines or call centers? Some speculate that if those jobs are automated, the workers will become unemployable. Others postulate that the very makeup of society will change when knowledge workers contribute to technology and productivity while others are not engaged in that process. The scenario also invites questions about the distribution of wealth, especially when some parts of the population are not contributing to it ... Despite some foretellers' projections, RPA will not cause global unemployment, with mankind becoming idle while machines do the work. Rather, by automating low-level activities, RPA will ultimately free employees to focus on higher-value work or discover innovative ways to provide value.
>
> How will you manage fallout from displaced labor? The automation of human jobs may cause some unrest, so prepare to have honest, open discussions with your organization. Resistance may come not only from the workers in automatable roles but also from directors who may fear erosion in their span of control, as they potentially go from managing employees to managing bots.[106]

The transition-manager's figleaf position continues to be that there will be some, better-quality jobs left behind after automation, yet the scale of these opportunities to work "hand-in-hand with robots" seems genuinely modest in comparison with the scope of the rising cluster of labor-displacing technologies. The Institute for Robotic Process Automation inadvertently captures the asymmetry quite neatly in its sanguine observation that while "it is expected that automation software will replace up to 140 million full-time employees worldwide by the year 2025, many high-quality jobs will be created for those who are able to maintain and improve RPA software."[107]

For the millions of workers living on the wrong side of this curve, the long-run effects of some mass, automated displacement to noshore threaten to be truly world changing. "How has science fiction," Brynjolfsson and McAfee have asked, "become business reality so quickly?" Their bestselling exploration of the "digital frontier" portrayed the cascading effects of the ICT

---

[105] Justice (2015: 4).

[106] Justice, C. and Salt, B. (2015) Employees: An endangered species? In KPMG, *Strategic Visions on the Sourcing Market 2016*. Amstelveen: KPMG, 29–34, pp. 31–2, emphasis added.

[107] Institute of Robotic Process Automation (2015) *Introduction to Robotic Process Automation: A primer*. New York: IRPA, p. 29.

revolution in epochal terms, historically commensurate with the forces of creative destruction unleashed, first, by the advent of steam power, and later, by electrification:

> The third industrial revolution, which is unfolding now, is fuelled by computers and networks. Like both of the previous ones, it will take decades to play out [and] it will lead to sharp changes in the path of human development and history. The twists and disruptions will not always be easy to navigate. But we are confident that most of these changes will be beneficial ones, and that we and our world will prosper on the digital frontier.[108]

For *Wired* blogger, Jason Kingdon, this robot-driven third industrial revolution evokes "a digital echo of Henry Ford's production line," as the Taylorist logic of fragmentation and routinization is taken to its (il)logical extreme—removing labor from production altogether.[109]

In white- and pink-collar job markets, routinization, automation, and relocation have long proceeded hand in hand. Back in the early 1960s, when across North America the movement began to separate back offices from front offices, the pattern was to relocate the feminized work of data processing "away from company headquarters [and out to] the low-rental industrial fringe of [the] city," a time when "the machine operator in the modern office [found herself working] under conditions similar to those of her blue-smocked sister in the plant."[110] These were also times, however, in which a generalized culture of technological optimism held sway. And so it was anticipated that the advance of automation in the office would yield not only benign but positive effects, shortening working hours and allowing for increased leisure time, "[s]ome urban planners and city managers foresee[ing] the need for more civic recreational services: parks, playgrounds, bowling alleys, fishing and boating facilities, skating rinks, libraries, art galleries, museums, auditoriums and theatres."[111] In the subsequent half century, the back office may have continued to move further back, as suburbanization was superseded by offshoring,[112] but the leisure dividend never did arrive.

---

[108] Brynjolfsson and McAfee (2012: 17, 76).

[109] Kingdon, J. (2013) How digital labor will drive the third industrial revolution. *Wired: Innovation Insights* blog, October 29, accessed at <http://insights.wired.com/profiles/blogs/how-digital-labor-will-drive-the-third-industrial-revolution?xg_source=activity#axzz2mjuFwYHc>, January 18, 2016, p. 1.

[110] Hoos, I. R. (1961) *Automation in the Office*. Washington, DC: Public Affairs Press, pp. 124–5. See also the discussion in Chapter 2.

[111] Hoos, I. R. (1961) *Automation in the Office*. Washington, DC: Public Affairs Press, p. 119.

[112] See Wilson, M. I. (1995) The office farther back: Business services, productivity, and the offshore back office. In P. T. Harker, ed., *The Service Productivity and Quality Challenge*. Dordrecht: Kluwer Academic Publishers, 203–24; Nelson, K. (1986) Labor demand, labor supply and the suburbanization of low-wage office work. In A. J. Scott and M. Storper, eds, *Production, Work, Territory*. Boston, MA: Allen and Unwin, 149–71.

Today, as the twin processes of transnational relocation and digitally enabled automation are pulling both costs and labor out of the back-office supply chain, the mood seems decidedly more pessimistic. When the outsourcing advisory firm, Gartner, applied its forecasting skills to the not so far away world of 2020, the images were not those of crowded art galleries and skating rinks but of ever more severe divisions of labor, society-wide waves of job displacement, and a growing threat of political instability. Reminiscent of the scenes rendered by Karel Čapek in *R.U.R.* a century earlier, the intensification and redistribution of stress was seen to be barely alleviated by the cold comfort of falling prices:

> Digitization is reducing labor content of services and products in an unprecedented way, thus fundamentally changing the way remuneration is allocated across labor and capital. Long term, this makes it impossible for increasingly large groups to participate in the traditional economic system—even at lower prices—leading them to look for alternatives such as a bartering-based (sub)society, urging a return to protectionism or resurrecting initiatives like Occupy Wall Street, but on a much larger scale.[113]

In this scenario, the hollowing-out economies of the global North would bear the brunt of the oncoming wave of disruption: "Mature economies will suffer most," Gartner concluded, because they will not have "the population growth to increase autonomous demand nor powerful enough labor unions or political parties to (re-)allocate gains in what continues to be a global economy."[114]

Meanwhile, elsewhere in the global economy, the mood has hardly been any less restive. The offshore beneficiaries of the early waves of relocated back-office functions, in India and the Philippines, have become acutely aware that their newly established industry has become a conspicuously vulnerable "aggregation point," if not target, for projects of automation. Here, the promise of liberation from menial toil rings just as hollow, but in a different way, because in the space of a generation not only new labor markets but new middle classes were constructed on the basis of the relocation of routinized employment tasks from higher-wage countries. Even if media scares of a coming outsourcing "apocalypse" are overstated, the quiet ascendancy of RPA has become a "worry for hundreds of mid-sized BPOs that currently rely on labour-based activities," as an Indian tech portal has reported, not to mention the hundreds of thousands of workers that have entered this industry.[115]

---

[113] Gartner (2013) Gartner reveals top predictions for IT organizations and users for 2014 and beyond. Gartner press release October 8, accessed at <http://www.gartner.com/newsroom/id/2603215>, January 18, 2016, p. 1.

[114] Gartner (2013) Gartner reveals top predictions for IT organizations and users for 2014 and beyond. Gartner press release October 8, accessed at <http://www.gartner.com/newsroom/id/2603215>, January 18, 2016, p. 1.

[115] CXOtoday News Desk (2014) IPsoft's Amelia: A threat to India's IT outsourcing? *CXOtoday* April 15, accessed at <http://www.cxotoday.com/story/chetan-dubes-amelia-a-threat-to-indias-it-

The work that the new generation of robotic systems does, outsourcing analyst Stephanie Overby has explained, tends to displace "the sweat shop tasks that occur in the back-office and IT," which in turn have long been a source of the industry's labor turnover problem, its image problem, and its FTE-constrained-growth problem.[116] Automation is an especially radical response to these "body-shop" problems, of course. It is a strategy, ultimately, for removing many of the bodies altogether. In the words of IPsoft's chief commercial officer, Jonathan Crane,

> Autonomics have the ability to absolve mankind of mundane chores...This is true not only in IT support, but in any systematic business process. The Indian vendors have thousands of staff doing similar work now with high rates of turnover and rising costs due to inflation. Autonomics are making the offshoring of tasks—so often considered the solution to optimize ITO and BPO tasks—irrelevant.[117]

While the offshore outsourcers may have been the pathfinders in the transnational project of "redividing" routinized labor—extruding back-office functions, rebundling tasks and systems, and streamlining all manner of business processes—there are some that are now arguing that this labor-arbitrage moment was but a transitional fix, en route to systemic automation. The alluring value proposition offered by companies like Blue Prism is that the outsourcing complex can finally move beyond lift and shift, finally getting away from the grind, and the noise, and the friction, and soar off instead into the clouds, where "a combination of smart people and dumb robots [can] get the work done."[118]

These visions of comprehensively automated, posthuman outsourcing may not come to pass, of course, or they will only be found in a few islands of innovation amid an ocean of business-as-usual labor arbitrage, but the ongoing conversation around these issues reveals at least two things. First, the experimental rollout of RPA systems will continue, in the wake of which these practices seem certain to spread at least incrementally. The outsourcing complex has itself become an adaptive, learning network, with the capacity to drive forward transformative projects of this kind, even if they do not come

outsourcing/>, February 18, 2016, p. 1; McLain, S. (2015) The seven signs of India's outsourcing apocalypse. *WSJ.com* July 13, accessed at <http://blogs.wsj.com/briefly/2015/07/13/the-seven-signs-of-indias-outsourcing-apocalypse-the-numbers/>, January 15, 2016.

[116] Overby, S. (2012) IT robots may mean the end of offshore outsourcing. *CIO Magazine* November 16, accessed at <http://www.cio.com/article/2390305/outsourcing/it-robots-may-mean-the-end-of-offshore-outsourcing.html>, January 18, 2016, p. 2.

[117] Quoted in Overby, S. (2012) IT robots may mean the end of offshore outsourcing. *CIO Magazine* November 16, accessed at <http://www.cio.com/article/2390305/outsourcing/it-robots-may-mean-the-end-of-offshore-outsourcing.html>, January 18, 2016, p. 2.

[118] Pat Geary, quoted in Global Delivery Report (2012) Will automation replace offshore BPO? *Global Delivery Report* November 28, accessed at <http://globaldeliveryreport.com/tag/robots/>, January 18, 2016, p. 2.

close to constituting an across-the-board paradigm shift. Only time will tell. But larger-scale movements are at least possible, and when it comes to highly standardized operations they can even be considered likely. Second, the very prevalence of RPA talk (not to say fear) is symptomatic of the perpetually restive mood of the outsourcing complex. Over the years, efforts to "humanize" the offshore outsourcing industry have met with little success.[119] Public-relations problems on the "outside," coupled with intractable challenges of dealing with actual humans on the "inside" (given the routinized, monotonous nature of so much outsourced work, the culture of permanent operational stress, and the high rates of labor turnover that follow from these conditions), together contribute to an entrenched sense of ennui amongst those tasked with the management of this work. Apparently stuck on the low road, drudgery has become a managerial condition too. As Phil Fersht of HfS Research has complained, the "outsourcing business is in danger of killing itself with boredom," confronting as it does the risk of losing touch with both humanity and value: "outsourcing organizations are heading towards a zombie state," he reports, because the "dull, repetitive tasks that often get offshored are leading to a condition where people are becoming demoralized and losing any interest they might have had in the tasks they routinely perform."[120] Others observe that these circumstances are producing "lethargy [across] the middle management layer," on top of the problems of alienation, weak attachment, and poor motivation on the shop floor.[121] It is not without significance that this is the zone where automation will strike, and where it stands a good chance of achieving real traction.

There is a new generation of change managers who clearly relish the opportunity to escape this daily grind altogether and instead apply their Six Sigma black-belt skills to the more exciting challenges of RPA deployments. For some of the industry's veterans this evidently gets the pulse racing again, taking them back to the early days of offshoring, when they had also been working at the cutting edge of both technological and organizational change.[122] Far from "humanizing" the outsourcing business, by building skills and valuing talent,

[119] Kripalani, M. (2006) Five offshore practices that pay off. *Business Week* January 30: 60–1.

[120] Quoted in Howlett, D. (2013) Welcome to Robotistan—the antidote to zombieism. *Diginomica* blog, November 10, accessed at <http://diginomica.com/2013/11/10/robotistan/>, January 18, 2016, p. 1.

[121] Howlett, D. (2015) Six barriers to change in the age of AaS and Robotistan. *Diginomica* August 26, accessed at <http://diginomica.com/2015/08/26/six-barriers-to-change-in-the-age-of-aas-and-robotistan/#.VrkbHvHf_Rs>, February 8, 2016, p. 3. See also Kuruvilla, S. and Ranganathan, A. (2010) Globalisation and outsourcing: Confronting new human resource challenges in India's business process outsourcing industry. *Industrial Relations Journal* 41(2): 136–53; Xiang (2007); Upadhya and Vasavi (2008).

[122] See, for example, Casale, F. (2015) Hard facts and hype: The data and the drama behind robotic process automation. In Institute of Robotic Process Automation, *Introduction to Robotic Process Automation: A primer*. New York: IRPA.

quite the opposite dynamic is now at work, at least in some organizations, as the debased currency of the FTE is traded away altogether. Outsourcing networks are now deeply engaged in the visualization and experimental production of what amount to post-FTE environments, by means of a quiet transformation that does not manifest as a single wave, but rather in myriad shifts and adaptations—one workplace, one contract, one engagement at a time. The workplace politics of this extended, multisite process of robotic displacement seem more likely to be diffuse and differentiated, instead of concentrated and contestable.[123] In the practiced mode of outsourced management, RPA deployments are ideally achieved with a minimum of "noise." The goal is to introduce this potentially highly disruptive technology in as non-disruptive a manner as possible. It is quite appropriate, then, that the posthuman work systems that are now being established are staffed by benign figures like IPsoft's virtual assistant, Amelia, or Xchanging's automated office-mate, Poppy. Perhaps the early field reports are true that the (retained) human staff at Xchanging's offices offered little or no resistance, some going as far as to greet "the robots as valued 'new hires,'" in the words of the LSE research team. Apparently, "[o]perations staff [at Xchanging] did not fear robotisation, but named and welcomed 'Poppy' as a team member."[124] More than this, Poppy's coworkers were soon coming up with suggestions for additional tasks that she and her virtual colleagues might take on. It is said that Poppy even received an invitation to the office party.

In a similar vein, Amelia "beguiles everyone she meets," it is said; fluent in more than twenty languages and holding down jobs, simultaeously, at Shell Oil, Accenture, and several other Fortune 100 companies, she maybe "starts as a child [but soon] becomes a PhD," learning at a rate that her human colleagues can only admire.[125] Amelia's rapid ascent to maturity is being watched especially closely in India, where it has been remarked that "if you lose your BPO job, you can blame it on Amelia."[126] Here it is recorded that intensive development work has meant that the disconcertingly "intense stare" originally associated with IPsoft's virtual assistant is a thing of the past; she can now call upon a wide repertoire of facial expressions appropriate to verbal responses,

---

[123] See Poster and Yolmo (2016).

[124] Willcocks and Lacity (2016: 113); Lacity, M. C. and Willcocks, L. (2015) What knowledge workers stand to gain from automation. *Harvard Business Review* June 19, accessed at <https://hbr.org/2015/06/what-knowledge-workers-stand-to-gain-from-automation>, January 14, 2016.

[125] Ankeny, J. (2015) Even better than the real thing. *Entrepreneur* 43(6): 34–43, p. 34; Jonathan Crane, IPsoft, quoted in Outsource (2015) Q&A: Jonathan Crane, IPsoft. *Outsource Magazine* June 10, accessed at <http://outsourcemag.com/qa-jonathan-crane-ipsoft-part-1/>, January 25, 2016.

[126] Nayak, V. D. (2014) If you lose your BPO job, blame it on AMELIA. *Economic Times* April 22, accessed at <https://prezi.com/9mzv8svuff8n/if-you-lose-your-bpo-job-blame-it-on-amelia/>, January 18, 2016.

based on the "emotional vectors of Pleasure, Arousal and Dominance."[127] There have been other significant changes in Amelia's life too. She was introduced to the world, early in 2012, as Eliza, a name that spoke to a resonant lineage, most immediately to the early 1960s and the revolutionary computing algorithm created by MIT's Joseph Weizenbaum, ELIZA the robotic doctor, whose programmed interactions with (imagined) psychotherapy patients anticipated not only the rise of artificial intelligence but also the codified scripts that would later form the basis of "customer management" systems in outsourced call centers.[128] Weizenbaum's own inspiration had been the character Eliza Doolittle in George Bernard Shaw's *Pygmalion*, the Cockney flower girl coached by a phonetics professor to pass as a duchess, in the process erasing every trace of her working-class accent—which in turn taps into the received genealogy of transformational morality tales that runs through *Rossum's Universal Robots* to *Frankenstein* all the way back to the mythological origins of Pygmalion in Ovid's *Metamorphoses*.[129]

When he was completing the work on his famous robot play, Karel Čapek recalled having been "seized by a dreadful fear, I wanted to warn against mass production and dehumanized slogans and, all of a sudden, I became anxious that it could happen, perhaps soon."[130] Similar premonitions of a "robot winter" have been issued, from time to time, during the century since, but none have proved to be especially reliable guides to the future. Of course, Čapek's first glimpses of what outsourcers would later know as Robotistan could not have been expected to have been accurate down to all of the technological details—imagining as he did a tropical island populated by universal robots, rather than a virtual domain orchestrated by software applications. But *R.U.R.* was nevertheless prophetic in other ways, notably in its depictions of transnationalized corporate power, of the unforgiving discipline of falling prices, and of the alienating effects of automation. Some of Asimov's forecasts would prove to be even closer to the mark. His vision of the robotic world was not one populated by "universal" mechanical servants; robotic automation would instead be a much more diffuse process, in which robots "fashioned for certain jobs" would gradually take over specific tasks, eventually being produced on an industrial scale by "matter-of-fact engineers." Seen

---

[127] Mishra, P. (2014) IPsoft's Amelia is a dream artificial intelligence creation. *Economic Times* December 14, accessed at <http://economictimes.indiatimes.com/magazines/panache/ipsofts-amelia-is-a-dream-artificial-intelligence-creation/articleshow/45529418.cms>, January 18, 2016, p. 1.

[128] Weizenbaum, J. (1966) ELIZA: A computer program for the study of natural language communication between man and machine. *Communications of the Association for Computing Machinery* 9(1): 36–45.

[129] Shanken, E. A. (2005) Hot to bot: Pygmalion's lust, the Maharal's fear, and the cyborg future of art. *Technoetic Arts* 3(1): 43–55.

[130] Karel Čapek, quoted in Bradbrook, B. R. (1998) *Karel Čapek*. Brighton: Sussex Academic Press, p. 45.

from this perspective, the path-enabling work of the offshore outsourcing industry over the past two decades—relocating and routinizing job functions, reintegrating them through long-distance networks—seems to have paved the way for just this kind of robotic re-engineering, which in the space of a few years has moved from an avant-garde idea to near-term program. And according to many of the opinion formers in the outsourcing business, it is fast becoming a restructuring imperative. The outsourcing complex has been constructed, over the period since the late 1990s, as an infrastructural network dedicated to the task of rolling efficiency gains and cost compression, organized primarily according to the interests of corporate buyers. Since it was premised on, and then constructed around "the idea that there is always a lower-cost location," in the words of business commentator Chris Niccolls, maybe it could have been anticipated that the long-run direction of travel was "towards Robotistan," which some anticipate will "outsourcing's final destination."[131]

---

[131] Niccolls, C. (n.d.) Robotistan: The final destination for outsourcing. *About.com*, accessed at <http://outsourcing.about.com/od/disruptive/a/Robotistan-The-Final-Destination-For-Outsourcing.htm>, January 15, 2016.

7

Conclusion

Beyond Offshore

A theme of this book has been that the move offshore, which began with the NIDL-era extension of manufacturing supply chains and which has since spread, in the wake of the ICT revolution, across swathes of the white-collar economy, represents an historical threshold moment with wide and deep implications for employment systems, corporate structures, management practices, regional development, and labor markets. More than a decade ago, Thomas Friedman's *The World Is Flat* anticipated the arrival of a new age of lateral, networked competition, but this was an idealized account of a transformation really only just getting started.[1] Global sourcing has proved to be a complex, cumulative, and involutionary process in which a tangle of locational, competitive, organizational, and "relocational" dynamics have come into play. To be sure, the crude pull of cheaper labor alternatives—what might be considered the original offshore impulse—remains in evidence, but this now coexists with the revalorization of nearshore locations, the selective integration of onshore and proximity-based operations, the consolidation of offshore centers of excellence, experiments in robotic automation, and much more.

More than an aggregate outcome of corporate decision-making, and more also than a transnational market in (work) tasks and (job) functions, the outsourcing complex now exhibits the form of an organizational platform, one that renders not only possible but practical historically new forms of "employment." The scare quotes are called for because the transactional task of "shipping jobs overseas" was really only the start; the work of the outsourcing complex is increasingly about the creation and propagation of new organizational and technical

[1] See Friedman (2005). See also Friedman, T. L. (2007) *The World Is Flat: Further updated and expanded.* New York: Farrar, Straus, and Giroux; Friedman, T. L. (1999) *The Lexus and the Olive Tree: Understanding globalization.* New York: Farrar, Straus, and Giroux; and Friedman, T. L. (1999) *Hot, Flat, and Crowded.* New York: Farrar, Straus, and Giroux.

capabilities, involving ongoing adaptions in the quantity and quality of labor inputs. Even if it is a space of persistent operational stress, the outsourcing complex has also become the site of a new *organizational fix* for corporations large and small, extending as it does the managerial repertoire while opening up new realms and registers for systematic restructuring. This is a new *spatial fix* as well, in that it enables the ongoing transformation of corporate systems and employment regimes in ways that promise truly to change the rules of the game. The future cannot be known, of course, but arguably the least likely scenario is a few minor perturbations en route to a new equilibrium. If there is a word for the normalized condition that is being enabled by the global build out of the outsourcing complex, "dislocation" might be it.

As a result, *Offshore* must remain a story without closure. There is no final stage, no settled geography, and no moment of equilibrium in the continuously restructuring world wrought by global outsourcing. The intersecting calculi of cost, competition, techno-organizational capabilities, and geographical location are always in motion, their dynamic interactions making for a perpetually restless landscape. In retrospect, the NIDL moment beginning in the 1970s and the ICT moment beginning in the 1990s marked successive step changes in this evolutionary/involutionary process. These were, in a sense, changes of gear, but the gears are still changing. Outsourcers are always on the lookout for the *next* shore. This is the shifting terrain that has been occupied— if far from conquered—by the outsourcing complex, the rationale of which is one of continuous restructuring. Once again, "dislocation" might be the most apt way to describe this (re)organizational rationale.

In one sense, the outsourcing complex can be seen as a cypher for the driving forces that are transnational labor-arbitrage, buyer-dominated contracting and price competition; in another, its mediating and matchmaking functions are undoubtedly generative as well, changing the game by creating new capacities, while also speaking to the considerable effort involved in holding these new global markets together. Constituted as a kind of networked platform, the outsourcing complex now performs an infrastructural role, as a spatial-organizational fix actively facilitating and extending a repertoire of long-, medium-, and shorter-distance engagements. It is the outsourcing complex that keeps this world in motion. In place of a conclusion, this closing chapter reflects on the future-making capabilities of the outsourcing complex, drawing together observations on the present structure, and mood, of the complex as well as some of its incipient organizational tendencies. The chapter then turns to the outsourcers' basic charge—the decomposition, migration, and recombination of tasks—through which the unstable political economy of global sourcing has been constructed. The book closes where it began, with the "redivision" of labor, an historic process that is being reworked in new ways in the age of globalized sourcing.

The Complex

An objective of this book has been to shed light on the operations of the outsourcing complex, conceived as a multifaceted cluster of economic actors, organizations, and networks that has come to play a catalytic role in the facilitation of global sourcing as an evolving field of corporate practice, competitive calculation, and organizational experimentation. Like so much of the world that is offshore—think of tax havens, detention sites, or the nominal headquarter locations of shell corporations—the transnational outsourcing complex occupies a space that is mostly out of sight, over the horizon, and barely within (regulatory) reach.[2] Yet at the same time it has a persistent presence, exerting an influence "at a distance" on the internal operations of corporations, and on their management and employment systems, not to mention on the structure of regional economies, and on the imaginaries of businesses and the general public. The outsourcing complex may be "out there," but it is also very much "in here."

The basis of the following narrative, Table 7.1 summarizes some of the principal features of the transnational outsourcing complex, connecting these in each case—for it is never still—with notable tendencies and developments. The fundamental work of the complex is that of intermediation, connecting the buyers and vendors of outsourcing engagements, facilitating the migration of tasks, and managing the ongoing relationships between contractors and providers, the underlying source of value being the premium attached to cross-border arbitrage (still mostly measured, bluntly, in terms of savings on direct labor costs). While some parts of the outsourcing industry have been striving, with a measure of success, to transcend the labor-arbitrage model that was its founding rationale, moving towards value-adding partnerships with corporate clients, these aspirations have been repeatedly frustrated by the preoccupation amongst corporate buyers for cost suppression, by an entrenched culture of price-based competition, and by crowding in the always expanding vendor market.

The utilitarian logic of tapping into cheap supplies of offshore labor—for that growing number of previously inhouse employment functions that can be decomposed, detached, and then delivered at a distance—seems to be irresistible. These are the foundations upon which the outsourcing complex, as a globalized delivery system and an agent of rationalization, has been constructed. This means that even as some lead firms and best-in-class providers have been able to move towards transformational (rather than merely transactional) forms of outsourcing, the gravitational pull of low-road

---

[2] For a wider discussion, see Palan (2003) and Urry (2014).

Table 7.1. The transnational outsourcing complex

	Principal features	Tendencies and developments
Operational rationale	Intermediation: facilitating the fragmentation, routinization, relocation, and (re)integration of work tasks Leveraging arbitrage across the borders of the firm and jurisdiction: for cost reduction, functional efficiency, and flexibility enhancement	From "your mess for less," with windfall gains in labor arbitrage, to more complex, value-adding operations From transactional to transformational outsourcing, as direction and aspiration, but with continuing reliance on routine processes; rise of labor-displacing automation
Politics and culture	Persistently negative public image, a vent for economic insecurities, prone to populist inflation Low corporate status, ambivalent identities, professional insecurity, minimalist sectoral organization	Corporate normalization and discreet expansion; bipartisan abrogation of policymaking responsibility Weak industry "voice," ongoing efforts to stabilize and recognize professional codes
Capital	Operational deconcentration onshore (following corporate disaggregation), reconcentration offshore (corporatization of supply chains) Relatively high barriers to entry, but weak brands/generic value propositions	Geographical diversification, including generalized movement in the direction of nearshore locations Augmentation of vendor-side capabilities, accompanied with transnationalization
Labor	Labor-cost arbitrage as a formative driver Routinization and deskilling; competitive disciplining of onshore and offshore labor	Moderate wage inflation in first-tier outsourcing centers fuels further decentralization Islands of offshore upskilling in an ocean of deskilling
Technology	ICT-facilitated expansion; fiber-optic and web-enabled connectivity Software-based monitoring, governance, and control	Cloud-based integration Accelerating robotic automation of already routinized operations
Markets	Subjection of externalized tasks to whip of price-based competition Corporate buyer dominance; crowded vendor markets	Persistent commoditization and undercutting Vendor-side concentration with low margins
Hierarchies	Lean strategies, based on core competences and outsourcing of secondary functions Flattened, stretched out, and intermediated hierarchies	Strategic focusing of core competences; from selective to systemic outsourcing Persistently destabilized corporate hierarchies
Networks	Volatile networks, always knotting and splitting, are marked with ongoing frictions as well as transnational flows Hybrid forms of expertise are enabled and shaped through networked relations between (contracting, competing, and collaborating) organizations	"Infrastructural" role of built-out outsourcing networks; becomes the source of network capabilities Strategic partnering (only) in blue-chip relationships, where it enables the mutual development of new capacities

competition remains pervasive. Sporadic upgrading, as a result, coexists with business-as-usual, lift-and-shift, your-mess-for-less, cost-cutting models of outsourcing, with value-adding innovations and high-road practices being constantly lost to the market. The cheap-labor rationale for outsourcing remains deeply entrenched, even as it has been repeatedly elaborated; cost suppression is a constitutive condition of the outsourcing complex. An equally persistent condition, however, is increased expectations on the part of corporate clients, in the form of enriched services and friction-free operations, even if they are rarely prepared to pay much (or any) more. And despite the fact that client expectations and project complexity have both been rising, tolerance of suboptimal performance is in very short supply, in a world of empowered buyers and fiercely competing vendors. Nevertheless, it remains bluntly true that cutting costs is "almost always the chief rationale" for outsourcing, as the no-nonsense observers at the *Economist* put it.[3] This fraught intersection, between escalating client demands and ongoing pressures for commodification, is the bind that defines so much of the outsourcing complex.

If this is how the outsourcing complex basically operates on the inside, its outlook and operations are also shaped by a generally hostile and unsympathetic world on the outside. Not without underlying cause, offshore outsourcing has become a political scapegoat for a host of anxieties around employment insecurity and the effects of trade liberalization. Ever since the Bush/Kerry presidential contest in the United States, when outsourcing first became an object of political spectacle, the response amongst those engaged in the business of outsourcing has been to recede further under the radar, recoiling from public scrutiny, even as underlying growth trajectories have hardly been impeded at all. (Meanwhile, for their part, those in positions of political leadership have singularly failed to grapple with the issue, beyond taking advantage of its inflammatory connotations for partisan purposes.) Low-profile modes of operation therefore coexist with a lingering sense of stigma.

These generally negative optics have done nothing to elevate the status of outsourcing in the corporate world itself, where this work is regarded as functionally necessary and prosaically demanding, but anything but a preferred destination for the most ambitious of high fliers. The managers of outsourced operations often grumble that they, and the challenging work that they do, are misunderstood. They must deal with their clients' less than top priority operations (their "mess"), while at the same time handling (indeed often taking the blame for) any problems that remain. This work may, in its own way, be essential, but it can also seem to be thankless. In a similarly unrequited search for respect, the providers of outsourced services may like to think of themselves as the strategic partners of their corporate clients, but instead are often treated as second-class citizens or low-status suppliers, best kept on a tight leash and safely of sight. So just as there are precious few public defenders of outsourcing, the designation "outsourcing professional" is an identity that only a few would actively choose. This is a

---

[3] Economist (2013) Outsourcing and offshoring: The story so far. *Economist* January 19, S5.

field dogged by professional insecurities, one expression of which is a persistent undercurrent of dissatisfaction with the industry's name and identity. In a formal sense, the (representative) organizational structures of the outsourcing business-cum-profession are relatively weak and "flat," even as its work has become increasingly regularized, indeed essential, as an actually existing domain of managerial practice and paraprofessional expertise.

In terms of the structure of capital, transnational outsourcing is predicated on the selective operational unbundling of tasks and employment systems in "onshore" organizations, in line with the well-established trend for "disaggregating" the corporation according to the principles of lean management. It is from this diverse array of secondary (or non-core) competences that outsourcing markets have been made. "Outsourcing may be called by many different names," an industry commentator has observed, and it has even been pronounced dead (in its 1.0 form) several times, "but the idea that there are other people, managers and locations outside of your firm that can do your work better, faster and for a better price is not going away."[4] Now that these "outside" markets have been established, the resulting archipelago of supply-chain and back-office economies has itself been subject to continuous waves of reorganization, corporatization, commodification, and relocation. The outsourcing complex now has its own complement of corporate giants, with workforces numbering in the tens of thousands and extending across many countries. Positioned alongside, and competing with, these multinational specialists is a formidable group of companies with origins in consulting, accounting, computing, and related fields that have diversified through the addition (or acquisition) of outsourcing divisions, subsidiaries, and practice fields, from Accenture to Kelly to IBM (see Table 4.2). Reflecting this diversification and deepening of outsourcing networks, the geographical structure of the outsourcing complex is not nearly so India-centric as it was in its formative years. The rise of the Philippines as a globally significant platform, to be joined by a range of nearshore locations across Latin America and Central and Eastern Europe, has contributed to the development of an increasingly multipolar outsourcing complex, with its own internal divisions of labor and functional specializations (see Figures 1.1, 5.1, and 5.2).

The work of the outsourcing complex is fundamentally concerned with leveraging arbitrage gains on behalf of corporate clients. The full cycle of this operation involves the extraction of work functions from client companies, their routinization, reorganization, and rebundling in offshore locations, and their effective reintegration into extended supply chains and back-office

---

[4] Niccolls, C. (n.d.) Outsourcing: Is this the end? *About.com*, accessed at <http://outsourcing.about.com/od/feasibility/a/Outsourcing-Is-This-The-End.htm>, January 12, 2016.

systems. What the outsourcers must strive for, in this context, is frictionless long-distance complementarity with the operational and strategic needs of their corporate clients, rigorously managing engagements so as to deliver year-on-year cost savings while minimizing "noise" and coordination problems. They generally have no choice but to operate in highly price-sensitive markets, where cost suppression translates into downward pressure on wages and the sweating of employees. While running extremely tight operations, with little in the way of untrimmed "fat," outsourcers must, on a daily basis, contend with barely satisfied corporate clients who demand nothing less than continuous improvement across all of the key performance indicators that regulate fees and contracts. The dashboards that monitor the performance of outsourcing engagements rarely display green lights from top to bottom; in the majority of these engagements *something* is not going well. And clients believe that they are paying, literally, to outsource these worries. The challenge of managing, governing, and sustaining such permanently stressed relationships is a chronic one, made even more difficult by largely unchecked pressures for frugality and commoditization.

Outsourcers do more than move jobs and tasks around in search of bottom-line savings. Theirs is a transformative presence. For example, it is rare, in practice, for the "same" job simply to be relocated, *in toto*, from one site to another or from onshore to offshore, since the act of relocation itself typically entails some degree of reorganization of the labor process and its accompanying organizational, social, and technical relations. More often than not, this will involve the establishment of more finely grained divisions of labor, and the standardization and deskilling of work tasks. Even though there are instances of upgrading in outsourced labor systems, as some lead firms have taken on increasingly sophisticated, complex, and value-adding operations, it is generally the case that the status, skill rating, degree of discretion, and of course level of remuneration in offshored jobs is lower. On the other hand, stress levels tend to rise along with the daily pressure to make targets. Offshore operations consequently struggle with persistent challenges of labor turnover and attrition, particularly where alternative employment opportunities are relatively plentiful, as they now are in many of the tier-1 outsourcing sites in India, a situation that has been driving wage inflation in many of these prime locations, fueling industry decentralization pressures. This means that while the top 50 or so most highly ranked outsourcing sites, worldwide (see Figure 1.1) may be comparatively stable, there is considerable volatility lower down the rankings, where there is a tendency for the geographies of the outsourcing complex to spread "outward," to new locations. In addition to the basic requirements for ICT and/or logistics connectivity, the underlying driver of these lateral movements to new sites and shores is, invariably, the availability, cost, capability, and pliability of local labor supplies. A growing cadre of consulting and advisory firms—today, key players in the outsourcing complex—have built practices around the continued monitoring, evaluation, and promotion of outsourcing sites.[5]

Outsourcing sites, of course, have to be fully connected to the grid. Location decisions are typically made at the nexus of labor (costs), organizational capabilities, and technological capacities. There is an unmistakable undercurrent of techno-determinism in many accounts of the supposedly revolutionary effects of ICTs, software automation, and digitization on outsourced and offshored work. Yet it is difficult to deny that these innovations have widened the *potential* locational reach of outsourced operations. Technical change, however, never occurs in isolation; its complex entanglement with parallel (and fundamentally enabling) processes of organizational and social change mean that predictions of a technologically flattened and perfectly integrated world are almost always exaggerated. The landscape of outsourced operations is far from flat, in fact, even if it is constantly being reanimated by shifting competitive dictates and by new technological capabilities, in the context of a downward pull on costs. Rather than being simply "liberated," locational decision making remains very carefully calibrated—maybe even more so, as the labor/technology mix changes. Some of the latest waves of innovation—most notably the introduction of RPA systems and related forms of software-based automation—seem to actually be *following* the networks and pathways established through earlier rounds of outsourcing. The work that the outsourcing complex does (breaking down tasks and detaching them from incumbent workers and organizations; streamlining, standardizing, and routinizing operations; digitizing channels of communication, monitoring, and control) effectively smoothes the way for subsequent automation, preparing the paths of least resistance. So while robots are hardly about to take over the world, they undoubtedly will become a significant presence in the channels that are cut and remade by outsourcing. The effects of RPA, in this respect, will not be locationally indiscriminate, but will instead tend to rework and react against the preexisting geographies of the outsourcing complex, where their labor-displacing effects are likely to be most concentrated.

Finally, Table 7.1 suggests that, as a heterogeneous organizational construction, the outsourcing complex exhibits a less than stable, hybrid form, combining elements of markets, hierarchies, and networks, conventionally understood. Powerful forces of commoditization, competitive instability, and a culture of rivalrous relations pervade the outsourcing complex, which emerged as a creature of transnationalization, liberalization, and marketization but which also tends to degrade and spoil the markets that it makes.

---

[5] See, for example, Tholons (2016) and Sethi, A. and Gott, J. (2015) *On the Eve of Disruption*. New York: A. T. Kearney.

The undercutting of costs and regulatory conditions was a founding principle for the outsourcing business, the premise upon which significant offshore growth was achieved. Competitive churning, contractual chiseling, and creeping commoditization continue to dog the sector as a whole, imposing limits on the potential for more collaborative and truly transformative approaches, indexing profit rates to the scale and growth of the outsourced headcount, and impeding innovation and value-adding maneuvers. Above all, the basic market condition of corporate-buyer dominance means that cost-cutting concerns remain inviolable, while contractual and organizational relationships are inescapably lopsided. Some in the industry go as far as to liken its relational culture to that of master and slave.[6]

Offshore outsourcing may itself be a function of the flattening, deconstruction, and stretching out of corporate hierarchies, but significant power asymmetries mark this nominally flatter world. To a significant degree, the outsourcing complex is an outgrowth of the managerial imperatives of wage suppression, deunionization, and labor control. This does not mean, however, that the network capabilities of the outsourcing complex are insignificant. Quite the contrary, the build out of a transnational infrastructure of provider networks has enabled new corporate capabilities, shifting the decision-making matrix around the location of functions, tasks, and activities in quite radical ways. Routine assembly work, back-office functions, and a host of other activities are these days only rarely colocated, onshore, with headquarters "control" functions, but by the same token they are unlikely to remain in their present locations—say in Shenzhen, Manila, Prague, or Dublin—for an indefinite period either. The movements out of higher-income countries that began with the NIDL in the 1970s, and which have been supercharged by the bundling of ICT and organizational innovations since the 1990s, may have at first resembled a more or less unidirectional offshore migration of jobs and functions, but most of this activity occurred in advance of the formation of an industry dedicated to the task of *permanent relocation*. This is the fundamental task of the outsourcing complex: to ensure the efficient delivery of offshore operations today, but also to sell the "next shore" to the corporate buyers of tomorrow. The maturation and consolidation of this complex means that the geographies of production, servicing, and employment are being rendered dynamic and mobile as never before—if far from indiscriminately so. The outsourcing complex has been a zone of stressed experimentation but also both an organizational and a spatial fix, transnational in reach.

[6] See HfS Research (2015) 80% of outsourcing relationships fail to deliver collaborative value...so what can we do? *Horses for Sources* blog December 15, accessed at <http://www.horsesforsources.com/failure-to-collaborate_121315>, December 27, 2015.

Migrating Tasks

The outsourcing complex can be hard to pin down. It is sprawling and decentered; it is amorphous and polymorphous; it is submerged and secretive; and it is, for want of a better word, complex. But if there is an essence buried somewhere at the heart of the outsourcing complex, this must surely be the corporate facilitation of the *migration of tasks*, first across the boundaries of an "original" employing organization and then, in the offshore variant of these operations, across a jurisdictional boundary or indeed ocean. Nowhere, perhaps, was the essential core of these functions more pithily (or aptly) exposed than in the case of an ill-fated attempt, just over a decade ago, to *patent* outsourcing. This episode, while providing an apt illustration of the outsourcing calculus of the time, can also be seen as an indicator of how the business was about to change.

In the period of relative calm that followed the anti-outsourcing storms of 2004–5, it was IBM that initiated a precocious move to secure patent protection for the methodology of outsourcing. The foundation of the company's claim to the United States Patent Office, labeled *Outsourcing of services*, was a diagnostic tool for assessing the viability and cost of "migrating" work tasks, presented as a supposedly distinctive "method for identifying human-resource work content to outsource offshore of an organization."[7] It was IBM's contention that:

> Determining which services are too complex and difficult to outsource and which are not . . . continues to be a challenge. In order to be successfully migrated to an outsourcing location, the tasks need to be able to be documented, repeatable, and able to be migrated at low risk to the corporation. Risk can be defined in terms of customer satisfaction, continuity of business, cost savings, business controls, and legal exposure to the corporation. No known solutions exist that both identify the universe of tasks performed and then select those tasks that are able to be consolidated and migrated.[8]

IBM's solution was a software algorithm designed forensically to analyze a client company's workforce, workloads, and work tasks in order to identify targets for cuts and outsourcing. Summarizing the context for their "invention," the IBM

---

[7] Behrmann, B. L. et al., International Business Machines Corporation, United States Patent Application, # 11/324958, p. 1, January 3, 2006, accessed at <http://appft1.uspto.gov/netacgi/nph-Parser?Sect1=PTO1&Sect2=HITOFF&d=PG01&p=1&u=%2Fnetahtml%2FPTO%2Fsrchnum.html&r=1&f=G&l=50&s1=%2220070162321%22.PGNR.&OS=DN/20070162321&RS=DN/20070162321>, March 15, 2016.

[8] Behrmann, B. L. et al., International Business Machines Corporation, United States Patent Application, # 11/324958, paragraph 0010, January 3, 2006, accessed at <http://appft1.uspto.gov/netacgi/nph-Parser?Sect1=PTO1&Sect2=HITOFF&d=PG01&p=1&u=%2Fnetahtml%2FPTO%2Fsrchnum.html&r=1&f=G&l=50&s1=%2220070162321%22.PGNR.&OS=DN/20070162321&RS=DN/20070162321>, March 15, 2016.

engineers observed that while "corporations have looked increasingly to out-sourcing of services, development, and manufacturing work as a strategy to reduce labor, administration, development, and manufacturing expense," problems of irreducible task complexity or botched implementation meant that there was often a great deal of underperformance, rising to outright failure, in pursuit of the managerial objective of reducing "overall end-to-end costs," defined as the basic goal of these projects.[9] Outsourcing initiatives had logically and properly begun, the IBM filing went on to explain, with the lowest-hanging fruit, with simple functions such as "low end services," recognizing that highly complex, discretion-based work might have to remain off limits. It was the space in between, populated by a wide range of intermediate tasks, that ought therefore to be the focus for the next round of workforce-restructuring efforts. Crucially, though, while the basic idea of outsourcing was seen to be "straight forward" enough, putting this idea to work had a habit of becoming "difficult" quite quickly, especially when it came to less than simple tasks.[10]

In the abstracted gaze typical of this form of business analytics, workers—where they figure at all—tend to appear as mere bearers of (harvestable) functional abilities, readied for conversion into the shadow currency of the outsourcing complex, the FTE. Correspondingly, the methodology for which IBM sought patent protection was targeted at breaking down that "portion of a human-resource within an organization [deemed appropriate for] outsour-cing," its objective being optimally to rationalize the "plurality of tasks being formed by a plurality of individual human resources" into portable "func-tional groups," primed for extraction and relocation through carefully staged transition plans, one department at a time.[11] These, in effect, were new tools for Taylorized scientific management, implemented in this case with a view to rationalization on a transnational scale. Along these same lines, IBM would soon append a related filing for a complementary device, this time a desktop calculator designed to match knowledge workers according to their

[9] Likewise, "It is a goal of the present invention to generate savings to the subject company," the patent claim stated. (Behrmann, B. L. et al., International Business Machines Corporation, United States Patent Application, # 11/324958, paragraphs 0004, 0083, January 3, 2006, accessed at <http://appft1.uspto.gov/netacgi/nph-Parser?Sect1=PTO1&Sect2=HITOFF&d=PG01&p=1&u=%2Fnetahtml%2FPTO%2Fsrchnum.html&r=1&f=G&l=50&s1=%2220070162321%22.PGNR.&OS=DN/20070162321&RS=DN/20070162321>, March 15, 2016.)

[10] Behrmann, B. L. et al., International Business Machines Corporation, United States Patent Application, # 11/324958, paragraphs 0006, 0005, January 3, 2006, accessed at <http://appft1.uspto.gov/netacgi/nph-Parser?Sect1=PTO1&Sect2=HITOFF&d=PG01&p=1&u=%2Fnetahtml%2FPTO%2Fsrchnum.html&r=1&f=G&l=50&s1=%2220070162321%22.PGNR.&OS=DN/20070162321&RS=DN/20070162321>, March 15, 2016.

[11] Behrmann, B. L. et al., International Business Machines Corporation, United States Patent Application, # 11/324958, paragraph 0013, January 3, 2006, accessed at <http://appft1.uspto.gov/netacgi/nph-Parser?Sect1=PTO1&Sect2=HITOFF&d=PG01&p=1&u=%2Fnetahtml%2FPTO%2Fsrchnum.html&r=1&f=G&l=50&s1=%2220070162321%22.PGNR.&OS=DN/20070162321&RS=DN/20070162321>, March 15, 2016.

"experience levels, salary, geographic location, job starting date and duration, and industry" with an on-call supply of so-called IGSIs—a customized metric for offshore labor derived from the acronym of IBM Global Services, India.[12]

Setting aside for the moment the fact that IBM's "inventions" were laying claim to what were already widely distributed industry practices, the ultimate fate of the company's filings had less to do with the technical merits of the analytics themselves than with public-relations optics. When news of IBM's move came to light, courtesy of the tech-industry website Slashdotters, the outcry was sufficiently loud (not to mention tinged with ridicule) that this, one of the world's most aggressive users of patent protection, chose to sheepishly withdraw the application.[13] While IBM's behavior on this occasion may have been somewhat frivolous, the company's attempt to codify, capture, and commercialize this fast-evolving corporate practice is symptomatic of an important moment in the evolution of the outsourcing business. It came around the end of the time when outsourcing represented the "easy out" for companies seeking to slash costs by way of a default, practically out-of-the-box solution that promised to deliver "an easy, and very temporary, way to improve profits without a lot of deep thinking."[14] This had been a time when "the cost of [offshore] operation was so much lower that even badly planned offshoring could absorb the mistakes and still show a significantly lower cost of operation," Chris Niccolls has explained, "At least for a while."[15]

After capturing these arbitrage windfalls from a raft of basically straightforward engagements, outsourcers would have to begin working a more difficult terrain. Offshore outsourcing is now less about eye-catching megadeals, and more about the everyday mid-management grind of *delivery*, usually on thin margins. The vendors, providers, and managers of outsourced services have been riding a growing market, but they have also been fighting a series of battles, some of which they continue to lose, against the serial underperformance of a large proportion of these long-distance engagements, against the souring and periodic rupture of client relationships, and against the creeping

---

[12] IBM patent applications, quoted in Mick, J. (2007) IBM tries to patent efficient job outsourcing. *Daily Tech*, October 1, accessed at <http://www.dailytech.com/IBM+Tries+to+Patent+Efficient+Job+Outsourcing/article9003.htm>, March 15, 2016.

[13] IBM explained that the filings had been made in error, since they violated a recently adopted policy of reducing the rate of "business method" patents in favor of those adjudged to contain significant technical merit. Williams, C. (2007) IBM drops attempt to patent outsourcing. *Register*, October 5, accessed at <http://www.theregister.co.uk/2007/10/05/ibm_patent_outsourcing_slashdot/>, March 15, 2016. See also Mishra, P. (2009) IBM to withdraw its patent for offshore outsourcing. *Economic Times* March 31, accessed at <http://articles.economictimes.indiatimes.com/2009-03-31/news/27639237_1_offshore-outsourcing-patent-application-ibm>, March 15, 2016.

[14] Buffington, J. (2007) *An Easy Out: Corporate America's addiction to outsourcing*. Westport, CT: Praeger; Niccolls, C. (n.d.) Outsourcing: Is this the end? *About.com*, accessed at <http://outsourcing.about.com/od/feasibility/a/Outsourcing-Is-This-The-End.htm>, January 12, 2016.

[15] Niccolls, C. (n.d.) Outsourcing: Is this the end? *About.com*, accessed at <http://outsourcing.about.com/od/feasibility/a/Outsourcing-Is-This-The-End.htm>, January 12, 2016.

degradation of outsourcing markets through margin erosion and commoditization. As a result, this has become a zone of managerial stress and competitive churn. And an exponential mode of growth has given way to a linear, incremental one: price discounting is endemic and the returns on scale economies are plateauing, as even the most innovative firms have struggled to uncouple revenue (and profit) generation from headcount growth.[16] This is why the early moves into robotic automation represent the thin end of what could become a rather large wedge, not just as a value-adding strategy, but as a means of transcending some of the inherent constraints of the prevailing labor-intensive business model, since this new generation of labor-displacing technologies is being advertised as "non-linearly scalable."[17] A key reason why major outsourcing firms are building RPA practices is to alleviate the lingering condition of "FTE dependency," while differentiating service offerings and working towards less transactional relationships with corporate clients. This evolutionary path will not be followed by every provider in the outsourcing business, but it is already established as a direction of travel for some. As Frank Casale explains:

> The decision to outsource has always been driven by the business need to lower costs and improve performance [yielding an] offshore delivery model that [drove] down costs by leveraging labor arbitrage ... Robotics represents the latest phase of outsourcing, a way to further save labor costs and improve work efficiency ... Because RPA software is a predictable expenditure, and at a fraction of the cost of an FTE with marginal cost for maintenance, companies can improve their agility and scalability without the need for recruiting and training. With a record number of contracts set to expire or renew in the next few years, robotic process automation presents the opportunity for companies to finally achieve their goal of decoupling revenue and headcount.[18]

If the object of the first generation of task-migration initiatives was to move work, selectively, to offshore locations, the strategy currently taking shape is one of decoupling from the headcount paradigm altogether. Instead of replacing onshore labor with cheaper labor, the next step for some outsourcers will be to remove labor altogether—what some are calling robot arbitrage.

---

[16] See Levy (2005), Manning et al. (2011), and Tornbohm, C. (2012) The future of BPO. *Outsource Magazine* 29: 34–5.

[17] Chetan Dube, IPsoft, quoted in Phadnis, S. (2013) "Blond humanoid" Eliza might take over low-end BPO work. *Times of India* September 17, accessed at <http://articles.timesofindia.indiatimes.com/2013-09-17/computing/42148094_1_infosys-bpo-chetan-dube-ipsof>, January 18, 2016.

[18] Casale, F. (2014) *Here Come the Robots: The emergence of robotic process automation and the beginning of the end of outsourcing as we know it*. New York: Institute of Robotic Process Automation, pp. 2–3.

There are some, like outsourcing guru Cliff Justice, who believe that this means that not only is the labor-arbitrage model visibly "dying," the employee itself might be "an endangered species."[19]

> The geographic discussion is giving way to automation. There is no "next India" or "next Philippines." Although [business process outsourcing] may have once been your most profitable strategy, today its costs have reached a point where the benefits of moving labor time zones away simply don't equal the hardships. And the economics and performance of technology [are such that RPA is] a viable alternative to low cost human labor.

> Labor arbitrage is, by definition, temporary. For one, wage inflation overseas eventually makes the cost savings of cheap offshore labor almost impossible to sustain, even with the shrewdest workforce management. What's more, while the labor cost curve will always escalate, inevitable performance problems driven by turnover and attrition mean that it might not always equate to an increase in productivity…

> The end of BPO and the rise of RPA are disruptive forces, upending industries, markets, and, potentially, whole societies. But they also present powerful opportunities for forward-looking, transformative enterprises [which are] changing their thinking and their models around outsourcing and technology capabilities [with some] shifting away from labor altogether.[20]

It may be not too fanciful to suggest that the IBM engineers who attempted to patent their company's model of outsourcing, just over a decade ago, saw a lot of this coming. They sensed that those were transitional times in what would become a long, and in some ways winding, evolutionary path during which corporations and service providers would experiment, learn, and adapt in the act of doing. The core objective of rolling rationalization would remain intact, but the means and methods would continue to evolve. "While the various embodiments of the invention have been illustrated and described, it will be clear that the invention is not so limited," the original IBM patent filing concluded, "Numerous modifications, changes, variations, substitutions and equivalents will occur to those skilled in the art without departing from the spirit and scope of the present invention."[21]

---

[19] Justice, C. and Salt, B. (2015) Employees: An endangered species? In KPMG, *Strategic Visions on the Sourcing Market 2016*. Amstelveen: KPMG, 29–34. See also Justice (2015).

[20] Justice (2015: 2, 5).

[21] Behrmann, B. L. et al., International Business Machines Corporation, United States Patent Application, # 11/324958, paragraph 0089, January 3, 2006, accessed at <http://appft1.uspto.gov/netacgi/nph-Parser?Sect1=PTO1&Sect2=HITOFF&d=PG01&p=1&u=%2Fnetahtml%2FPTO%2Fsrchnum.html&r=1&f=G&l=50&s1=%2220070162321%22.PGNR.&OS=DN/20070162321&RS=DN/20070162321>, March 15, 2016.

Dividing Labor

As the originators of the NIDL thesis long ago put it, "the division of labor should be understood as an on-going process, and not as a final result."[22] As Doreen Massey emphasized, moreover, the act of separating tasks and dividing labor spatially was always more than a matter of making new geographical patterns; it entailed transformed "relations between activities in different places, new spatial patterns of social organisation, new dimensions of inequality and new relations of dominance and dependence."[23] The outsourcing industry has been making and remaking labor markets across an ever expanding portfolio of offshore locations for decades now. As the very term "offshore" implies, this is a *relational* process, one that has been shaped, symbiotically, with the restructuring of "onshore" employment regimes and job markets. As Chapter 6 indicated, estimates of the *combined* effects of late-generation outsourcing, labor-displacing automation, and global economic integration have a tendency quickly to become science fictional in their scale, scope, and implications. There have been many waves of internationalization and globalization before, of course, but the rapid growth and consolidation of the outsourcing complex has coincided with the ascendancy of genuinely transnational forms of labor-market restructuring, as offshore, near-shore, onshore, and noshore economies are being rolled out and recombined in historically new ways. These (mutual) transformations are being driven by iterative and integrated logics, even if their outcomes can appear to be disintegrated and dissipated.

In the blue-skies visions of strategy-consulting firms like McKinsey, globalizing labor markets are now poised for truly radical change, as the cumulative effects of trade liberalization, offshore outsourcing, ICT-enabled automation, and large-scale economic migration drive an unprecedented wave of transnational integration in employment systems, with significant consequences for jobs, wages, and organizational structures in advanced and developing countries alike. In high-income economies, a new cluster of disruptive technologies, including advanced robotics and the automation of knowledge work, have been identified as the root causes of "sweeping change[s]" in corporate structures and in the nature (and location) of work.[24] Here, employment prospects are forecast to be "weakest in low-skill production and transaction occupations (assembly workers or customer service representatives), where tasks [can] be automated or transferred to low-cost locations," while labor demand is expected to hold up rather better in sectors like healthcare,

---

[22] Fröbel et al. (1980: 45).   [23] Massey (1984: 8).
[24] Manyika, J., Chui, M., Bughin, J., Dobbs, R., Bisson, P., and Marrs, A. (2013) *Disruptive Technologies*. San Francisco, CA: McKinsey Global Institute, pp. 6–7.

food preparation, and higher-level management, in other words precisely those "roles that cannot be automated or easily moved."[25]

Drawing on less proprietary sources of evidence, a widely discussed research project at Oxford University has vividly substantiated several of these claims. The product of a sign-of-the-times collaboration between an economist specializing in the future impacts of technology, Carl Benedikt Frey, and a member of Oxford's Robotics Research Group, Michael A. Osborne, this research revealed that 47 percent of total employment in the United States— something in the region of 70 million domestic jobs—should be considered to be at "high risk" of automation within the next one to two decades, enabled by the plummeting costs of "computer capital" and the rise of a Kondratiev-like cluster of innovations in machine learning and mobile robotics. According to this analysis, those exposed to short-term risk of computerized displacement would include "most workers" in transportation and logistics, "the bulk of office and administrative support workers," a large portion of the (remaining) blue-collar production workforce, along with a "surprising[ly] substantial share of employment in services, sales and construction occupations."[26] A rump of relatively "secure" jobs, on the other hand, would be found in the higher echelons of corporate and financial management, and in education, healthcare, and the arts and media, which were expected to be relatively impervious to automation by virtue of their association with "knowledge of human heuristics [and] the development of novel ideas and artifacts."[27] These findings are broadly consistent with those of the research program on the effects of automation and routinization, or what is known as skill-biased technical change, which have been identified as a leading cause of wage and employment polarization in the United States.[28]

Until quite recently, the suggestion that "computers might significantly disrupt human labor markets [has been] on the fringes," Farhad Manjoo has observed, it having been the case that the majority of economists have not been "taking these worries seriously."[29] Stagnating wages and stubborn inequalities in the U.S. labor market, however, have caused these questions to surge towards the top of the agenda, informing a growing consensus that

[25] Dobbs, R., Madgavkar, A., Barton, D., Labaye, E., Manyika, J., Roxburgh, C., Lund, S., and Madhav, S. (2012) *The World at Work*. San Francisco, CA: McKinsey Global Institute, pp. 7, 24.

[26] Frey and Osborne (2013: 38). See also Frey, C. B. and Osborne, M. (2015) *Technology at Work: The future of innovation and employment*. London: Citi GPS.

[27] Frey and Osborne (2013: 40).

[28] Autor, D. H. and Dorn, D. (2013) The growth of low skill service jobs and the polarization of the US labor market. *American Economic Review* 103(3): 1553–97; Acemoglu, D. and Autor D. (2011) Skills, tasks and technologies: Implications for employment and earnings. In Ashenfelter, O., ed., *Handbook of Labor Economics*, Vol 4B. Amsterdam Elsevier, 1043–171.

[29] Manjoo, F. (2011) Will robots steal your job? *Slate* September 26, accessed at <http://www.slate.com/articles/technology/robot_invasion/2011/09/will_robots_steal_your_job.single.html>, January 18, 2016, p. 3.

the coming wave of labor-displacing technologies will bring significant, long-run consequences.[30] Affirming the argument that outsourcing and automation have begun to work in tandem, these investigations have revealed that, when it comes down to the characteristics of particular jobs, "many tasks that are candidates for computer substitution are also candidates for offshoring."[31] Recall that on the basis of detailed job-content analyses (similar to Frey and Osborne's method), the most authoritative assessments of the number of jobs *potentially* offshorable from the United States (i.e. deliverable at a distance) have come in with an upper range of 30–40 million.[32] It was on the basis of these calculations that Alan Blinder forecast that the United States should prepare for a "nasty transition" through the course of what would amount to a global "re-division of labor," inaugurating new and sharp distinctions between a mostly immovable cluster of jobs requiring physical interaction, personal touch, or face-to-face contact, many of them in the less well-paid services (like table waiting or hairdressing), and those jobs (or fragments of jobs) that could be delivered electronically over long distances.[33] This new divide will not only cut through sectors like healthcare (family-practice medicine being locationally sticky, while the analysis of radiological charts is being offshored), but much more broadly, it also threatens to upend conventional human-capital and indeed social hierarchies (given that some of the work performed by credentialed employees will become newly vulnerable to offshore outsourcing. It is true that, to a substantial degree, there will remain a cluster of highly remunerated jobs, characterized by creativity and/or complexity, that are likely to be relatively immune to *both* automation and offshoring—although there is an emerging theme across data-crunching exercises as well as cultural commentary that this "protected" job market is not nearly so large as was once believed.

For the most part, mainstream economists do not have much truck with these projections, clinging firmly to the faith that the highly flexible U.S. labor market will be able roll with whatever is thrown at it. The classic skeptics' response posits, as Exhibit A, the transition from an agricultural to a manufacturing-and-services economy over the past 200 years, one that saw the number of farm jobs fall by around 99 percent, followed by vigorous growth

---

[30] See Roosevelt Institute (2015) *Technology and the Future of Work: The state of the debate.* New York: Open Society Foundations; Levy, F. and Murnane, R. (2013) *Dancing with Robots: Human skills for computerized work.* Washington, DC: Third Way; Zysman, J. and Kenney, M (2015) *Where Will Work Come from in the Era of the Cloud and Big Data.* New York: Roosevelt Institute; West, D. M. (2015) *What Happens if Robots Take the Jobs? The impact of emerging technologies on employment and public policy.* Washington, DC: Brookings Institution.

[31] Levy, F. and Murnane, R. (2013) *Dancing with Robots: Human skills for computerized work.* Washington, DC: Third Way, p. 13.

[32] See Jensen and Kletzer (2010) and Blinder and Krueger (2008, 2013).

[33] See the further discussion in Chapter 3.

in new (though previously unimaginable) employment sectors elsewhere in the economy, from auto assembly to telesales.[34] The updated version of this we-have-seen-it-all-before argument draws on what would seem to be an ill-advised historical analogy: orthodox trade economists will claim that the U.S. labor market has "adapted" relatively well to the wave of deindustrialization that began in the 1970s, in response to which Alan Blinder has found it necessary to counter that "I, for one, am not convinced that the transition from manufacturing to services (which is still going on) has been that smooth."[35] In social and spatial terms, the transition away from manufacturing employment in the United States has most certainly not been smooth, even if aggregate figures may give the impression that "compensatory" employment growth has occurred. Obviously, there is no eternal economic law that guarantees such growth, that the new jobs will be comparable in terms of wages, benefits, and security, or that upside growth will compensate those individuals and communities that actually lost the jobs. As Gary Marcus has argued,

> [T]here is no causal mechanism, physical, economic, sociological, or legal, that guarantees that new jobs will always come into existence. Adam Smith's invisible hand seems to offer the promise that (at least over the long haul) markets will set prices in rational ways. That doesn't mean, though, that there will always be remunerative, let alone satisfying work for human beings to do.[36]

Similar arguments apply to the question of *where* jobs will be lost and created, both globally and interregionally, processes that are likewise governed neither by convenient axioms of compensatory growth nor by immanent laws of long-run equilibrium.

Task fragmentation and routinization are important drivers of these processes of non-compensatory restructuring, especially now that offshoring and automation have begun to reinforce one another. "Routine tasks can easily be broken down into a clear set of steps," Oldenski writes, "which can then be programmed into computer code (in the case of skill biased technology change) or communicated to someone located in another country (in the case of offshoring)."[37] It is becoming increasingly evident that, together, these processes are playing a significant role in the hollowing out of employment and wage structures in the United States, as separable and fragmentable

---

[34] See the discussion in Blinder (2009: 50). For a pop-cultural version of these arguments, see Kelly, K. (2012) Better than human. *Wired* December 24, accessed at <http://www.wired.com/2012/12/ff-robots-will-take-our-jobs/>, February 17, 2016.

[35] Blinder (2009: 28). Compare with Bhagwati et al. (2004) and Lawrence, R. Z. (2009) Comments. In B. M. Friedman, ed., *Offshoring of American Jobs*. Cambridge, MA: MIT Press, pp. 91–100.

[36] Marcus, G. (2012) Will a robot take your job? *New Yorker* December 29, accessed at <http://www.newyorker.com/news/news-desk/will-a-robot-take-your-job>, February 17, 2016.

[37] Oldenski, L. (2014) Offshoring and the polarization of the US labor market. *Industrial and Labor Relations Review* 67(3): 734–61, p. 735.

tasks are outsourced, exported, or automated, leaving behind a polarized array of complex and touch-based jobs, including janitors, financiers, carers, truck drivers, and surgeons.[38] These workers are finding themselves at opposing ends of an increasingly capital- and profit-intensive economy, one that is marked, not coincidentally, by a consistently falling labor share of national income. Prior to the mid-1980s, labor's share of national income in the United States had been so stable, hovering around 64 percent, that its constancy had become a principal stylized fact of macroeconomics. It has since dropped around six percentage points, and shows no signs of recovery, most of this reduction being accounted for by the effects of "increased globalization, vertical specialization, and offshoring."[39] This fortifies what have become, in effect, some of the leading stylized facts of post-Fordist economics, concerning secular increases in labor-market inequality and the long-run erosion of the "middle" of the employment structure.[40] And it is consistent with the course of what has been an anemic "recovery" from the Great Recession in the United States.

What the well-established repertoire of offshore outsourcing strategies and the new generation of automation techniques share, in this context, is a distinct facility for realizing the managerial goal of instantaneous, on-call flexibility, delivered at minimal cost. They also offer the promise of an unwavering—sleepless, faultless, and interruption-free—task focus. Around twenty years ago offshore outsourcing became the favored strategy for the establishment of around-the-clock call-center operations and overnight back-office processing; today, new capabilities in robotic automation are opening the path to yet more unimpeded forms of on-demand, 24/7 task intensification. Compared to the easily scalable and increasingly adaptable platoons of software robots, human workforces begin to look frail, limited, and inefficient. And even the cheapest human labor can appear to be expensive and unreliable. The problem with human workers, Frey and Osborne observe in their account of the new economics of computerization, is that they "must fulfill a range of tasks unrelated to their occupation, such as sleeping, necessitating occasional sacrifices in their occupational performance."[41]

Fear of offshoring may have preceded, by a decade or so, the actual advance of the practice as a measurable force in labor-market restructuring. The robot

---

[38] See Oldenski, L. (2012) The task composition of offshoring by US multinationals. *International Economics* 131(3): 5–21; Oldenski, L. (2014) Offshoring and the polarization of the US labor market. *Industrial and Labor Relations Review* 67(3): 734–61.

[39] Elsby, M. L., Hobijn, B., and Şahin, A. (2013) The decline of the U.S. labor share. Paper presented at the Brookings Panel on Economic Activity, September 19, Brookings Institution, Washington, DC, p. 28.

[40] See Harrison and Bluestone (1988), Harrison (1994), Cappelli et al. (1997), Peck (2002), and Theodore (2016).

[41] Frey and Osborne (2013: 16).

panics of the past few years may follow a similar course. One difference, however, is that the outsourcing complex was constructed contemporaneously with the first of these episodes; today, it exists as a consolidated infrastructural network readied to realize the objectives of the second. Winifred Poster and Nima Yolmo have argued that what has made outsourcing distinctive, historically speaking, is its demonstrated capacity for "push[ing] the boundaries of what can (and should) be considered labour."[42] This was achieved, initially, by breaking down the boundaries of the late twentieth-century enterprise, and then by building new business models to capture gains from cross-border arbitrage. Deskilling and decentralization were the dominant dynamics. Jobs were not being "killed" as such, but they were being restructured and relocated—indeed restructured not least *through* relocation. Acutely aware of the political taint of "shipping jobs overseas," corporations learned to be efficiently discreet about a practice that has become all but ubiquitous, under circumstances where the imperatives of cost control and organizational flexibility were sacrosanct. It remains to be seen whether the current round of experiments in automation—governed by these same principles—will precipitate a trickle or a flood of robotic deployments. Whatever happens, though, it will likely happen quietly.

---

[42] Poster and Yolmo (2016: 583).

Bibliography

Note on the arrangement of references in the bibliography and footnotes: not all the references cited in the footnotes appear here. Bibliographical details are provided below for more substantial sources and those to which frequent reference is made. More specific citations, website and press material, and ephemera are detailed only in the footnotes for each chapter.

Armbrüster, T. (2006) *The Economics and Sociology of Management Consulting.* Cambridge: Cambridge University Press.

Ashley, E. (2008) *Outsourcing for Dummies.* Hoboken, NJ: Wiley Publishing.

Barnet, R. and Müller, R. (1974) Global reach: II. *New Yorker,* December 9: 100–59.

Barthelemy, J. (2001) The hidden costs of IT outsourcing. *MIT Sloan Management Review* 42(3): 60–9.

Bhagwati, J., Panagariya, A., and Srinivasan, T. N. (2004) The muddles over outsourcing. *Journal of Economic Perspectives* 18(4): 93–114.

Blinder, A. S. (2009) Offshoring: Big deal, or business as usual? In B. M. Friedman, ed., *Offshoring of American Jobs.* Cambridge, MA: MIT Press, 19–60.

Blinder, A. S. and Krueger, A. B. (2008) *Alternative Measures of Offshorability.* Cambridge, MA: National Bureau of Economic Research.

Blinder, A. S. and Krueger, A. B. (2013) Alternative measures of offshorability: A survey approach. *Journal of Labor Economics* 31(S1): S97–S128.

Bluestone, B. and Harrison, B. (1982) *The Deindustrialization of America: Plant closings, community abandonment, and the dismantling of basic industry.* New York: Basic Books.

Brittain-Catlin, W. (2005) *Offshore: The dark side of the global economy.* New York: Picador.

Brynjolfsson, E. (2014) *The Second Machine Age: Work, progress and prosperity in a time of brilliant technologies.* New York: W. W. Norton.

Brynjolfsson, E. and McAfee, A. (2012) *Race against the Machine.* Lexington, MA: Digital Frontier Press.

Buffington, J. (2007) *An Easy Out: Corporate America's addiction to outsourcing.* Westport, CT: Praeger.

Caincross, F. (2001) *The Death of Distance.* London: Orion.

Cappelli, P., Bassi, L., Katz, H., Knoke, D., Osterman, P., and Useem, M. (1997) *Change at Work.* New York: Oxford University Press.

Carmel, E. and Abbott, P. (2007) Why "nearshore" means that distance matters. *Communications of the ACM* 50(10): 40–6.

Coe, N. M. and Yeung, H. W-C. (2015) *Global Production Networks: Theorizing economic development in an interconnected world*. Oxford: Oxford University Press.

Corbett, M. F. (2004) *The Outsourcing Revolution: Why it makes sense and how to do it right*. Chicago, IL: Dearborn.

Couto, V., Mani, M., Sehgal, V., Lewin, A. Y., Manning, S., and Russell, J. W. (2008) *Offshoring 2.0: Contracting knowledge and innovation to expand global capabilities*. Durham, NC: Duke University CIBER and Booz Allen Hamilton.

Dicken, P. (1986) *Global Shift*. London: Harper and Row.

Dicken, P. (2015) *Global Shift*. New York: Guilford.

Dobbs, L. (2004) *Exporting America*. New York: Warner Business.

EIU (Economist Intelligent Unit) (2008) *Offshoring 2.0: Aligning business and technology*. London: EIU.

Engardio, P. (2006) The future of outsourcing. *Business Week* January 30: 50–8.

Farrell, D., ed., (2006) *Offshoring*. Cambridge, MA: Harvard Business School Press.

Frey, C. B. and Osborne, M. A. (2013) The future of employment: How susceptible are jobs to computerisation? Working paper, Oxford Martin School and Department of Engineering Science, University of Oxford.

Friedman, T. L. (2005) *The World Is Flat*. New York: Farrar, Straus, and Giroux.

Fröbel, F., Heinrichs, J., and Kreye, O. (1980) *The New International Division of Labor*. Cambridge: Cambridge University Press.

Gereffi, G. (2006) *The New Offshoring of Jobs and Global Development*. Geneva: International Labour Organization.

Gereffi, G. (2014) Global value chains in a post-Washington consensus world. *Review of International Political Economy* 21(1): 9–37.

Gereffi, G., Humphrey, J., and Sturgeon, T. (2005) The governance of global value chains. *Review of International Political Economy* 12(1): 78–104.

Grossman, G. M. and Helpman, E. (2002) Outsourcing in a global economy. NBER working paper #8728. Cambridge, MA: National Bureau of Economic Research.

Grossman, G. M. and Rossi-Hansberg, E. (2008) Trading tasks: A simple theory of offshoring. *American Economic Review* 98(5): 1978–97.

Harrison, B. (1994) *Lean and Mean: The changing landscape of corporate power in an age of flexibility*. New York: Basic Books.

Harrison, B. and Bluestone, B. (1988) *The Great U-Turn: Corporate restructuring and the polarizing of America*. New York: Basic Books.

Hätönen, J. and Eriksson, T. (2009) 30+ years of research and practice of outsourcing: Exploring the past and anticipating the future. *Journal of International Management* 15(2): 142–55.

HfS Research (2012) *A Blueprint for the Industry Known as "Outsourcing."* Boston, MA: HfS Research.

IAOP (International Association of Outsourcing Professionals) (2010) *Outsourcing Professional Body of Knowledge*. Zaltbommel: Van Haren.

IAOP (2015) *Outsourcing Talent 2015*. Poughkeepsie, NY: IAOP.

IEDC (International Economic Development Council) (2015) *Defining the Reshoring Discussion*. Washington, DC: IEDC.

Javalgi, R. G., Dixit, A., and Scherer, R. F. (2009) Outsourcing to emerging markets: Theoretical perspectives and policy implications. *Journal of International Management* 15(2): 156–68.

Jensen, J. B. and Kletzer, L. G. (2010) Measuring tradable services and the task content of offshorable services jobs. In K. G. Abraham, J. R. Spletzer, and M. Harper, eds, *Labor in the New Economy*. Chicago, IL: University of Chicago Press, 309–35.

Justice, C. (2012) *The Death of Outsourcing*. Houston, TX: KPMG.

Justice, C. (2015) *Bots in the Back Office: The coming wave of digital labor*. Houston, TX: KPMG.

Kipping, M. (2002) Trapped in their wave: The evolution of management consultancies. In T. Clark and R. Fincham, eds, *Critical Consulting: New perspectives on the management advice industry*. Oxford: Blackwell, 28–49.

Lacity, M. C. and Rottman, J. (2012) Rural sourcing and impact sourcing. In M. C. Lacity and L. P. Willlcocks, eds, *Advanced Outsourcing Practice*. New York: Palgrave Macmillan, 143–68.

Larsen, M. M., Manning, S., and Pedersen, T. (2013) Uncovering the hidden costs of offshoring: The interplay of complexity, organizational design, and experience. *Strategic Management Journal* 34(5): 533–52.

Leamer, E. E. (2007) A flat world, a level playing field, a small world after all, or none of the above? A review of Thomas L. Friedman's "The World Is Flat." *Journal of Economic Literature* 45(1): 83–126.

Levy, D. L. (2005) Offshoring in the new global political economy. *Journal of Management Studies* 42(3): 685–93.

Linder, J. C. (2004) *Outsourcing for Radical Change: A bold approach to enterprise transformation*. New York: AMACOM.

Mankiw, N. G. and Swagel, P. (2006) The politics and economics of offshore outsourcing. *Journal of Monetary Economics* 53(5): 1027–56.

Manning, S., Lewin, A. Y., and Schuerch, M. (2011) The stability of offshore outsourcing relationships: The role of relation specificity and client control. *Management International Review* 51(3): 381–406.

Massey, D. (1984) *Spatial Divisions of Labour*. London: Macmillan.

McKenna, C. D. (2006) *The World's Newest Profession: Management consulting in the Twentieth Century*. Cambridge: Cambridge University Press.

Mullin, R. (1996) Managing the outsourced enterprise. *Journal of Business Strategy* 17(4): 28–36.

Nadeem, S. (2011) *Dead Ringers*. Princeton, NJ: Princeton University Press.

Neo Group (2015) *Trends and Opportunities in Latin America: A growing market for world-class global services*. Walnut, CA: Neo Group.

O'Mahoney, J. and Markham, C. (2013) *Management Consultancy*. Second edition. Oxford: Oxford University Press.

Oldenski, L. (2014) Offshoring and the polarization of the U.S. labor market. *Industrial and Labor Relations Review* 67(3): 734–61.

Oshri, I., Kotlarsky, J., and Wilcocks, L. P. (2011) *The Handbook of Global Outsourcing and Offshoring*. Basingstoke: Palgrave Macmillan.

Palan, R. (2003) *The Offshore World: Sovereign markets, virtual places, and nomad millionaires*. Ithaca, NY: Cornell University Press.

Peck, J. (1992) Labor and agglomeration: Control and flexibility in local labor markets. *Economic Geography* 68(4): 325–47.

Peck, J. (1996) *Work-Place: The social regulation of labor markets*. New York: Guilford.

Peck, J. (2001) *Workfare States*. New York: Guilford.

Peck, J. (2002) Labor, zapped/growth, restored? Three moments of neoliberal restructuring in the American labor market. *Journal of Economic Geography* 2(2): 179–220.

Peck, J. (2010) *Constructions of Neoliberal Reason*. Oxford: Oxford University Press.

Peck, J. (2016) The right to work, and the right at work. *Economic Geography* 92(1): 4–30.

Peck, J. and Theodore, N. (1998) The business of contingent work: Growth and restructuring in Chicago's temporary employment industry. *Work, Employment and Society* 12(4): 655–74.

Peck, J. and Theodore, N. (2002) Temped out? Industry rhetoric, labor regulation, and economic restructuring in the temporary staffing business. *Economic and Industrial Democracy* 23(2): 143–75.

Peck, J., Theodore, N., and Ward, K. (2005) Constructing markets for temporary labour: Employment liberalisation and the internationalisation of the staffing industry. *Global Networks* 5(1): 1–24.

Phillips, S. (2012) *The Moral Case on Outsourcing*. Portland, OR: Alitum Press.

Pollin, R. (2003) *Contours of Decent: U.S. economic fractures and the landscape of global austerity*. London: Verso.

Poster, W. R. and Yolmo, N. L. (2016) Globalization and outsourcing. In Edgell, S., Granter, E., and Gottfried, H., eds, *Sage Handbook of the Sociology of Work and Employment*. London: Sage, 576–96.

Scott, A. J. (1988a) *Metropolis: From the division of labor to urban form*. Berkeley: University of California Press.

Scott, A. J. (1988b) *New Industrial Spaces: Flexible production organization and regional development in North America and Western Europe*. London: Pion.

Slaby, J. R. (2012) *Robotic Automation Emerges as a Threat to Traditional Low-Cost Outsourcing*. Boston, MA: HfS Research.

Sutherland, C. (2013) *Framing a Constitution for Robotistan*. Boston, MA: HfS Research.

Theodore, N. (2016) Worlds of work: Changing landscapes of production and the new geographies of opportunity. *Geography Compass* 10(4): 179–89.

Theodore, N. and Peck, J. (2002) The temporary staffing industry: Growth imperatives and limits to contingency. *Economic Geography* 78(4): 463–93.

Tholons (2013) *Top 100 Outsourcing Destinations*. New York: Tholons.

Tholons (2016) *Top 100 Outsourcing Destinations*. New York: Tholons.

Uchitelle, L. (2007) *The Disposable American: Layoffs and Their Consequences*. New York: Vintage.

Upadhya, C. and Vasavi, A. R., eds (2008) *In an Outpost of the Global Economy*. London: Routledge.

Urry, J. (2014) *Offshoring*. Cambridge: Polity.

Willcocks, L. P. and Lacity, M. C. (2016) *Service Automation: Robots and the future of work*. Stratford-upon-Avon: Steve Brookes Publishing.

Xiang, B. (2007) *Global "Body Shopping."* Princeton, NJ: Princeton University Press.

Yeung, Henry W-C. and Coe, N. M. (2015) Toward a dynamic theory of global production networks. *Economic Geography* 91(1): 29–58.

Index

Index

outsourcing
  advisors *see* advisors, outsourcing
  analysts *see* analysts, outsourcing
  complex *see* complex, outsourcing
  costs *see* cost suppression; costs of
    outsourcing
  definition of *see* Definition, of outsourcing
  Hall of Fame (IAOP) 99–100
  Market *see* global sourcing market, value of;
    market, outsourcing
  sites of 3–4, 150, 151 *see also* Tier 1
    outsourcing locations; Tier 2 outsourcing
    locations
Outsourcing Professional Body of Knowledge
  (IAOP) 92, 103–4, 224
Overby, Stefanie 54, 121, 197

Pactera 102
Philippines 82, 143, 164–5, 169, 177, 187, 196,
  207, 215
Poland 21, 145, 152–3, 177
polarization *see* inequality; labor markets
polling data *see* opinion poll data
Poppy (Xchanging) 166–7, 199
Poster, Winifred 5, 56, 221, 226
postfordism 27, 47, 220
proximity, economics of 130, 147–9,
  152, 160
proximity development centers 149, 202
PRT Corporation 146–7
principal-agent problem 124
private-equity business 19, 63, 67–8, 73, 76–9
profession, outsourcing 8, 12–13, 20, 48–9, 51,
  54, 92, 96–9, 101–5, 137, 205–7 *see also*
  certification; complex, outsourcing; IAOP
professionalization *see* profession, outsourcing

rationalization 11, 103, 105, 180, 184, 204,
  212, 215 *see also* lean production;
  reorganization; standardization
relationship management 50, 55, 95, 98,
  113–18, 213–14 *see also* governance, of
  outsourcing; intermediation
relocation 22, 25–6, 56, 179, 195–6, 202, 205,
  207–8, 210, 221 *see also* locational calculus;
  locational decision-making
reorganization 207–8 *see also* fix,
  organizational
reshoring 130–1, 143
restructuring 5, 17–18, 22, 27, 35, 42, 63, 67,
  78–9, 130, 162–3, 171, 187, 201, 203,
  219–21
rightsizing 14, 52, 173 *see also* downsizing;
  lean production
robophobia 21, 168
robot arbitrage *see* arbitrage, robot
robotic process automation *see* RPA

robotics 172, 177, 183, 190, 214, 216–17
  see also automation; autonomics; RPA
robotistan 171, 177–9, 182, 184, 188, 200–1
robots 21, 165–6, 169, 172–6, 180–1, 189–92,
  195, 197, 199–200, 209, 220
Romania 145, 152–3
Romney, Mitt 19, 59, 62–85, 89–90 *see also*
  Bain Capital
Rossum's Universal Robots see *R.U.R.*
Routinization 11, 16, 22, 95, 125–6, 176, 179,
  195, 197–8, 201, 205, 209, 219 *see also*
  deskilling; standardization
RPA (robotic process automation) 18,
  21–2, 165–6, 171, 178–82, 184–5, 193–4,
  205, 214
RSI (Rural Sourcing Inc.) 132–3
R.U.R (Rossum's Universal Robots) 190–2,
  196, 200
rural sourcing 127–9, 133–6, 138–9, 141–4,
  161–2
Rural Sourcing Inc. *see* RSI

Safire, William 25, 48
Salt, Bernard (KPMG) 194, 215
Santos, Juan Manuel 159
SAP 119, 144, 157
Schlesinger, David 45–6
Schoenberger, Erica 34, 42
scientific management 52, 212
service level agreements *see* SLAs
shared services 51, 152, 176, 182, 207
skill-biased technical change 217, 219
Slaby, James (HfS) 174–7, 180, 226
SLAs (service level agreements) 111,
  121–2, 186
Slashdotters 213
software automation 18, 21–2, 165, 168, 172,
  174, 177, 181, 194, 209, 220 *see also*
  automation; autonomics; RPA
spatial divisions of labor 17, 34, 216 *see also*
  division of labor; NIDL
spatial fix *see* fix, spatial
standardization 10, 16, 35, 125, 178, 181,
  208–9 *see also* routinization
stress, managerial 9–11, 105, 198, 208, 214
Sturgeon, Timothy 44, 70, 224
supply chains 16–17, 26–7, 34, 36, 39–40, 96,
  131, 145–6, 207
  buyer dominated 20, 96, 112, 123, 142, 210
  management of 4, 17–18, 51–2, 163, 173
Sutherland, Charles (HfS) 185, 188, 226
swivel chair problem 174, 184, 191

Tata Communications Transformation
  Services 28, 102, 149, 157, 162
Taylorism 52, 195, 212
TCS 149, 157–8, 170

Printed and bound by CPI Group (UK) Ltd, Croydon, CR0 4YY